The Art of Command in the Civil War

The Art of Command
in the Civil War

EDITED BY STEVEN E. WOODWORTH

UNIVERSITY OF NEBRASKA PRESS   LINCOLN AND LONDON

Philip L. Shiman, "Engineering and Command: The Case
of General William S. Rosecrans, 1862–1863," adapted from
Engineering Sherman's March, forthcoming from Louisiana
State University Press, material used by permission of publisher.

Library of Congress Cataloging-in-Publication Data
The art of command in the Civil War
edited by Steven E. Woodworth.
p.   cm.
Includes bibliographical references (p.   ) and index.
ISBN 0-8032-4785-0 (alk. paper)
1. United States – History – Civil War, 1861–1865 – Campaigns.
2. Command of troops – History – 19th century.
3. Generals – United States – History – 19th century.
4. Generals – Confederate States of America – History.
5. United States. Army – History – Civil War,
1861–1865.   6. Confederate States of America.
Army – History.   7. Military art and science –
United States – History – 19th century.
I. Woodworth, Steven E.
E470.A76   1998
973.7′3 – dc21   98-19543
CIP

For John Y. Simon, teacher and scholar

Contents

Introduction

"Everything is very simple in war," wrote nineteenth-century German philosopher Carl von Clausewitz, "but the simplest thing is difficult." The basic solution to many a strategic or tactical problem may be, in an academic sense, fairly obvious. Yet as this sage veteran of the Napoleonic Wars pointed out, actually making things happen in such a way as to bring about victory is a difficult matter indeed.[1]

A constant temptation for those who study war—and particularly the exercise of command—is to fall into the error of thinking that the problems confronting a historical commander were really easy ones. "Monday-morning quarterbacks" have their academic counterparts in next-century historians, who, if they are not careful, can begin to think that the solutions to a Civil War general's problems lay close at hand and were to be had for the grasping. Such misconceptions are particularly hard to avoid if latter-day scholars allow themselves to conceive of the war as a sort of chess game—neat, orderly, quiet, and rational. Calm, comfortable, and unhurried, chess players study the situation at length and without disturbance. They then make their moves carefully, based solely on their own calculations of how best to win. Pieces may be moved with precision and complete predictability over a neat grid of right angles and perfect squares. A very small amount of reflection should be adequate to convince us that the game of chess bears only the vaguest theoretical resemblance to the hard business of war. A little more reflection should assure us that military command is not solely, perhaps not even mostly, a matter of strategy and tactics either.

To be successful, an army commander must manage to relate well to his nation's commander in chief and such other political powers as may affect his operations and the conduct of the war. This may very well include the newspapers and public opinion. He must select loyal and efficient subordinates, secure their appointment, inspire their cooperation and that of such less-than-inspiring specimens as politics may force him to retain under his command, and somehow contrive to get the very different minds of all these men working together in harmony. He must see to the training, organization, discipline, equipping, and supply of his army and have his orders carried out in all of these areas and others too. He must endeavor to get valid information about his enemy, knowing that a fair proportion of the raw information he receives will be egregiously false, some of it probably deliberately so, and any of it dangerously likely to feed either his fears or his hopes till they become the means of his destruction. He must endeavor to prevent the enemy's learning his own strength, plans, and dispositions. In all of this he will be overworked, sleep deprived, harassed, frazzled, and under constant tension, knowing that the fate of his country and his whole reputation are riding on nearly his every decision. And he will have the dubious pleasure of working with other men whose personalities are equally on the ragged edge and for similar reasons. If he gets through all of this successfully, he may have a chance to attempt to exercise some strategy and tactics.

The purpose of this book is to explore a few of the factors that make the exercise of command a vastly more complicated and interesting process than a game of chess. In his essay, Craig L. Symonds deals with one of the foremost problems confronting generals at the highest levels of command—the need to relate well with the commander in chief and the rest of the civil government. His is a case study in how such matters should *not* be handled. Joseph E. Johnston's poor relations with Confederate president Jefferson Davis were a major factor in his lack of success as a commander. These relations, in turn, were effectively poisoned by Johnston's relationship with Louis Wigfall, one of Davis's bitterest enemies in the Confederate congress. For Johnston the relationship grew out of naïveté, even deliberate obtuseness, and blighted his career. Wigfall, for his part, had no scruples about using Johnston as a political club with which to beat the president. Symonds's study provides valuable new insights into the perplexing question of how a general of Johnston's obvious military ability could fail to achieve battlefield success.

Military intelligence was a subject afforded little attention in the training of America's army officers prior to the Civil War, nor was it pursued with systematic efficiency during the conflict. George McClellan put a railroad detective on his staff—with unfortunate results—and various Southern generals received information from a number of romantic if not always very militarily profitable Southern belles-turned-spies. Yet as William B.

Feis makes clear in his essay on Ulysses S. Grant's use of intelligence in the Belmont campaign, those generals who knew how to gather and analyze intelligence efficiently possessed an important advantage in their operations. Not only does Feis's essay demonstrate the significance of Grant's skill in the area of military intelligence, it also reveals that an awareness of this aspect of command—long overlooked by scholars of the war—sheds a fascinating new light on the entire concept and purpose of Grant's brief foray at Belmont, Missouri. What was previously thought a mere incident of the war's early days becomes a significant early indicator of the character of Ulysses S. Grant and his manner of making war. Thus in this case particularly, going beyond the mythical chessboard-war yields a new level of understanding about the conflict as it actually happened.

Donald E. Collins's essay explores a different area of difficulty for Civil War officers, particularly Confederate ones: dealing with desertion. By the latter stages of the war, desertion from the Southern armies had reached massive and disastrous proportions. Even in late 1863 and early 1864 it was beginning to take on ominous dimensions. Preventing desertion is arguably the most fundamental aspect of maintaining discipline in an army. Few troops posed more difficulties for Confederate officers in this respect than some of those conscripted from North Carolina. Unenthusiastic about the conflict brought upon them by the hot tempers of their proud neighbors to the north and south, many Tarheels desired nothing so much as to be able to sit the war out in peace. Commanding in North Carolina during the winter of 1863–1864, George Pickett had to deal with this aspect of command. His solution was drastic and generated much controversy then and since.

Philip L. Shiman addresses another neglected yet important facet of the task that Civil War commanders had to perform if they were to achieve success, that of the application of engineering to war. If armies were to move, they had to have roads and bridges—and maps, if they were not to get lost. If they were to achieve success in battle, they would often need fortifications or the means of attacking them. If they were to eat, they would require an entire network of roads, railroads, and navigable waterways to bring up rations, along with forts or blockhouses to defend those supply lines. It was an unglamorous side of war, but no general would succeed without mastering it at least to some degree. One who did so to an unusual extent was William S. Rosecrans, and Shiman examines this general's application of these skills.

Selection of the right sort of subordinate officers is another aspect of successful command that is often overlooked by modern students of the Civil War. In "T. J. Jackson and the Value of 'The Right Sort of Man,'" award-winning Civil War historian William J. Miller examines the famous Stonewall Jackson's approach to this facet of the art of military command. Miller shows how Jackson based his personnel decisions not only on a man's possession of the necessary professional attainments but also the personal traits—above all the strength of character and the firm moral fiber—required to work effectively with his fellow officers and his commander and to overcome unforeseen obstacles. Focusing especially on the case of staff member Jedediah Hotchkiss, Miller shows that in Jackson's efficient and highly successful system personal character was not only relevant but was the chief consideration in selecting "the right sort of man."

Brooks D. Simpson deals with the political aspect of generalship, but unlike Craig Symonds's study of the unfortunate Confederate general Joseph E. Johnston, Simpson's piece shows us how a general successfully dealt with politics. He does this by taking a new look at Ulysses S. Grant's grand campaign of 1864. Simpson makes clear that Grant's task was by no means as simple as historians have sometimes represented it to be. The new Federal commanding general had to face significant political restraints and restrictions on his freedom of action, and he was forced to try to use a number of very inferior subordinate generals simply because those men possessed too much political clout for the administration to risk wounding their overblown egos in an election year. In marked contrast to Joseph E. Johnston, Grant made his way successfully through the political thicket that confronted him, and Simpson shows us how.

Few Civil War generals come in for more abuse than the hapless Braxton Bragg. Disgruntled subordinates and politicians took up the hue and cry against him less than six months after he rose to command of the Confederate Army of Tennessee, and the condemnation has never let up since. Bragg was indeed unsuccessful as a commander but not for the reasons often claimed. A skillful strategist, Bragg was as good a tactician as many a more successful Civil War general (it was not, after all, a war characterized by its brilliant tactics). What ultimately denied success to an otherwise very promising commander lay in the other skills that a winning general needed but he lacked. My own essay in this volume will seek to identify at least some of the missing ingredients in Bragg's generalship by looking at a revealing but little-studied campaign. The Tullahoma campaign of June 1863 has been much ignored, largely because it was overshadowed by the nearly simultaneous Vicksburg and Gettysburg campaigns and because its effects were not, as successful Union general William S. Rosecrans observed, "written in letters of blood." Yet it reveals as clearly as any operations of the Army of Tennessee the reason Bragg's skills failed to produce the effect they should have. The unfortunate general was faced with nearly insurmountable political problems both in his relations with his commander in chief and with his subordinates. His unsuccessful efforts to overcome these obstacles provide a striking contrast to Grant's success in the 1864 campaign.

Thus, these essays represent a beginning in the exploration and mapping out of a larger and more complex landscape on which we can expand our understanding of Civil War generalship. The contributors hope they will point the way to new and more rewarding directions in the study of command.

Notes

1. Carl von Clausewitz, *On War,* ed. Anatol Rapoport (New York: Penguin, 1968), 164.

1 / No Margin for Error: Civil War in the Confederate Government

CRAIG L. SYMONDS

Historians have often attributed the failure of the Southern Confederacy to win its independence to its inferiority in available manpower and to other equally tangible factors such as inadequate industrial support, weak internal transportation, and a dearth of naval facilities. Indeed, for more than a generation after the end of the war, Union numerical and matériel superiority seemed, to Southern observers at least, to constitute a full explanation for Confederate defeat. A bronze memorial to Lee's army erected at Appomattox in 1926 by the United Daughters of the Confederacy emphasizes—and indeed exaggerates—the underdog status of the Southern armies overwhelmed, finally, by sheer numbers:

HERE ON SUNDAY APRIL 9, 1865
AFTER FOUR YEARS OF HEROIC STRUGGLE
IN DEFENSE OF PRINCIPLES BELIEVED FUNDAMENTAL
TO THE EXISTENCE OF OUR GOVERNMENT
LEE SURRENDERED 9000 MEN THE REMNANT
OF AN ARMY STILL UNCONQUERED IN SPIRIT
TO 118000 MEN UNDER GRANT[1]

The purpose of such exaggerated references to numerical disparity, of course, is to make the point that it was not for lack of courage or boldness that the South failed—the U. D. C. wanted it clearly understood that defeat was the result of Union brute force.

Ironically, the claim that the South was hopelessly overmatched from the outset exposes Southern leaders to the charge of what Henry Steele Commager called "criminal imbecility" for undertaking an unwinnable war. But while the leaders of the secession movement may have been guilty of many things—hubris among them—a Southern war of independence was not unwinnable. The North did have unquestioned manpower and matériel advantages, to be sure, but its military objective—conquering, occupying, and controlling some 750,000 square miles of enemy territory—was a far more daunting task than the Southern objective of outlasting the Northern will to fight. Moreover, Southerners were acutely aware that history was full of examples of weaker powers overcoming long odds to win. They had to look no further than the American Revolution to provide themselves with an inspirational symbol of the triumph of will over numbers. By itself, therefore, brute force is not a sufficient explanation of the war's outcome.[2]

A second explanation is that defeat was a product of a failure of will—precisely that aspect of the struggle in which Southerners felt most confident. In 1950 E. Merton Coulter argued that the South lost the war because of a collapse of Southern morale, worn to the breaking point by four years of casualties and deprivation. Though many, such as President Jefferson Davis, remained determined and unrelenting to the last, the Confederacy itself was beaten, not only in the field, but in its collective heart. This was not a popular notion among the champions of the Lost Cause; it was precisely the view that the U. D. C. sought to dispel when it erected the plaque at Appomattox claiming that Lee's vastly outnumbered army was "still unconquered in spirit."[3]

Coulter was certainly correct in claiming that Southern morale had been crushed by 1865. But as an explanation for the defeat of the Confederacy this—like the brute force explanation—is not fully satisfactory simply because Southern morale, good or bad, was itself a product of military success or failure. The collapse of Southern will was largely a result of defeat rather than the cause of it. Of course, will was a critical factor in one respect. Contrary to Southern expectation, Northern will survived early defeats and repeated disappointment long enough for Union matériel superiority to assert itself. Once again, while the eventual collapse of Southern will was a critical factor in determining the outcome of the American Civil War, it is not a comprehensive explanation for Confederate defeat.

A third factor is the argument of David M. Potter and others that the South fell victim to its own internal divisions and to inadequate leadership at the top. According to this view, the South might have triumphed despite its inferior numbers and Northern staying power if it had been able to sustain a united front and efficiently channel its energies. Instead, it dissolved into petty disagreements about the perquisites of power—struggles between the government at Richmond and the governors of various states and conflicts between the commander in chief and his generals in the field.[4]

Jefferson Davis is unavoidably the centerpiece of this argument. Indeed, a few disappointed Southerners such as Edward A. Pollard, the bitter and unforgiving publisher of the *Richmond Examiner*, blamed the South's defeat entirely on what he asserted was the manifest incompetence of its president. Though Pollard was hardly an unbiased observer, most historians have treated Davis roughly, even while recognizing the extraordinary difficulties he faced. Partly this is because, whatever his gifts as chief executive, Davis suffers in any comparison with his counterpart north of the Potomac. In dealing with internal dissent, political factionalism, and difficult generals, Davis's prickly micromanagement served him less well than did Lincoln's flexible pragmatism.[5]

Other historians minimize the role of internal politics or discount them altogether. James M. McPherson cites what he calls the "fallacy of reversibility" to discredit the assertion that faction was decisive in the South's defeat. He notes that "bitter division and dissent" were as widespread in the North as in the South. If discord, obstreperous generals, and a beleaguered executive explain Southern defeat, why didn't the North collapse under the same burden?[6]

Unquestionably, both Lincoln and Davis faced daunting difficulties. Both men had to orchestrate the unprecedented mobilization of manpower and resources, both resorted to equally unprecedented suspensions of civil liberties, and both faced troublesome internal political opposition. Lincoln was bedeviled by the Democrats, most of whom sought to ensure that the war did not become a social or political revolution, and by the Radicals within his own party who were just as determined that it should. For his part, Davis had no formal political opposition, and he did not have to worry about reelection, but he did face a bitter and acrimonious backstairs campaign conducted by his political foes, many of whom were men with (in George Rable's words) "imposing egos and an appalling inability to cooperate," who often seemed more interested in humiliating Davis than in defeating the Yankees. And he did, after all, have to orchestrate a total war while presiding over a government whose very raison d'être was the maintenance of a weak central authority.[7]

Both presidents also had to deal with self-important, politically motivated, or simply less-than-competent general officers. If Davis had P. G. T. Beauregard, Gustavus Smith, Mansfield Lovell, and Joseph E. Johnston,

Lincoln had Benjamin Butler, John C. Frémont, Franz Sigel, and George B. McClellan. And in the North as well as in the South, these unhappy generals often joined forces with political foes of the administration. While Davis's foes within the ranks of his own generals became stalking-horses for his political enemies in Richmond, at least none of them became his opponent in a general election as McClellan did against Lincoln in 1864.[8]

But the fact that both chief executives—Lincoln as well as Davis—faced significant internal factionalism and dissent does not invalidate the argument that internecine warfare within the Confederate government was instrumental, even critical, in the South's defeat. The "fallacy of reversibility" is valid only if other factors are reversed as well. Factionalism was more costly to the South than to the North precisely because of the South's tiny margin of error. Lincoln's government and the Northern will to continue the war could survive the inefficiency produced by internal faction and bickering because of the North's tangible superiority in manpower and resources. The Confederacy had no such margin for error. Its defeat, therefore, was a *combination* of its tangible weaknesses and its internal factionalism, which together bred defeat and disappointment and which in turn led to the collapse of will.

Assessing the role of faction in Confederate defeat begins with a consideration of Jefferson Davis. Davis had undisputed skills as a soldier and politician, but many of his personal characteristics proved to be liabilities for the chief executive of a confederated government. His tendency to judge men largely by their personal loyalty, his obsession with detail, his perception of himself as a military strategist—all these created problems for him as president. Even more important, many (if not most) of those who emerged as Davis's political foes were constitutionally unsuited to be team players. For the most part they were men who had devoted their political careers to opposition and obstruction; decades of fending off perceived Yankee threats had imbued them with an instinct to attack rather than to accommodate. Given these circumstances, it is not surprising that Davis had difficulty with men like Robert Barnwell Rhett of South Carolina, Louis T. Wigfall of Texas, and William Lowndes Yancey of Alabama—even his own vice president, Alexander Stephens of Georgia. These were men with strong personalities, and because they shared their criticism of Davis with each other, their friendship groups became informal political alliances within the Confederacy.[9]

Thomas L. Connelly and Archer Jones have unraveled these factions in their book *The Politics of Command* (1973) and described them as competing and overlapping power blocs. These blocs had no formal structure or official status; they existed at all because the lack of party structure in the Confederacy denied them a constitutionally acceptable outlet for their criticism. As a result, much of the opposition to the government took on a decidedly personal tone and seemed to Davis little short of disloyalty. Since the entire life of the Confederacy was consumed by war, these alliances, or factions, often manifested themselves in the advocacy of one strategy over another, or more often, one general over another. Thus, political faction became inextricably tied into civil-military relations when political leaders became vocal advocates for field generals as a means of influencing national politics.[10]

Davis's generals, too, manifested a wide variety of personality traits: Beauregard's flamboyance, Lee's tact, Hood's brashness, and Bragg's inability to get along with just about everyone. But none of Davis's generals caused him more anguish than Joseph E. Johnston. The relationship between Davis and Johnston was a curious one that provides particular insight into the political fabric of the wartime South and into the factions that kept the Confederate government at war with itself. While personal animosity and a disagreement about strategic alternatives constituted the melody of the feud, politics was a constant counterpoint.[11]

Davis and Johnston had had problems even before the war. As secretary of war in the 1850s, Davis had declined to confirm Johnston's claim to a colonelcy. But this early disagreement did not preclude an amicable working relationship during the war. One of Davis's first questions after assuming the burden of the presidency in 1861 was "Where is Joe Johnston?" After the victory at Manassas, the relationship between the two men was positively cordial. Their relationship became strained later that summer when Davis ranked Johnston fourth—behind Samuel Cooper, Sidney Johnston, and Lee—in his formal nomination of general officers to the Confederate congress. Angry and hurt, Johnston first complained and then he sulked. His petulant reaction planted the first seeds of doubt in Davis about Johnston's reliability, but even then he maintained confidence—or at least a hope—that Johnston could be effective in the field. When, after the Battle of Seven Pines outside Richmond, the badly wounded Johnston was carried from the field on a litter, Davis bent over him with genuine concern, filled with evident anxiety for Johnston's recovery. The decisive turning point in their relationship came only a few days later. While Johnston's old friend and classmate Robert E. Lee fought what came to be known as the Seven Days' Battles, Louis Wigfall and his wife Charlotte stopped by the Richmond home where Johnston was recuperating to pay a courtesy call.

Wigfall was the midwife of Confederate faction. Originally from South Carolina, he had developed a reputation there as a heavy drinker, a frequent gambler, and an occasional brawler. After declaring bankruptcy in 1848, he moved to Texas where he recouped his fortunes and won election to the United States Senate. A strong supporter of secession, he returned to Charleston in April to witness the first shots of the war, and in May he shared a carriage with Davis during the Confederate president's triumphal arrival in Richmond. He lobbied hard for a brigadier's commission, which he eventually got, but he was disappointed not to be invited to join Davis in his dash to the Bull Run battlefield in July. Soon afterward, he resigned his commission in order to take a seat in the Confederate senate where, after a brief honeymoon, he quickly established himself as a thorn in the side of the administration.[12]

The source of Wigfall's animosity toward Davis was a combination of his disappointment in not being accorded the status of close adviser and a social tiff between their wives. Gossipmongers reported to Varina Davis that Charlotte Wigfall had referred to her as a "coarse western woman," and the ensuing coolness between the women soon enveloped their husbands. Even though much of that was still in the future when Wigfall and his wife stopped by to visit the wounded Johnston after the Battle of Seven Pines, his relationship with the Confederate president had already begun to sour.[13]

During his visit, Wigfall invited Johnston to move into the Wigfall home on Grace Street during his recovery. At the time such an offer must have seemed to Johnston no more than the product of generous compassion; it is at least possible that he did not consider the larger ramifications of his decision. But it was inevitable that his acceptance of that invitation would finalize his breach with the president. By setting up quarters in the camp of the enemy (so to speak), Johnston all but announced his alliance with the president's foes.

Johnston's personal popularity made him particularly useful to Wigfall, who subsequently cited what he trumpeted as Davis's ill treatment of Johnston to discredit the administration. Most of the time, Wigfall's support for Johnston was less a measure of his respect for the general or of his confidence in Johnston's military skill than a means of attacking the president's conduct of the war. Connelly and Jones note perceptively that "Wigfall often seemed more interested in how Johnston could promote the anti-administration position in Congress rather than evincing interest in the general himself." Likewise, George Rable has noted that Wigfall and his allies "seemed more eager to attack the administration than to promote Johnston's strategic views."[14]

Perhaps the greatest irony in the relationship between Davis, Wigfall, and Johnston is that it seems to be definitive proof of the old adage that politics makes strange bedfellows. The "enemies," that is, Davis and Johnston, were in fact very much alike, while the "friends," that is, Wigfall and Johnston, were very nearly opposites. Both Davis and Johnston were sensitive men (one is tempted to say touchy), and during the Civil War they both felt underappreciated. Each believed that he sacrificed himself to the greater good of the country he served. Like most self-perceived martyrs, they were fundamentally lonely men who needed friends to sustain them in difficult times. Perhaps because of that neither man was particularly well served by those they counted as "friends." Davis certainly gained nothing politically and very little personally for his loyalty to Judah Benjamin, Lucius Northrop, or John C. Pemberton for example. And though Johnston was grateful for Wigfall's sympathy and support, in the end, that relationship was a major factor in his professional undoing.[15]

As for Wigfall and Johnston, they could hardly have been more different. Johnston was quiet—even shy—often blushing during public appearances. In his dealings with others he was an open book, unable to disguise either his opinions or his emotions. By contrast, the London *Times* reporter William Howard Russell described the calculating Wigfall as likely "to conceal [his] expression beneath half-closed lid." Johnston was strait-laced in his personal habits; a stickler about matters of protocol, manners, and conduct; and a careful dresser who was more than a bit vain about his looks. He seldom drank, and never to excess, and ate sparingly. Wigfall lived large and had a well-earned reputation for overindulging both at the table and with the bottle. What bound these two antipodes together was not personal chemistry but circumstance and opportunity.[16]

Johnston had known Wigfall briefly during the few months that the senator had spent as the commander of a brigade of Texas troops in Johnston's army, but it was not until he moved into the Wigfall home in June 1862 that he became publicly associated with Wigfall and his faction. Lydia Johnston and Charlotte Wigfall became fast friends, and they entertained jointly—so frequently, in fact, that their residence was considered by many to be a social rival of the Confederate White House presided over by Varina Davis.

Of course, the rivalry between the Wigfalls and the Davises was more than social, and so too was the association between Wigfall and Johnston. Wigfall did not break openly with Davis until after Johnston moved into his home, but when he did he took advantage of Johnston's presence to draw out the general's strategic views and obtain confirmation of his own opinions about Davis's shortcomings. In that respect, they fed off each other. Indeed, their bond of mutual antagonism to Davis both defined and delimited their relationship, for they had virtually nothing else in common.

It is clear what Wigfall got from the relationship—Johnston was politically useful to Wigfall and his allies in the Confederate senate—but what did Johnston get out of it? Most likely, Wigfall's compliments and solicitations fed Johnston's desperate need for official approval and acceptance—something he did not get enough of from Davis. Wigfall was an attentive admirer at a time when Johnston felt aggrieved by the way the administration had treated him. The thought that he was being used by Wigfall apparently never entered his conscious mind—he either didn't see it or wouldn't see it. He was guilty of more than naïveté in this relationship; his correspondence with Wigfall suggests a certain deliberate self-deception. He saw Wigfall only as a personal ally and chose to ignore the senator's broader political agenda. Moreover, he never figured it out. Many years after the war, while organizing his papers, Johnston came across a letter from Wigfall and jotted in the margin: "a distinguished C. S. Senator and my devoted friend." Such unreflective loyalty is similar to Davis's stubborn fidelity to unpopular men like Judah Benjamin and Lucius B. Northrop.[17]

As the months passed and Wigfall emerged as Davis's most vocal critic, Johnston became involved in events of a decidedly political character. In November of 1862, he accepted an invitation to attend a public breakfast in honor of Senators Henry Foote and William Yancey, two more of Davis's congressional foes. The declared purpose of the event was a reconciliation between the two men who had been privately feuding for months. But what reconciled them was their common opposition to Davis, and the unmistakable subtext of the breakfast was public opposition to the administration. By his presence, Johnston announced his association with the enemy—at least as far as Davis was concerned.[18]

In spite of all this, Davis appointed Johnston to the command of the western theater later that same month. Johnston would have no direct command of troops; instead, he would be responsible for coordinating the movements of two armies: Braxton Bragg's Army of Tennessee and John C. Pemberton's Army of Mississippi. Johnston was unhappy with his new assignment, not only because it did not include direct command of an army, but also because his authority did not extend to Theophilus Holmes's army across the Mississippi in Arkansas. Johnston believed that making the trans-Mississippi a separate command theater threw away the opportunity to coordinate the movements of Confederate forces on both sides of the river. Historians have argued, and continue to argue, about whether Davis's command structure was realistic and workable or whether Johnston was simply unable or unwilling to make it work. Lydia Johnston was convinced that Davis had devised these arrangements for the express purpose of making her husband a scapegoat. She wrote to Charlotte Wigfall that her husband was being "shabbily used" by the "great commander in chief." Wigfall and his friends seized upon this issue to assail the president. Throughout the spring, Wigfall took it upon himself as chairman of the powerful Military Affairs Committee to block a number of presidential initiatives, ostensibly in the interest of protecting military prerogative, but also simply to effect small public humiliations on the president. Johnston's apparent connivance in these minor events further undermined Davis's swiftly eroding faith in Johnston's reliability or fidelity.[19]

In May 1863, after five months of long-distance bickering about the command structure, Davis ordered Johnston to quit his headquarters at Chattanooga and go to Mississippi to take personal direction of the defense of Vicksburg. Johnston arrived in the Mississippi state capital at Jackson on May 13, the day after Grant interposed his forces on the road between Jackson and Vicksburg, effectively cutting Johnston and his small force off from Pemberton's army near Vicksburg. Johnston wired Richmond that he was "too late." Johnston did try to effect a coordinated attack on one element of Grant's forces, but his effort failed partly because of the difficulty of communicating with Pemberton and partly because Pemberton and Johnston had very different views of the proper strategic response to the crisis. Johnston wanted Pemberton to fight his way east or north in order to maintain his freedom of movement so that he could attach his forces to those under Johnston and thereby retain the possibility of confronting Grant on something like equal terms. Pemberton, unwilling to abandon Vicksburg, delayed and agonized, then struck south rather than east, and finally retreated inside the city's defenses to withstand a siege.[20]

Davis held Johnston personally and, indeed, almost solely responsible for the subsequent fall of Vicksburg. While Pemberton was besieged, Johnston and his small army remained in the vicinity and did nothing, as Davis saw it, to effect the relief of the city. Johnston was still loitering nearby in July when Pemberton's starved garrison marched out of Vicksburg to surrender. Davis was hugely disappointed. It seemed to him that Johnston had done little, if anything, to prevent the disaster. If a general failed after doing all that he could, that was one thing, but to fail to try was unacceptable. Davis might have been willing to forgive Johnston even his political associations with Wigfall and his cronies if he had believed that the general was doing all in his power to achieve victory. But in Mississippi, as on the Virginia Peninsula, it seemed to Davis that Johnston was simply too passive. When Josiah Gorgas, the Confederate chief of ordnance, remarked to Davis that Vicksburg had fallen for want of provisions, Davis spat back: "Yes, for want of provisions inside, and a general outside who wouldn't fight."[21]

That same month Davis demoted Johnston to a small command encompassing only Mississippi and southern Alabama. Davis probably would have preferred to dismiss him altogether, and he laid the groundwork for such a move by promoting Daniel Harvey Hill to lieutenant general. Hill went to Bragg as a corps commander thereby enabling Bragg to detach William Hardee to assume command in Mississippi. But Davis stopped short of dismissing Johnston outright, for he knew how popular "Ole Joe" was in the country—more popular among much of the civilian population than was Davis himself. And he knew, too, that Wigfall and his allies would make Johnston's dismissal a cause célèbre, thus fracturing the Confederacy at a time when unity was essential.[22]

Unity did not concern Wigfall. Since he saw Davis as the principal impediment to a Confederate victory, he was eager to do whatever was necessary to discredit the president and weaken his power. The fall of Vicksburg gave Wigfall new opportunities to criticize the administration. With the clear intention of embarrassing Davis, Wigfall introduced a resolution in the Confederate senate to publish all the correspondence concerning the Vicksburg campaign, including Johnston's report. His expectation was that the public would side with Johnston, thus undermining Davis's ability to direct and define Confederate strategy.

But two could play at that game. Someone in the Confederate White House leaked a copy of Pemberton's report (which Johnston had not seen because Pemberton had submitted it directly to Richmond rather than through the theater commander) to the friendly *Richmond Sentinel*. As might be expected, Pemberton's report cast all the blame for the fall of Vicksburg on Johnston. The *Sentinel* blasted Johnston's inaction and pointed an accusatory editorial finger at Ole Joe: "For nearly seven weeks he sat down in sound of the conflict, and he fired not a gun . . . he has done no more than to sit by and see Vicksburg fall, and send us the news." Davis could not have expressed it better himself.[23]

Even before Vicksburg's fall, Wigfall had warned Johnston that in view of the administration's enmity, he should keep copies of all his official papers in case he had to defend himself from unfair attacks. At the same time Wigfall urged Johnston to "send me copies to be used when & as I see fit." Without demur, Johnston provided them. No doubt he would have claimed that he was merely responding to a request from a government official, but while Johnston may have been politically naïve he was no fool, and he had to know that Wigfall intended to use the documents as political weapons. To his brother Beverly, Johnston wrote, "There is no reason why I should be a martyr."[24]

In receipt of Johnston's papers, Wigfall reported back: "I showed your letter to Semmes of Louisiana, Barnett of Kentucky & others who were friends of yours, who promised to see that justice was done to you." Feeling triumphant, Wigfall confronted Secretary of War James Seddon and claimed that once Johnston's papers were published, "the wisdom of his views and the stupidity of Davis [would] be exposed."[25]

As always, Wigfall was motivated throughout this episode more by antagonism toward Davis than by friendship for Johnston. To Johnston he explained that "the safety of the country requires that he [Davis] should be taught that he has no monopoly of bad temper, that if he puts himself out to disoblige others, others will disoblige him." When Johnston responded that disobliging Davis was not the ultimate goal, Wigfall sent him a lesson in politics: "Not having been in Richmond for more than a year," Wigfall wrote, "you are not likely to know that state of affairs there. Davis's bad judgement of men & bad temper together will ruin the country unless he is controlled."[26]

Johnston's relationship with Wigfall utterly poisoned his relationship with Davis. The dispute in the summer and fall of 1861 over Johnston's rank, which had marked the beginning of their strained relationship, might never have blossomed into a full-fledged war if it had not been fertilized by the political dimension supplied by Wigfall's advocacy of Johnston's cause. By the fall of 1863 the personal war between Davis and Johnston had become such an obsession for both of them that it threatened to eclipse the war each was conducting with the enemy. In August, Wigfall wrote Johnston gleefully that Davis "was blind as an adder with rage & ready to bite himself." That fall, Mary Chesnut confided to her diary that "the president detests Joe Johnston for all the trouble he had given him. And General Joe returns the compliment with compound interest."[27]

And yet only two months later, Davis appointed Johnston to command the Army of Tennessee. He had little real choice. He had resisted the flood of complaints against Bragg for months (many of them from Wigfall and his allies in the Confederate congress, others from officers within the army), and after the debacle on Missionary Ridge in November he knew that he could no longer keep Bragg in command without risking open revolt. Ironically, Johnston had supported Bragg in this controversy, insisting that Bragg was a competent general who should be sustained. Because Wigfall and his friends sought to discredit Davis by attacking Bragg, they were disappointed and angered when the president's allies cited Johnston's support for Bragg. Wigfall complained to Johnston that he was undermining the efforts of his "friends" to get rid of Bragg and put Johnston in his place. Proving that he was not completely naïve, Johnston wrote back: "the friends who have been irritated by my expressions of opinion are less my friends, I take it, than the President's enemies." Though Wigfall did not respond directly to this observation, it is easy to imagine him reading the letter and saying aloud, "Well, of course."[28]

In the end, Davis was forced to give in to Wigfall and his "friends" and appoint Johnston to take Bragg's place. There was no one else. Lee wouldn't leave Virginia, Beauregard was worse than Johnston, Hardee wouldn't take the job, Longstreet was back in Virginia; every subordinate commander in the theater recommended that Johnston be named to the position. However unpopular he was with the administration, Johnston's name, at least, retained a certain value to the army. In December, Davis swallowed hard and made the appointment.

Wigfall was triumphant. "Davis has at last been forced to do you justice," he wrote to Johnston. For his part, Johnston refused to gloat. Far too late in the game, he now assumed the role of the apolitical military professional. To Wigfall he responded, "The president is, by the constitution, the judge of the Military Merit of the officers. I shall, therefore, while the war last, serve to the best of my ability, wherever he may place me."[29]

Johnston's conduct of the ensuing campaign in north Georgia in 1864 remains controversial. In his postwar *Narrative* (1874), Johnston claimed that he had a fully matured plan to trade space for time, saving the blood of his soldiers until he had an opportunity to inflict a decisive defeat on an enemy drawn deep into inhospitable country. It is more likely that he did not conceive of the campaign in such terms until late May after Sherman had already flanked him out of three strong defensive positions and after he had retreated nearly a hundred miles into central Georgia. Nevertheless, the plan that he articulated in his memoirs has attracted a number of defenders who argue that Davis, and not Johnston, should bear responsibility for the failure of the campaign: first, for refusing Johnston's repeated requests for cavalry attacks against Sherman's supply lines and, second, for dismissing Johnston in July and replacing him with John Bell Hood.[30]

It is at least possible that a whole-hearted commitment to Johnston's strategy of cutting Sherman's supply lines might have made a difference in that campaign. But it was never tried because Davis no longer had any faith in Johnston's promises or recommendations. By the time the north Georgia campaign got underway in May 1864, the civil war within the Confederate government had so poisoned the relationship between Davis and Johnston that there was no confidence left on either side. If Robert E. Lee been the one to request cavalry support, Davis would have responded with alacrity, for Lee had won Davis's respect and confidence not only by deeds in the field but by his professional and solicitous demeanor. But as far as Davis was concerned, neither Johnston's track record as a field commander nor his questionable association with Wigfall had earned him the right to expect the blind support of the administration. Davis therefore rejected Johnston's requests and eventually relieved him of command, turning the army over to John Bell Hood.

The fall of Atlanta in the late summer of 1864 was a deathblow to the Confederacy. Not only did it deprive the South of an important manufacturing and transportation center, it discredited Lincoln's political opponents in the North who insisted that the war was stalemated and thereby helped assure Lincoln's election victory that fall. Arguments about how Atlanta was lost—and about who should bear the blame for it—fill countless pages. Some blame Davis for relieving Johnston in the midst of the campaign; many more blame him for leaving Johnston in command as long as he did. Hood, whose costly assaults bled the Army of Tennessee to a shadow of its former self, is another favorite culprit. And, of course, there is William Tecumseh Sherman whose methodical determination wore down both Southern generals. But one factor insufficiently considered in many of these assessments is the critical role of political faction. To assess the sources of Confederate defeat, it is not merely the actions of Davis or his generals that must be examined but the erosion of the command relationship within the Confederacy, a relationship weakened, if not destroyed, by Davis's political foes, including Texas senator Louis T. Wigfall.

The Davis-Johnston feud was partly personal—both men were sensitive and therefore likely to take offense easily. The feud was partly about strategy—the two men did have real differences of opinion about the best way to defend the Confederacy. But it was also about politics. Johnston's willingness to accept aid and comfort from Davis's political foes was both unprofessional and self-destructive. It undermined his credibility with the government and helped ensure he would be ineffective in the field. If it is too much to assert that their personal civil war was a major factor in Confederate defeat, at the very least the poor relationship between Davis and Johnston, greatly exacerbated by Wigfall and his allies in the Confederate congress, contributed to the internal disintegration that, when combined with the South's narrow margin for error, hastened the demise of the Confederacy.

Notes

1. I am indebted to Tracy Chernault and Joseph Williams of the Appomattox Court House National Historical Park for information about the history of the U. D. C. marker at Appomattox. The last line—"TO 118000 MEN UNDER GRANT"—has been effaced from the existing marker but is still legible. Thanks, as well, to members of the works-in-progress seminar of the history department at the Naval Academy who critiqued this paper in an earlier form.

2. A good summary of this issue appears in Richard E. Beringer, Herman Hattaway, Archer Jones, and William N. Still Jr., *Why the South Lost the Civil War* (Athens: University of Georgia Press, 1986). They argue that "the weakness of southern nationalism" was "the proximate cause of Confederate defeat" (p. 3). The Commager quotation is from "How 'The Lost Cause' Was Lost," *New York Times Magazine*, August 4, 1963, 10.

3. E. Merton Coulter, *The Confederate States of America: 1861–1865* (Baton Rouge: Louisiana State University Press, 1950).

4. David M. Potter, "Jefferson Davis and the Political Factors in Confederate Defeat," in *Why the North Won the Civil War*, ed. David Donald (Baton Rouge: Louisiana State University Press, 1960), 91–112. Potter goes so far as to suggest that "it hardly seems unrealistic to suppose that if the Union and the Confederacy had exchanged presidents with one another, the Confederacy might have won its independence" (p. 109).

5. Edward A. Pollard, *The Lost Cause: A New Southern History of the War of the Confederates* (Richmond: n.p., 1866). Consistent with his animus against

Davis, Pollard was also a devoted supporter of Joseph E. Johnston whom he called "the military genius of the Confederacy" (p. 44).

6. James M. McPherson, "American Victory, American Defeat," in *Why the Confederacy Lost*, ed. Gabor Boritt (New York: Oxford University Press, 1992), 25.

7. George Rable, *The Confederate Republic: A Revolution against Politics* (Chapel Hill: University of North Carolina Press, 1994), 111.

8. See, for example, T. Harry Williams, *Lincoln and His Generals* (New York: Random House, 1952), and Steven E. Woodworth, *Jefferson Davis and His Generals: The Failure of Confederate Command in the West* (Lawrence: University Press of Kansas, 1990). Bell Wiley labeled the tendency of Confederate leaders to promote personal agendas over the common good as "Big-man-me-ism." Bell I. Wiley, *The Road to Appomattox* (Memphis: Memphis State University Press, 1956), vol. 1, 518.

9. William C. Davis, *Jefferson Davis: The Man and His Hour* (New York: Harper Collins, 1991), especially chapter 23; Rable, *Confederate Republic*, especially chapter 6.

10. Thomas Lawrence Connelly and Archer Jones, *The Politics of Command: Factions and Ideas in Confederate Strategy* (Baton Rouge: Louisiana State University Press, 1973), especially chapter 3.

11. Craig L. Symonds, *Joseph E. Johnston: A Civil War Biography* (New York: W. W. Norton, 1992), especially chapters 13 and 16.

12. Alvy King, *Louis T. Wigfall: Southern Fire-Eater* (Baton Rouge: Louisiana State University Press, 1970).

13. Mary Chesnut, *Mary Chesnut's Civil War*, ed. C. Vann Woodward (New Haven: Yale University Press, 1981), 136 (diary entry of August 8, 1861).

14. Connelly and Jones, *Politics of Command*, 59; Rable, *Confederate Republic*, 198.

15. Davis, *Jefferson Davis*; Woodworth, *Jefferson Davis and His Generals*; Symonds, *Joseph E. Johnston*.

16. William Howard Russell, *My Diary North and South* (New York: Alfred A. Knopf, 1988), 87.

17. Undated postwar annotation on letter of Johnston to Wigfall dated April 5, 1864, Wigfall Family Papers, Library of Congress, Washington DC, (hereafter cited as WF).18. Thomas C. DeLeon, *Belles, Beaux, and Brains of the 60s* (New York: G. W. Dillingham, 1907), 402.

19. Johnston to James A. Seddon, May 13 and 16, 1863, U.S. War Department, *The War of the Rebellion: A Compilation of the Official Records of the Union and Confederate Armies*, 128 vols. (Washington DC: Government Printing Office,

1881–1901), 1st ser., vol. 24, pt. 1, pp. 215–16 (hereafter cited as OR; all references are to series 1 unless otherwise noted); Lydia Johnston to Charlotte Wigfall, December 25, 1862, and January 1, 1863, WF. In April, for example, Wigfall reported negatively on a bill requested by Davis to confer the rank of brigadier general on the chief of the Bureau of Ordnance and the chief of the Engineer Bureau. *Journal of the Congress of the Confederate States of America*, 7 vols. (Washington DC: Government Printing Office, 1904 [1968]), vol. 3, 336.

20. Davis to R. E. Lee, May 31, 1863, OR 25, pt. 2: 841–42.

21. Josiah Gorgas, *The Civil War Diary of General Josiah Gorgas*, ed. Frank Vandiver (University: University of Alabama Press, 1947), 50.

22. Special Order 176, July 25, 1863, OR 23, pt. 2: 931. Robert G. H. Kean, *Inside the Confederate Government: The Diary of Robert Garlick Hill Kean, Head of the Bureau of War*, ed. Edward Younger (Baton Rouge: Louisiana State University Press, 1957), 83 (entry of July 26).

23. *Richmond Sentinel*, July 9, 1863.

24. Wigfall to Johnston, June 15, 1863 and March 18, 1863, Joseph E. Johnston Papers hereafter referred to as JO, numbers 294 and 300, Henry E. Huntington Library, San Marino, California (hereafter referred to as HEH); Joseph E. Johnston to Beverly Johnston, February 19, 1864, WF.

25. Wigfall to Johnston, August 9 and 11, 1863 (JO 295), HEH; *Richmond Examiner*, July 25, and August 8, 1863.

26. Wigfall to Johnston, March 19, 1864 (JO 301), HEH.

27. Wigfall to Johnston, August 11, 1863, WF; Chesnut, *Mary Chesnut's Civil War*, 482–83 (diary entry of October 1863).

28. Johnston to Wigfall, December 27, 1863, WF.

29. Wigfall to Johnston, December 18, 1863 (JO 298), HEH; Johnston to Wigfall, December 27, 1863, Louis T. Wigfall Papers, Library of Congress, Washington DC.

30. Joseph E. Johnston, *Narrative of Military Operations during the Civil War* (New York: DaCapo Press, 1874). For a defense of Johnston, see Gilbert Govan and James W. Livingood, *A Different Valor: The Story of General Joseph E Johnston, C. S. A.* (Indianapolis: Bobbs-Merrill, 1956).

2 / Grant and the Belmont Campaign: A Study in Intelligence and Command

WILLIAM B. FEIS

"There are no more important duties which an officer may be called upon to perform," asserted West Point professor Dennis Hart Mahan, "than those of collecting and arranging the information upon which either the general or daily operations of a campaign must be based."[1] In this passage the foremost military theoretician in the United States before the Civil War described the centrality of intelligence, or the collection, analysis, and use of military information, in wartime. Information about the enemy's capabilities and intentions provides the foundation upon which a commander formulates plans for battles and campaigns. After all, noted the nineteenth-century military thinker Antoine Henri Jomini, "how can any man say what he should do himself, if he is ignorant [of] what his adversary is about?"[2] At the outbreak of the Civil War, however, Union and Confederate military leaders faced serious challenges with regard to intelligence. Both armies lacked formal organizational and operational guidelines, seasoned personnel, and prior experience in these complicated matters. Most Civil War officers learned about the intelligence "business" on the job, relying upon intuition and common sense to meet their information needs. Because of the importance of this command function, how a commander found, interpreted, and utilized intelligence to make decisions, especially given the adverse conditions, offers another perspective from which to view command and leadership during the war. According to two recent intelligence scholars, "by comparing what a given officer believed with his actions one can reconstruct his calculus of military actions and his nature as a commander."[3]

This essay will examine Brig. Gen. Ulysses S. Grant's intelligence operations prior to the Battle of Belmont on November 7, 1861, and assess how military information influenced his decision making during the campaign. Not only was this engagement his debut as a combat commander, but the preceding campaign also served as his introduction to large-scale intelligence operations. Like many of his brother officers, Grant had little experience with information gathering and had even less time to familiarize himself with this vital yet complicated pursuit once the shooting started. Basically, intelligence operations consist of three interrelated stages: collection, analysis, and usage. Establishing collection methods requires a high degree of ability, but collating and analyzing the often contradictory reports, usually under pressure, demands even more expertise, especially since this phase is highly susceptible to the whims of perception, subjectivity, and wishful thinking. After crossing this interpretive minefield, utilizing the resultant assessment as a basis for decisions requires by far the most talent and skill. But proficiency at any one of these stages never guarantees success at another level, even a lower one.[4] By war's end, Grant had become fairly adept at all levels of the process although not always at the same time. But in the fall of 1861 he had yet to devise a campaign or conduct operations based upon the information he collected. Belmont gave him that opportunity.

What makes the study of the Belmont battle from an intelligence perspective even more intriguing is that, according to Grant, two crucial pieces of information propelled him into battle that day. For a multitude of reasons, however, these reports were not the true catalysts. Instead, the mass of information Grant accumulated during the two months preceding the battle helped put him on the road toward Belmont. Thus, a logical starting point for an analysis of Grant's decision is September 1861, when he assumed command of the District of Southeast Missouri headquartered at Cairo, Illinois. Between September and November he assembled a rudimentary intelligence service and collected information on Maj. Gen. Leonidas Polk's forces manning the stout defenses of Columbus, Kentucky (appropriately nicknamed the "Gibraltar of the West"), and on Southern detachments posted directly across the river near the tiny hamlet of Belmont, Missouri. To understand why Grant chose to assail Belmont on November 7 we must proceed down the same path he followed in reaching that conclusion, taking note of the information and perceptions that informed that decision and ultimately propelled him downriver to look for a fight.

The Intelligence Background: September 1–October 31, 1861

On September 1, 1861, Maj. Gen. John C. Frémont, head of the Union's Western Department based in St. Louis, assigned Grant, a brigadier general since August 5, to command the newly formed District of Southeast Missouri, comprising the strategic area bordering neutral Kentucky along the Mississippi River on the east and abutting Confederate Arkansas to the south. All of Missouri south and east of Ironton and southern Illinois fell within the district's boundaries, including major garrisons at Bird's Point and Cape Girardeau in Missouri and at Mound City, Illinois. Moreover, Grant's command guarded eastern Missouri and the mouth of the Ohio River, protected the overland approaches to St. Louis and its railroad connections, and occupied an important strategic position from which to observe events in Kentucky and, if necessary, to confront Confederate forces along the Mississippi should that state's neutrality end. On September 4, Cairo, Illinois, became part of the district, and because of its strategic location at the confluence of the Mississippi and Ohio Rivers, Grant established his headquarters there. The Ohio native's star had risen quickly, and he now oversaw more men (over thirteen thousand) and territory than in any of his previous postings.[5] With great challenges and important decisions looming ahead, perhaps Grant experienced the same anxiety described by another officer who faced the awesome responsibility of command for the first time. "Although I knew I could and would fight with the 'sabre,'" this officer observed, "I feared that I could not fight with the Spy Glass." Only time would tell whether General Grant would wield the sword and the spyglass with equal skill.[6]

The new district commander had barely settled in when a monumental political-military crisis arose in Kentucky. On September 4, the same day that Grant established headquarters at Cairo, Confederate forces under Brig. Gen. Gideon J. Pillow crossed the Mississippi River and marched into Kentucky, thereby trampling the Bluegrass State's avowed neutrality. By nightfall, Pillow had occupied the important river towns of Hickman and Columbus.[7] Two days later, Grant heard from one of Frémont's spies that the Confederates were moving toward Paducah, a town located at the confluence of the Ohio and Tennessee Rivers around twenty miles east of Cairo. In Confederate hands, Paducah would pose a significant threat to Grant's left flank, southern Illinois, and the upper Ohio Valley. With a great deal at stake and figuring that the Confederates had already settled the neutrality issue, Grant hurriedly assembled an expeditionary force, steamed upriver to Paducah, and claimed the town for the Union, all without prior authorization from department headquarters.[8] Thus, within a few days of his elevation to district command, Grant made his first important contribution, denying the enemy a strategically important position while securing what would become the staging point for later advances into the heart of the Confederacy. Moreover, he had also demonstrated a willingness to act "on his own hook" should the need arise.

After leaving sufficient forces to garrison Paducah, Grant returned to Cairo triumphant yet aware that much larger and more difficult tasks lay ahead. Despite his recent success, the Federals were not much closer to their goal of loosening the Confederates' grip on the Mississippi River. The most immediate obstacle was Columbus, Kentucky, a key Southern river fortress and terminus point of the logistically important Mobile & Ohio Railroad. After seizing the town, Polk began transforming Columbus, nestled among high bluffs that overlooked a large stretch of the river and surrounded by rugged and naturally defensible terrain, into a key bastion anchoring the left flank of the Confederate defensive line in the West. Stout fortifications on the heights, appropriately named the Iron Banks, bristled with a vast array of artillery that stood like silent sentinels commanding the river.[9]

On the Missouri bank and in the shadow of the Columbus guns lay Camp Johnston, a small Confederate post situated near Belmont to protect the ferry landing and the line of communication with Kentucky. More importantly, however, this Southern toehold on the western bank offered a convenient portal into southeast Missouri and a staging area for offensive operations against Cairo, Cape Girardeau, or St. Louis. In Confederate hands Columbus and Belmont not only posed a formidable impediment to a Federal advance downriver but also threatened the tenuous Union presence in southeast Missouri, a region already menaced by guerrillas and bushwhackers, pro-Confederate Missouri state troops under Brig. Gen. M. Jeff Thompson, and Maj. Gen. William J. Hardee's troops posted south of the Arkansas border at Pitman's Ferry.[10]

Both Grant and Frémont respected Columbus's defensive strength and its potential to impede Union operations along the Mississippi. Moreover, they also realized that the Belmont camp represented a dangerous breach in their Missouri defenses. Nevertheless, the Confederates reached Columbus first and made clear their intention to stay, prompting Grant to press for an immediate advance before the position became impregnable. Confident that Frémont shared his concerns, the Cairo commander eagerly informed department headquarters of his willingness to organize and lead an expedition against the Confederate position.[11]

Frémont at first concurred with his subordinate's appraisal of the situation and on September 8 presented a plan that called for Union forces to expel the enemy from southeast Missouri and then move to capture Columbus. He proposed dispatching troops from Paducah, now a separate command under Brig. Gen. Charles F. Smith, toward "the rear and flank of Columbus" while Grant drove Thompson and any other Confederate forces out of Missouri. Once this phase was complete, Frémont envisioned a combined assault by Smith and Grant on Columbus. After capturing the Confederate stronghold, the department commander hoped to seize Hickman and eventually move on to Memphis, predicting that the result of his grand offensive "would be a glorious one to the country."[12]

Unfortunately for Frémont, General Sterling Price, who led an army of pro-Confederate Missouri state troops, forced the Pathfinder down a more conservative trail. Price's August 10 victory at Wilson's Creek in southwest Missouri and the subsequent Union withdrawal toward the Missouri River had opened half of the state to invasion. In September Price moved to capitalize on this situation. Wary of the deteriorating situation in the western counties and unwilling to risk a reverse on the Mississippi until he had subdued Price, Frémont quickly shelved his grand offensive indefinitely. On September 10 he ordered Grant to remain on the defensive in Kentucky and limit his activities in Missouri to chasing guerrillas.[13] At least for the present, the advance on Columbus would have to wait.

While awaiting further orders, Grant and his small staff, including his newly arrived adjutant, Captain John A. Rawlins, organized and prepared the Cairo troops for action. Part of the duties at Cairo included the construction of an intelligence apparatus to insure a constant flow of information to headquarters. When Grant assumed command in Cairo on September 4, his predecessor, Colonel Richard J. Oglesby, had already laid the groundwork for an information service, including a stable of civilian informants roaming the countryside south of Cairo and other "secret service" employees.[14] Upon this foundation Grant assembled his own intelligence system with access to both active and passive sources of information.[15] Active sources tapped by Grant included spies operating in Columbus, scouts (civilians employed by the army to gather information) roaming near enemy lines, and, most important of all, reconnaissance patrols. Ideally, scouts and spies were recruited from Unionist ranks in the South because of their familiarity with the "movements, feelings, [and] habits" of the people. "We must use men who have been in rebeldom to do our work effectively," noted one Federal officer.[16] Typically, reconnaissance expeditions, composed primarily of infantry units because of a shortage of cavalry, originated from Grant's outposts closest to enemy territory. For example, patrols from Bird's Point in Missouri, led by such able officers as Oglesby and Colonel W. H. L. Wallace, monitored the no-man's-land in the Charleston-Belmont vicinity and, among other duties, attempted to verify or dispel rumors concerning Confederate troop movements from Columbus. Along the Kentucky shore, patrols sent from the Union outposts at Fort Holt and Fort Jefferson watched for enemy activity in the rugged wilderness north of Columbus.[17]

The land-based reconnaissances received assistance from the Union navy plying the Mississippi above Columbus. The gunboats *Tyler*, *Lexington*, and *Conestoga*, under the overall direction of Captain Andrew Hull Foote, performed many duties for the army.[18] They supported amphibious landings and protected reconnaissance parties on land by distracting the Columbus river batteries. The brown-water navy also reconnoitered above Columbus and Belmont, at times supplying information on the number and types of guns in Columbus and on the size of the military encampments surrounding the city. Foote's gunboats also performed "reconnaissance-by-fire" missions to determine the location of Confederate forces in the deep woods along the river. The explosion of an eight-inch shell in the middle of camp "was not a very pleasant introduction to the Gun Boats," remarked one Confederate whose bivouac the navy discovered in this manner.[19] Besides causing Polk's men on the western bank some anxious moments, the Federal navy played an important role in Grant's intelligence scheme.

Although much less dramatic, Grant also obtained intelligence from passive sources, which included prisoners of war, deserters, civilians, refugees, escaped slaves, intercepted correspondence (both civilian and military), and newspapers. Experience dictated, however, that the information derived from these sources be evaluated with care. Colonel Lew Wallace, stationed at Paducah, provided an enlightening commentary on the dangers associated with relying too heavily upon these sources. "Now I may be listening to a story of the advance of the enemy," he complained, "an hour hence I shall be as reliably told that Columbus is evacuated and the Confederates gone to New Orleans." "The truth is," he continued, "those who tell us know nothing; those who do know will not tell."[20] On the other hand, civilians, refugees, and runaway slaves could provide accurate appraisals of recent enemy activity in the area, furnish information on the location and condition of roads, and report on the nature of the terrain. Prisoners of war and enemy deserters, if questioned properly, could also supply insights into the enemy's order of battle, an important facet of combat intelligence. Additionally, since the practice of exchanging prisoners of war remained in vogue, returning Union prisoners sometimes furnished news and observations from behind Confederate lines. At Cairo, however, Grant was not yet in the habit of questioning everyone—regardless of age, gender, or race—who entered Union lines from enemy territory.[21]

Over the next two months Grant relied heavily upon his emerging intelligence system to keep abreast of Confederate activities on three different fronts. First, through reconnaissances and scouts he watched for troop movements between Columbus and Belmont that might presage a Confederate invasion of southeast Missouri. Second, his scouts and spies monitored military activity in Columbus, noting any threatening movements toward Paducah. Deserters from Polk's army also provided insights on these matters. Third, his operatives kept a close eye on Thompson's forces in southeast Missouri and on Hardee's troops stationed south of the Missouri-Arkansas border. Aside from Polk in Columbus, Thompson and Hardee were the only immediate threats in Grant's district. With an efficient intelligence system, Grant wanted to prevent the Confederates from surprising him, particularly from Belmont, but also hoped to uncover an opportunity to strike Columbus.

On September 10, Grant's embryonic information service faced its first test when a gunboat commander reported that transports laden with Southern troops had crossed to Belmont and estimated that at least three thousand troops, mostly cavalry, now occupied Camp Johnston.[22] Although concerned, Grant doubted that Polk would embark on an offensive in Missouri so soon after invading Kentucky. "My impression is that they want time to prepare for defense," he reasoned. Even if the Confederates advanced, he believed the most likely target would be Paducah since that position, in Union hands, posed the most substantial threat to Columbus and to Confederate control of western Kentucky. Moreover, many Southerners believed that the recent invasion of Kentucky remained incomplete until the Confederacy's sphere of influence reached to Paducah and the Ohio River. After determining that neither Cairo nor Paducah were in danger at that moment, however, Grant advocated taking the initiative instead of waiting on Polk to make up his mind. "If it was discretionary with me," he told Frémont, "I would take Columbus."[23]

Later that day a Union spy spirited out of Columbus a copy of Polk's General Order 19, dated September 7. This important document confirmed Grant's assessment that Polk was too preoccupied with regrouping, organizing, supplying, and resting his command to execute a major offensive. As Grant knew well from his experiences with recently acquired Paducah, transitioning from invasion to occupation was no easy task, and Polk, attempting to defend both Columbus and Hickman, had his hands full. Grant also divined from this document that the Southern commander had recalled the troops he had posted toward Paducah.[24] To Grant, the Confederates in Columbus, overwhelmed with preparations to receive an attack, had little time or energy to initiate one. This interpretation became a common and dominant thread woven throughout Grant's later assessments of enemy movements and intentions.

The knowledge that Polk and Pillow were the principal officers in Columbus also contributed to Grant's pacific picture of the enemy. Polk's military reputation had suffered as a result of his hasty and, to many, ill-conceived invasion of Kentucky that placed the onus of violating that state's neutrality squarely on the South. Some complained of his failure to capture Paducah and cement Confederate control of western Kentucky. Characterized as a "vain cadet," the Episcopal bishop had few admirers in blue or gray, with the notable exception of his most powerful supporter, Jefferson Davis.[25] His lackluster subordinate, Gideon Pillow, aroused even more visceral reactions from those who knew him. Like many officers familiar with Pillow's background, Grant openly despised the haughty Tennessean. His incompetence in military affairs, revealed during the Mexican War when he placed a ditch on the wrong side of his fortifications, earned him the derision of West Pointers, while his unwarranted arrogance merited the contempt of most everyone else. One officer claimed that Pillow was "as consum[m]ate an ass, as any army, modern or ancient, has ever been inflicted with." When he heard that Pillow had earned a command in southeast Missouri early in the war, Grant predicted he "would not be a formidable enemy." This rather unflattering view of his opponents would have an impact on Grant's future behavior. "Knowing Polk's caution and believing Pillow to be a fool," argued one historian, led Grant to take risks he might not have if faced with a more competent adversary.[26]

Despite Grant's negative opinion of Polk and Pillow and his growing conviction that they presently pursued a defensive strategy, September 11 brought news that contradicted this image. A Confederate deserter stated that five thousand troops had crossed to Belmont recently and that some officers in Columbus talked about attacking Bird's Point and Cairo soon. In response, Grant dispatched infantry patrols and a gunboat toward Belmont for verification. Colonel Oglesby, in charge of the column sent from Norfolk, returned on September 16 and reported that the size of the Camp Johnston garrison, around three thousand men, remained unchanged. More importantly, he neither heard of nor observed any activity in the camp that foretold of a major advance.[27]

In fact, Grant believed so fervently that his adversary thought only in terms of defense that before these reconnaissance patrols could even report his thoughts had already turned toward plans for a Union offensive. On September 12, Grant offered headquarters a two-pronged plan aimed at clearing the Confederates out of Missouri and ultimately turning Columbus. First, he proposed that Smith's Paducah forces turn the Confederate left flank by attacking Union City, Tennessee, a key supply depot twenty miles south of Columbus, and sever Polk's communications. Second, Grant planned for another flanking force on the Missouri shore, presumably under his command, to march on Belmont under the protection of the gunboats. With their supply lines cut and threatened on both flanks, Grant believed Polk "would be forced to leave Columbus."[28] Although reminiscent of his own earlier plan to capture the Confederate stronghold, Frémont did not comment on his subordinate's proposition.

After hearing more news of Confederate activity on September 15, Grant's attention shifted from grand offensive schemes to defending his command. Recent rumors claimed that Polk had evacuated Columbus, but from the sketchy information Grant had no idea whether the Southern forces were "marching upon Paducah or leaving Kentucky altogether."[29] Although doubtful that his adversary had any offensive inclinations, Grant needed the services of his scouts and spies now more than ever. Unfortunately, he faced a crisis on that front. Earlier in the month, Grant had requested more money for secret service operations and had also asked permission to maintain and control his own secret service budget. However, department headquarters issued no reply. When the latest rumors surfaced on September 15, Grant again contacted St. Louis, this time using the seriousness of the present crisis as a pretext. "It is highly necessary to get information which cannot be obtained from our own reconnoitering parties," he complained, "[but] without money to pay, the services of citizens cannot much longer be obtained." He feared that, without proper compensation for the risks they incurred, particularly those who resided behind enemy lines, his sources would likely return home in silence. Frémont finally granted his request, but three days—and the crisis—had passed before Grant received the needed funds for intelligence operations.[30]

Despite his monetary troubles, Grant searched diligently for any information that might shed light on the supposed evacuation of the Columbus garrison and its possible destination. Finally, he learned from both a deserter and from one of his spies, known only as "Mr. L.," that on September 14 ten thousand troops under General Albert Sidney Johnston, the new commander of the Confederacy's Department No. 2, had left Columbus, now headquarters of the "First Division" commanded by Polk, and marched toward Mayfield, Kentucky. According to both sources, his ultimate objective was the capture of Paducah.[31] Combined with the unconfirmed reports of the evacuation of Columbus, Grant should have been duly alarmed at these ominous developments. Initially, however, he remained suspicious of the news brought by the agent and deserter, stating that "I do not think this movement [on Paducah] has been made."[32] Nevertheless, Grant remained cautious, and over the next several days both he and Smith accelerated defensive preparations. On September 20 Grant's intelligence finally brought welcome news that the Confederates at Mayfield had returned to Columbus. Although this crisis had seemingly passed, more trouble loomed ahead.[33]

In reality, Southern forces had indeed occupied Mayfield just as Grant's sources had claimed but in nowhere near the strength reported. The force depicted as an army led by Johnston was actually only two regiments under Brig. Gen. Benjamin F. Cheatham on a defensive mission to secure Polk's right flank. Similarly, what Grant saw as the termination of the "offensive" against Paducah was in reality the retreat of Cheatham's column toward Columbus, a move prompted by the lack of fresh water and supplies in Mayfield.[34] The supposed large-scale offensive push reported by Grant's intelligence had never entered Polk's thoughts. In fact, at that moment the bishop general feared that Union forces in Paducah were poised to attack him, not the reverse, which led to Cheatham's foray to Mayfield. The Confederate withdrawal only strengthened Grant's perception that the enemy remained in a defensive mode.[35]

Before long, however, another challenge to that belief emerged. On September 23 a spy in Columbus warned that Polk had dispatched more troops to Belmont, prompting Grant once again to send the reliable Colonel Oglesby with a patrol toward the Confederate camp.[36] But the patrol found that now only twenty-five hundred of Thompson's guardsmen occupied Belmont, meaning that no infusion of troops from Columbus had occurred. In addition, Oglesby downplayed the threat posed by these current occupants of Camp Johnston, observing that Thompson's bivouac appeared quiet with no sign of any preparations commensurate with a pending offensive. The results of the reconnaissance once again confirmed Grant's suspicions that the enemy remained "confined to their encampments at Columbus and Belmont."[37]

Despite the district commander's assessment and the confidence he placed in Oglesby's judgment, the latest rumor of Confederate forces crossing into Missouri had caused great trepidation in St. Louis, especially in light of events in western Missouri. In late September, Sterling Price's state troops had ventured as far north as the Missouri River and had captured the Union garrison at Lexington, a loss that reverberated throughout the Western Department.[38] With the fate of his command as well as that of the Union cause in Missouri at stake, John C. Frémont was undoubtedly the most apprehensive of all. In response to the crisis, he left for western Missouri on September 24 to direct operations against Price personally, leaving his adjutant, Captain Chauncey McKeever, in charge of departmental affairs in St. Louis.[39] Fearful that recent events might encourage Polk either to reinforce Price or to attempt to expel Union forces from southeastern Missouri or Paducah, Frémont directed Grant and Smith to remain on the defensive and work together to "control" any Confederate incursions against their positions. Although he gave them some latitude to attack if the chance arose, Frémont was quick to clarify that "at present I am not in favor of incurring any hazard of defeat." Suspending all offensive operations along the Mississippi River, the Pathfinder embarked on a mission to salvage western Missouri and his own increasingly battered reputation.[40]

At the time, Grant concurred with his superior's decision to delay an assault on Columbus but for different reasons. While the department commander feared a simultaneous advance against Cairo and Paducah in support of Price's operations, or vice versa, Grant believed that Polk favored strengthening, not abandoning, his works, thereby surrendering the initiative to the Federals. But Grant faced acute manpower and supply shortages that delayed an advance on the stronghold. He possessed sufficient forces to defend Cairo, he complained, but not enough for "an aggressive movement against the large force now occupying Columbus." Moreover, the possibility that Frémont might appoint a more senior officer to lead the campaign in the interim also weighed heavy on Grant's mind and only added to his anxiety and restlessness. Grant summed up his frustration in a letter to his wife. "All is quiet here now," he remarked, but just "how long it will remain so is impossible to tell." One thing was certain, he added, "If I had troops enough[,] not long."[41]

The prospects for an advance in the near future, however, depended upon Frémont's success against Price. Until these two forces had locked horns in southwestern Missouri, Columbus would have to wait. Frustrated by the inertia gripping the District of Southeast Missouri, Grant fixed his gaze upon Columbus, confident that only the want of men and supplies and Frémont's obsession with Price prevented him from reducing the "Gibraltar of the West" to rubble.[42]

Even though Frémont's priorities had shifted westward, the possibility that Polk might reinforce Price kept the department commander glancing nervously toward Columbus. Before long he saw something that concerned him, and on September 28 he sent Grant an urgent warning that, based upon his sources, the Confederates had evacuated Columbus, crossed to Belmont, and planned to assail Ironton or Cape Girardeau. More in touch with the true situation, however, the Cairo commander replied confidently that, on the contrary, "Evrything [sic] here is quiet [with] no rumors to disturb it." A few days later he completely dismissed Frémont's report as idle gossip. "There is no enemy on the Missouri side of the river . . . except Jeff Thompsons force at Belmont." As for this latter contingent, Grant believed that even a small Union force could "easily drive them from [the] vicinity."[43]

The district commander had barely quashed this latest rumor when news about increased Confederate activity in Kentucky grabbed his attention. On September 30 a wounded Confederate prisoner let slip that a large column under Pillow had departed Columbus for Paducah. Lacking any contradictory evidence, Grant remained somewhat cautious and traveled up the Ohio River to assist Smith with defensive preparations. Once again, the Confederate attack failed to materialize. However, when Grant returned to Cairo he received a report of Southern troops crossing to Belmont intent upon capturing Cape Girardeau. But Grant's operatives and Smith's scouts soon unearthed no corroborative evidence showing any Confederate movements toward either Paducah or Belmont. Once again, Grant's intelligence had reaffirmed his belief that Polk remained on the defensive. As a result, on October 4 he wrote that the enemy had "no concerted plan to attack [Cairo], Cape Girardeau or Paducah."[44]

Despite Grant's recent assurances, the tide of rumors refused to ebb. On October 6, he again received news from department headquarters that Johnston was at Belmont with a large force preparing to attack Cape Girardeau. Unfortunately, Grant confessed that this latest report baffled him. He had received no "reliable" intelligence for the past two days that shed light on this alleged movement, primarily because the gunboats were all out of service, his scouts had returned empty-handed, and one of his spies, from whom he expected a "full & accurate report," had yet to return. "I always try to keep myself posted as to [the enemy's] movements but I am at a loss for the last few days," he complained.[45] Facing a critical information shortage, Grant dispatched an infantry patrol toward Belmont and sent Johnston Brown, a trusted Union scout, to "ascertain the position . . . of the enemy." But until more evidence arrived, Grant held to his original view that "the enemy have no present intention of moving on Cape Girardeau" and that if the Confederates planned to attack anywhere (which he doubted), Paducah would likely top their list.[46]

The next day Grant finally received reliable intelligence that supported his basic assessment, although it also contained indications of a possible advance against Paducah. The intelligence originated with Smith who reported that a priest, whose flock included officers and men in Columbus, had learned that Polk planned to attack Paducah in the next few days. But when he relayed this information to Grant, Smith appeared reluctant to place much credence in it, stating that he forwarded the report "for what it is worth," a common phrase used to express doubt about the reliability of a report. In fact, Smith was not alone in his skepticism. Some of his subordinates also played down the possibility of an attack on Paducah. Colonel Lew Wallace may have summed up the prevalent feeling among the Paducah garrison at the time. "While we don't remit our vigilance," he observed, "we are not greatly concerned."[47] Although certainly not ignoring the possibility of a Confederate advance to the Ohio River, Grant held fast to his original assessment, proclaiming that the Southerners were still "fortifying strongly and preparing to resist a formidable attack and have but little idea of risking anything upon a forward movement."[48]

In the meantime, Grant also monitored the movements of Thompson and Hardee. Throughout September Grant had watched Thompson, not a difficult task considering his force of around twenty-six hundred men had not, for the most part, ventured far from Belmont. But on October 1, Thompson's brigade departed for New Madrid to resupply and prepare for an advance on Cape Girardeau.[49] Jeff Thompson had earned a ghostlike reputation in the region, especially among the footsore Union infantrymen sent after him who, more often than not, came away empty-handed. After just such a mission, one tired soldier complained that "there seems to be nothing reliable about any of the reports we have of him." Unfortunately for Thompson, this time he fooled no one. The same day he departed Belmont, a deserter told Grant of the move, and subsequent information, gleaned from prisoners and civilians in the area, corroborated the story.[50]

Unaware that Grant was on his trail, Thompson departed New Madrid for Cape Girardeau, reaching Sikeston on October 4. Although only thirty miles shy of his objective, Thompson canceled the assault because of inadequate manpower and headed west toward the safety of the swamps. Grant learned of the Confederates' arrival in the Sikeston area and then confirmed their hasty retreat to the west. As a result of Thompson's precipitate withdrawal, the Cairo commander concluded once and for all that "there is [now] no force . . . threatening Cape Girardeau."[51]

Finding retreat distasteful, however, Thompson attempted to salvage something from his aborted mission and turned north toward Fredericktown, sending his infantry toward that town while he led his cavalry on a bridge-burning expedition. After skirmishing with Union forces on October 17, Thompson, with his infantry and cavalry back together, occupied Fredericktown, about twenty-five miles east of Ironton. But with fewer than two thousand men and new recruits scarce, he proposed to hold the town only "until the enemy discovers my weakness."[52] However, Grant knew all along that Thompson's depleted brigade numbered less than three thousand men and, armed with this information, ordered Colonel Joseph Plummer and forty-five hundred men to find and destroy the Swamp Fox. Taking his task seriously, Plummer's men routed Thompson's forces on October 21 and sent them retreating southward toward Greenville and Bloomfield. Claiming that Plummer's Fredericktown victory had "crushed out the Rebellion in South East Missouri," from late October on Grant saw Thompson as little more than a minor nuisance.[53]

During September and October Grant also observed Hardee's activities in northeast Arkansas. Busy recruiting, training, and supplying his brigade, Hardee had not ventured far from Pitman's Ferry since late August. That changed on September 17, after Polk, fearing a Union attack from Paducah and searching for reinforcements, requested Hardee's presence in Columbus. After several delays, "Old Reliable" Hardee and his four-thousand-man brigade finally trudged out of their camps, crossed the Mississippi, and on October 6 reached Columbus. Unfortunately for Polk,

Johnston had decided that central Kentucky needed Hardee's troops more than Columbus and ordered the brigade to join Brig. Gen. Simon Bolivar Buckner's army at Bowling Green. With little rest in between, Hardee's footsore column finally reached central Kentucky around October 13.[54]

Grant first learned of Hardee's departure from Pitman's Ferry on September 28, although initially he seemed skeptical of the report, probably doubting that the Confederates would leave northern Arkansas so exposed.[55] However, on October 16 Brig. Gen. William T. Sherman, the Union commander facing Buckner in central Kentucky, confirmed that Hardee had reached Bowling Green. Two days later, a "secret agent" corroborated this news. Although Hardee's transfer relieved pressure on Grant, it caused new headaches for his fellow Ohioan. Sherman already believed that Buckner possessed superior numbers and intended to attack Louisville; the news of Hardee's arrival further convinced him of impending disaster. From his perspective, the Confederate legions gathering to the south appeared formidable, although Buckner's forces, even with the addition of Hardee, numbered far fewer than the Union commander believed. Moreover, the Confederates, just as fearful of Sherman as he was of them, entertained few thoughts of an advance on Louisville. Nevertheless, Sherman's paranoia was at fever pitch and, feeling cut off and doomed, he implored Grant to rattle the gates of Columbus and relieve the pressure on central Kentucky.[56]

The Cairo commander offered to cooperate with Smith in an effort to aid Sherman, even though his forces were already dangerously dispersed, his manpower resources low, and his men ill armed. "If you have any plan to propose I am ready to cooperate to the extent of my limited means," Grant informed the Paducah commander, adding that he could provide up to five thousand troops for the campaign. As usual, however, department headquarters refused to endorse the proposal.[57] But, by this time, Grant had already forfeited nearly all hope of leading an advance on Columbus anytime soon, bemoaning that "the fates seem to be against any such thing." In his own defense, however, he offered the weakened condition of his command as the primary reason "for my not being in Columbus to-day instead of where I am." Excuses aside, with Hardee gone, Thompson on the ropes, and Polk idle, Grant's desire to seize the initiative still burned. "What I want," he proclaimed, "is to advance."[58]

In spite of the dismal outlook for a Union advance down the Mississippi, after learning on October 25 that Johnston had gone east to inspect the defenses at Cumberland Gap Grant's offensive zeal flared again. Combined with intelligence showing that only ten to fifteen thousand troops remained in Columbus, Grant discerned an emerging pattern in Confederate behavior, specifically, the tendency to weaken the left flank on the Mississippi to shore up the center and the right at Bowling Green and Cumberland Gap.[59] Convinced now more than ever that the Confederates in Columbus had neither the will nor the manpower for an offensive campaign, Grant once again lobbied headquarters for permission to advance. "Such [drafts] have been made upon the force at Columbus for the Green River country [central Kentucky] and possibly other parts of Kentucky," Grant told Frémont, "that if Genl Smith and my command were prepared [Columbus] might now be taken." Although Grant then promptly retreated from his proposal, citing inadequate supplies, arms, and transportation as the chief impediments to success, he had put Frémont on notice that an opportunity was at hand, and only headquarters could provide the logistical support required to capitalize on it. Had Frémont authorized an advance that day, the Cairo commander would undoubtedly have overlooked these complaints and forged ahead. But this request, like those before it, elicited no response from Western Department headquarters.[60]

By the end of October, a certain view of the military situation in southeast Missouri and Kentucky had taken shape in Grant's mind. First, Grant believed that Thompson represented only a minimal threat after his thrashing at Fredericktown and that the Swamp Fox had put considerable distance between himself and Union forces in the region. The Cairo commander also knew that Hardee's forces had been transferred from northern Arkansas to central Kentucky. Only Belmont and New Madrid remained as symbols of Confederate authority in southeast Missouri.

As for western Kentucky, Grant's assessment centered on his fundamental belief that Columbus had suffered serious manpower losses to Buckner's command that, in turn, had sapped what little enthusiasm the Bishop General had for any offensive ventures. In essence, the ever-cautious Polk waited for the Federals to dash themselves against the rocks of his Gibraltar and spent his time and resources preparing for that event. The first evidence that Grant leaned toward this perception had come on September 9 when he interpreted Polk's General Order 19 as a defensive manifesto. Whether prescience or wishful thinking on Grant's part, the resulting picture of a defensive-minded foe persisted and became a common denominator in later intelligence analyses. Thus, the more Grant assumed that Polk had eschewed the offensive option, the more this judgment shaped his ongoing assessment of the overall situation. Using an earlier example, when he learned on October 6 of the supposed Confederate advance on Paducah, Grant held firm to his impression that the enemy had no such designs. Despite having information that contradicted this view, he maintained that "my beleif [sic] is that the attack will not be made for the present," an opinion based on little more than his own intuition.[61] When he heard on another occasion that Johnston had occupied Belmont with a large force, he again deferred to this perception, despite possessing "no reliable intelligence" to support it.[62] Napoleon once commented that "in war everything is perception" but warned against "making pictures," or fixating upon a certain view of the enemy. In this case, however, Grant's perception of the enemy's intentions, originating in September and buttressed by the bulk of his intelligence, proved correct. By early November, detaching troops from Columbus had become anathema to Polk, who warned of "the serious consequences" resulting from such a policy. More importantly, the Bishop General was thinking only in terms of defense, just as Grant had predicted. Until Frémont authorized an attack on Columbus, however, Grant's optimistic assessments mattered little.[63]

The Battle of Belmont

On November 1 Frémont surprised the Cairo commander with orders to make demonstrations toward Charleston and Norfolk, Missouri, and Blandville, Kentucky, although the instructions were silent on the purpose behind the operation. Urging him to keep in constant motion before these towns, Frémont wanted Grant to occupy the enemy's attention but specifically forbade him from attacking any point. In conjunction with these demonstrations, Smith received instructions to move columns toward Columbus in a menacing fashion but was also prohibited from seriously engaging the enemy "without special orders." Unlike Grant's directive, however, Smith's orders explained the rationale behind the saber rattling on both sides of the river. Reflecting Frémont's fixation on western Missouri, the combined movement was designed to "occupy the enemy in the Mississippi Valley" in case Polk attempted to reinforce Price.[64]

The next day, however, Grant gained another task on top of the demonstration. Thompson had supposedly resurfaced near the St. Francis River, sixty-two miles southwest of Cairo, and Frémont instructed the Cairo commander to drive him into Arkansas. Even though Grant viewed the Swamp Fox, still stinging from the beating he took on October 21, as a minor threat, he nevertheless dispatched Oglesby with four thousand men and Plummer with another three thousand in pursuit. Instead of merely pushing these forces out of the state, as Frémont's orders directed, he instructed Oglesby to locate and "destroy" Thompson's command.[65] With these columns underway, Grant returned to his preparations for the upcoming demonstration.

On November 5, however, Grant indicated that he had more in mind than a mere demonstration. On that day he informed Smith of his intention to "menace Belmont," a position well south of the objectives stipulated in Frémont's November 1 directive. The next evening two Union brigades, nearly three thousand men, boarded transports at Cairo, steamed downriver, dropped anchor along the Kentucky shore a few miles above Columbus, and under the watchful eyes of the gunboats waited silently for the dawn.[66]

Early on November 7, Grant's men disembarked three miles above Belmont and began their march toward the Confederate camp. Occupied by one infantry regiment, a battalion of cavalry, and an artillery battery and commanded by Colonel James C. Tappan, Camp Johnston came alive at the news of the Federals' approach. When word of the attack reached Polk's headquarters, however, the Confederate commander convinced himself that the ruckus on the opposite shore was merely a diversion masking an assault upon Columbus. Until he determined otherwise, Polk decided to keep his troops concentrated on the Kentucky side. He did send four of Pillow's Tennessee regiments, about twenty-five hundred men, across to support Tappan. These troops had received the order to reinforce Camp Johnston just as they were departing Columbus for Clarksville, Tennessee. In a move to strengthen the defenses further east, Johnston had ordered Pillow's entire division (five thousand men) to northern Tennessee, causing a further drain on the ranks in Columbus. The gunfire across the river interrupted their journey, and four regiments disembarked to meet the Unionists. The newly reinforced Belmont garrison, now totaling around three thousand men under Pillow's direct command, formed in time to meet the initial Federal assault at mid-morning.[67]

After savage fighting between equally green volunteer armies, the Federals flanked the Southerners, forced them back through Camp Johnston, and threatened to drive them into the river. With victory in their grasp and exhilarated by their first combat, many of the pursuing Union soldiers ignored their officers' pleas and commenced looting the Southern encampment. In the interim, Pillow's men huddled along the river bank or fled up-river. Meanwhile, Smith's demonstration against Columbus had fallen far short of Grant's expectations. The Federals prowling in the vicinity sty-mied Polk for awhile, but when they failed to close on Columbus he deter-mined that Smith's forces had aborted their attack on the fortress city and finally dispatched reinforcements to Pillow's beleaguered command. Once on the west bank, the fresh troops under General Frank Cheatham chased the Federals back to their transports waiting upriver. As the Federals cut their way out, Grant himself barely escaped capture. Under fire from the shoreline, the transports managed to slip away from shore and return to Cairo. The retreat from Belmont resulted in the withdrawal of all Federal columns operating in southeast Missouri and western Kentucky and ended the first major Union action in the region since the capture of Paducah.[68]

Grant Justifies His Attack

After the battle Grant crowed about his "complete" victory and claimed that he had "accomplished all that we went for, and even more," somehow forgetting about his panic-stricken retreat, which had left the enemy in possession of the field. His triumphant rhetoric failed to quell a storm of criticism that met him the moment he stepped off the *Belle Memphis* in Cairo. "We have met the enemy and they are not ours," trumpeted one newspaper correspondent, echoing the sentiments of many in the North. Others berated the general for fighting a battle that had "cost many good lives and resulted in very little, or nothing." A soldier in Oglesby's com-mand spoke for many when he stated simply that "Grant got whipped at Belmont."[69]

Over time, historians joined this debate and raised serious questions concerning Grant's actions that day. Ranging from commendatory to con-demnatory, scholars have attempted to unravel the mysteries of Belmont and extract something meaningful from the sacrifice. While one author viewed the battle as a "folly" defying military logic because "it was so ludi-crous and its outcome so disastrous," another declared that Belmont illus-trated "a few of the qualities which carried Grant to eventual victory" (i.e., initiative, aggressiveness, determination) and established him as a fighting general. One historian claimed that Grant's day at Belmont "was rounded out in such a way that gives it a good place in military history." The author of the only monographic treatment of the battle asserted that Grant learned valuable lessons about command and leadership that day, noting that "he had done well; he would do better."[70]

At some point in their treatises these historians grappled with Grant's after-action reports containing the justifications and objectives behind the attack. On November 10 Grant sent Frémont the first brief account of the battle. Overall, he claimed that he attacked Belmont for two basic reasons. First, he wanted to prevent Polk from sending troops into Missouri to reinforce Price's army in the southwest. Second, he hoped to intercept an enemy force supposedly sent from Columbus to strike the columns under Oglesby and Plummer hunting Thompson west of Belmont.[71] For some unknown reason, however, Grant deemed this report unsatisfactory and later submitted a more detailed sketch, complete with official correspondence and certain insights absent from the original summary. The revised report, dated November 17, 1861, supplanted the earlier version and became the general's official rendition of the campaign. Consistent with the first report, he again stressed that preventing troops in Columbus from reinforcing Price and protecting his columns were the key motivations behind the attack. But unlike his earlier report, this time he explained how he arrived at these objectives and, ultimately, why he attacked Belmont.[72]

Regarding the reinforcements heading for Price, a movement that in reality never occurred, Grant stated that he first learned of it from a November 5 telegram from Frémont, which he also claimed authorized him to proceed with the demonstration ordered on November 1. But Grant failed to provide a verbatim copy of this telegram, an unusual oversight considering its importance to his case. Not only has the telegram itself failed to materialize, neither Grant's headquarters correspondence nor Frémont's letterbooks contain any record of it. The absence of this key document and the lack of corroborating testimony affirming that Frémont's staff even sent the message or that Grant received it leaves little doubt that the telegram never existed. On the other hand, even if the mysterious telegram had reached Grant, it is doubtful that he would have accepted it without question given his strong belief that Polk had neither the desire nor the manpower to support Price's operations.

In addition, Grant's prebattle correspondence, particularly that in which he discussed his plans, contains no mention of this movement or that interrupting the western flow of reinforcements was a main reason for his attack. Not until the day after the battle—and in his second telegram to Frémont—did Grant refer to Price or to any efforts to reinforce him. In this dispatch, Grant provided an estimate of Federal casualties and the number of Confederate prisoners in his possession. He then told of how both he and McClernand had lost their horses to enemy fire. After this piece of trivia Grant noted, as an afterthought, that "prisoners taken report that a large force [was] prepared to . . . join Price." The attack on Belmont, he claimed, "will no doubt defeat this move." Curiously, Grant did not seem to be in any hurry to relay this news to Frémont who, given his fixation upon Price's army and the thrust of his alleged November 5 directive, would have wanted to know immediately about this ominous development. More importantly, however, nowhere in his correspondence—either before or immediately after the battle—did Grant indicate that the prevention of this supposed movement had been the primary motivation behind his actions all along.[73]

By nightfall of November 8, however, this postbattle discovery had somehow become a preengagement objective in Grant's account. In a letter to his father he stated for the first time that a primary goal behind the Belmont expedition was to prevent reinforcements from joining Price but made no mention of any orders directing him to do so.[74] But even though Grant had apparently stumbled upon this information after the battle, the news that he had indeed thwarted Price's reinforcement gave his attack, so far devoid of any other tangible results, a much nobler purpose as well as the appearance of success. From then on, Grant let his post-Belmont revelation stand as an essential element in his decision to assail the outpost.

The origin of Grant's second stated objective, the protection of Oglesby's and Plummer's columns sent in pursuit of Thompson, appears dubious as well. On November 6 troops from Cairo boarded the transports and steamed downriver, stopping for the night along the Kentucky shore. According to Grant, at 2:00 AM the next morning a messenger from Colonel W. H. L. Wallace arrived in the general's cabin aboard the *Belle Memphis* and relayed news from a "reliable Union man" in Charleston that Confederate troops had crossed to Belmont recently to hunt down the Union columns chasing Thompson. "This move," wrote Grant in his official report, "seemed to me more than probable" and ultimately drove him "to attack vigorously at Belmont."[75] Unfortunately, like the November 5 telegram, no other corroborative evidence has surfaced to verify the contents of the 2:00 AM message or prove its existence.

Wallace's role as the purveyor of the information also casts doubt upon the validity of the Cairo commander's story on this point. Although Wallace and his troops were in Charleston that night, en route to join Oglesby's column, his post-Belmont correspondence discredits his superior's version of his involvement in sending the message. On November 14 Wallace blasted Grant for engaging in such a foolish and costly engagement and rendered perhaps the most stinging indictment of his conduct. He maintained that Grant "had not the courage to refuse to fight" even though the "advantages were all against him & any permanent or substantial good [was] an utter impossibility." "True [Belmont] demonstrated the courage and fighting qualities of our men," he continued, "but it cost too much." These statements appear odd coming from the officer who supposedly provided the information that initiated the very attack he now condemned. Moreover, Wallace gave no indication that he knew of the alleged Confederate move to Belmont or that he had transmitted this important news to his superior that night. In fact, had he known that Confederate troops were moving west from Belmont, he neglected to impart this news even to Oglesby, the one officer who truly needed to know. Nevertheless, even if Wallace had supplied the information, the news would have had little impact. Grant had already determined to attack Belmont before the transports departed Cairo.[76]

Finally, the fact that the November 5 telegram and the 2:00 AM intelligence report first appeared in Grant's official report, which was not composed until May 1864 and backdated to correspond with the battle, also makes them suspect. Written primarily by Rawlins and Lt. Col. Theodore S. Bowers, these staff officers relied upon memory and an assortment of documents to reconstruct what had transpired nearly three years earlier, thereby subjecting the report to the whims of clouded recollections, the absence of key actors (W. H. L. Wallace died in April 1862), and interpretations tainted by hindsight. Judging from the harsh treatment Grant received for Belmont, the report was possibly an attempt by Grant's staff to settle the controversy and deflect any further criticism from their boss, now head of all Union armies, by offering a more detailed explanation. Unfortunately, in their attempt to set the record straight, his subordinates only confused the issue more by offering unsubstantiated evidence to demonstrate that their commander had exhibited wisdom and prudence, not insubordination. Perhaps Grant scholar John Y. Simon offered the best advice on how to deal with the November 5 telegram and the 2:00 AM intelligence report, as well as the justifications that supposedly emerged from them. "Recognizing their questionable origins," he cautioned, "we can better understand the battle by ignoring both."[77]

Following that advice remains unsatisfying, however, unless another explanation for Grant's decision can be found. Put another way, if Grant's postbattle rationale for assaulting Belmont is discarded, why did he risk lives and his career on a venture that had no perceivable purpose? Surely his desire to "bloody" his men cannot by itself account for his decision. Why, then, did U. S. Grant fight at Belmont? Professor Simon once again offers wise counsel: "The answer must be found in [Grant] himself, and no simple answer will do."[78]

Why Did Grant Fight at Belmont?

Factoring Grant's prebattle perceptions into his decision-making calculus produces a compelling alternative to the general's explanation for the attack. As examined earlier, his interpretation of Confederate intentions, based upon a mixture of intelligence, assumptions, and intuition, had remained fundamentally unchanged since September. Combined with other factors, this mental image probably influenced Grant's final decision and propelled him toward Belmont. On November 5 the Cairo commander outlined his plans for the upcoming operation and, in the process, revealed that he intended to do more than merely amuse the Columbus garrison with a pointless demonstration. Unaware that Smith was already under orders to demonstrate against Columbus, Grant asked the Paducah commander to support his operations in Missouri by sending a reconnaissance-in-force toward the Confederate stronghold. Grant hoped Smith's move would divert Polk's attention and prevent him from "throwing over the river much more force than they now have" at Belmont, thereby allowing the troops from Cairo time "to drive those [forces] they now have [there] out of Missouri." To accomplish this part of the plan, Grant was assembling an expeditionary force to "menace Belmont." Saying nothing about reinforcements heading for Price but recognizing the vulnerability of the contingent pursuing Thompson, Grant informed Smith that the primary objective of this dual movement was to "to prevent the enemy from sending a force to fall in the rear of those now out from this command."[79]

The next day, however, Grant had changed his mind. Instead of protecting Oglesby and Plummer, he moved toward diverting these troops for use in his operations against Belmont. Later that day, he went even further. The latest intelligence showing a depletion of the Columbus garrison by transfers to central Kentucky combined with two months of false alarms had vindicated Grant's long-held view that Polk had neither the forces nor the desire to venture into Missouri. Seeing an opportunity to seize the initiative along the Mississippi, Grant ordered W. H. L. Wallace to intercept Oglesby and instruct him to break off his pursuit of Thompson (Plummer would continue the chase) and turn southeast toward Confederate-held New Madrid, roughly twenty-five miles southwest of Belmont. His instructions suggest that he expected the combined Oglesby-Wallace column to be in the field for several days, perhaps anticipating extended operations beyond the Belmont engagement.[80] Once underway toward New Madrid, Grant told Oglesby to contact him at Belmont, indicating that he intended to be in control of the town by that time.

Thus, instead of mindlessly chasing Thompson, whom he saw as a minor threat anyway, or exhausting his men marching about the countryside in harmless demonstrations, Grant saw an opportunity to drive the enemy from southeast Missouri, which both he and Frémont believed was a necessary prelude to a campaign against Columbus. When Oglesby, after receiving his new orders from Wallace, boasted that his command "could march to Memphis," he undoubtedly understood that Grant had in mind more than mere saber rattling.[81] Restless from months of inactivity and perhaps fearing that another chance might not come along, Grant forged ahead, believing the results would justify the risks. Charles W. Wills, a soldier in Oglesby's brigade, came close to deciphering Grant's intentions: "I think the Paducah forces were to take Columbus, Grant was going to swallow Belmont, we were to drive all the guerrillas before us to New Madrid, and then with Paducah forces and Grant's we were to take Madrid and probably go to Memphis or maybe join Frémont."[82] Grant's drive to seize or to make opportunities and, as one historian noted, his willingness to "try conclusions" would become hallmarks of his generalship.[83]

Grant's attack on Belmont, therefore, constituted one phase of a larger plan to reclaim the western bank of the Mississippi River from Belmont to New Madrid for the Union. Although Columbus had been his preferred goal all along, clearing the Missouri shore from Belmont to New Madrid also promised significant rewards without the attendant risks of an assault on Polk's fortifications. If successful, the movement might aid in turning the Columbus position, thus avoiding a costly attack into the teeth of its defenses. While pursuing this mission, however, Grant stretched Frémont's original directive and disobeyed the order prohibiting an attack. But this sort of behavior was nothing new for the district commander. Two months earlier Grant had seized Paducah without authorization, a move fraught with far more political and military risks than the assault on Camp Johnston.

The plan to capture Belmont and New Madrid and to drive the Southerners out of southeast Missouri had not originated with Grant. As early as September 5 Frémont had indicated his desire to expel Southern forces from southeastern Missouri, ordering Grant to capture Charleston, Sikeston, and Belmont and "follow the retreating Rebels to New Madrid." In his grand offensive scheme announced three days later, Frémont declared that Grant's primary objectives were to control the west bank opposite Columbus and to capture New Madrid, thereby dislodging the enemy from the region, while forces from Paducah flanked Columbus. Once this phase of the operation was complete, the department commander hoped to launch a combined attack on Columbus and Hickman as part of a drive down the Mississippi Valley toward Memphis. Although his fixation on southwestern Missouri checked the plan in mid-September, Frémont fully intended to "move on Memphis" after defeating Price.[84] Grant's actions on November 6–7 must be viewed within this context. He was not blindly moving downriver "looking for a fight" anywhere he could find it but was essentially following a general course plotted by the Pathfinder in early September. With Thompson on the run, Polk on the defensive, and the Confederate leadership fixated on central Kentucky, Grant saw an opportunity. Thus, when Frémont ordered demonstrations on November 1, the district commander set in motion the plan hatched in September in hopes of regaining the initiative in the Mississippi Valley. Although these same orders forbade an attack, his desire to advance outweighed his fear of insubordination.

Grant's hunger for the initiative also factored into events on November 7. He believed that when two opponents fielded armies of inexperienced volunteers to delay an offensive for the sake of more drill and discipline gained nothing since the enemy would utilize the time for similar purposes. As a result, whichever side seized the initiative first ultimately gained the upper hand. And since the Union carried the burden of forcing open the Mississippi while the Confederates had only to hold their ground, an offensive, in Grant's mind, became a question of when, not if.[85] From the day he assumed command at Cairo the district commander waited anxiously for Frémont to unleash him. Moreover, his intelligence-driven perception that the Confederates in Columbus posed only a minimal offensive threat heightened his awareness of the opportunity presented to him in early November. Regardless of whether this "picture" of the enemy situation drove his intense longing to advance or vice versa, the decision to attack Belmont was undoubtedly born of this relationship.[86]

The assault on Belmont also made sense for other reasons. First, to Union officials, this enemy outpost represented a dangerous chink in the Federal armor in southeastern Missouri, and eliminating it offered the surest way to neutralize a potential problem. Second, the Confederate troops occupying the camp also presented an inviting target for Grant, especially since a sizable expanse of water stood between the garrison and support from Columbus. Union intelligence had also shown that only a small force, typically no more than three thousand troops, occupied Belmont at any one time. By November 7, the odds were even better because Grant knew that Thompson, the last known occupant at Camp Johnston, had evacuated the area. Third, in order for the New Madrid phase of the plan to succeed, Grant had to protect Oglesby's flank as he moved south toward his objective, and assailing the Belmont garrison would attain that end. And fourth, from the earlier Union occupation of Belmont and numerous reconnaissances in that direction, essentially dress rehearsals for the real event, the district commander gained knowledge of the roads and terrain in the area. Although in the shadow of the Columbus guns, Belmont remained a vulnerable and inviting target.[87]

More importantly, Grant had also gleaned from his intelligence that the Confederate high command had thinned the ranks in Columbus, leading him to conclude that Polk's main worry was ensuring the safety of Columbus. If threatened on both sides of the river, his ever-cautious adversary would probably remain behind his defenses, conserve his manpower, and leave Camp Johnston to its own fate, especially if the scuffle across the river only masked a main thrust against Columbus. In the final analysis, the odds were good that Polk would not risk the "Gibraltar of the West" to save a minor outpost, thereby allowing Grant's forces to seize the western bank with little interference from Kentucky. Although Polk did send troops to rescue Belmont, his initial hesitation showed that Grant's assumptions had merit.[88] Finally, with Belmont and New Madrid in Union hands, and with Smith threatening Polk on his Kentucky flank, the possibility remained that this combined offensive might turn Columbus and force its abandonment, a scenario that Grant had envisioned as early as September 12.

Overall, Grant's use of intelligence during the Belmont campaign marked him as a superior commander among his early war contemporaries, especially when compared with Maj. Gen. George B. McClellan's handling of intelligence on the Peninsula the following year. Contrary to the arguments that bad intelligence precipitated the Battle of Belmont, Grant actually based his decision to assault the outpost on good intelligence tempered by a perceptive reading of the enemy's condition and intentions as well as the likely behavior of their commanders. Belmont was actually his bid to initiate the long-awaited campaign to open the Mississippi Valley and, in his view, to start winning the war before it became too costly. Thus, instead of a fruitless battle brought about by flawed information, as some have argued, Belmont was actually a potentially profitable engagement born of two months of intelligence work, Grant's remarkable prescience and flexibility, and his unwavering belief in the initiative as a decisive element in war.

Notes

The author would like to thank Mrs. Cecile Guthrie for her kind support and for honoring him with the Gerry D. Guthrie Fellowship, which made this essay possible.

1. Dennis Hart Mahan, *An Elementary Treatise on Advanced-Guard, Out-Post, and Detachment Service of Troops and the Manner of Posting and Handling Them in Presence of the Enemy* (New Orleans: n.p., 1861), 73.

2. Baron Antoine Henri Jomini, *Summary of the Art of War*, trans. Captain G. H. Mendell and Lieutenant W. P. Craighill (Westport CT: Praeger, 1971), 268.

3. Civil War commanders used the words *information* and *intelligence* interchangeably, and I have followed their example. For a definitive analysis of military intelligence in the Civil War, see Edwin C. Fishel, "Myths That Never Die," *International Journal of Intelligence and Counterintelligence* 2 (1988): 27–58; John Ferris and Michael I. Handel, "Clausewitz, Intelligence, Uncertainty, and the Art of Command in Military Operations," *Intelligence and National Security* 10 (1995): 14.

4. Civil War intelligence expert Edwin C. Fishel discussed this concept in a letter to the author, February 29, 1992.

5. John Y. Simon, ed., *The Papers of Ulysses S. Grant*, 20 vols. to date (Carbondale: Southern Illinois University Press, 1967–), vol. 2, 163 (hereafter cited as PG). For the geographical dimensions of the district, see Frank J. Welcher, *The Union Army, 1861–1865: Organization and Operations* (Bloomington: University of Indiana Press, 1993), vol. 2, *The Western Theater*, 155.

6. Donald J. Stanton, Goodwin F. Berquist, and Paul C. Bowers, eds., *The*

Civil War Reminiscences of General M. Jeff Thompson (Dayton OH: Morningside, 1988), 90, emphasis in original.

7. On the Confederate invasion of Kentucky, see U.S. War Department, *The War of the Rebellion: Official Records of the Union and Confederate Armies*, 128 vols. (Washington DC: Government Printing Office, 1881–1901), 1st ser., vol. 4, pp. 179–95 (hereafter cited as OR; all references are to series 1 unless otherwise noted); Steven E. Woodworth, *Jefferson Davis and His Generals: The Failure of Confederate Command in the West* (Lawrence: University Press of Kansas, 1990), 38–39; Woodworth, "'The Indeterminate Quantities': Jefferson Davis, Leonidas Polk, and the End of Kentucky Neutrality, September 1861," *Civil War History* 38 (1992): 289–97; Nathaniel Cheairs Hughes Jr. and Roy P. Stonesifer Jr., *The Life and Wars of Gideon J. Pillow* (Chapel Hill: University of North Carolina Press, 1993), 194; Thomas L. Connelly, *Army of the Heartland: The Army of Tennessee, 1861–62* (Baton Rouge: Louisiana State University Press, 1967), 51–55; and Joseph H. Parks, *General Leonidas Polk, C.S.A.: The Fighting Bishop* (Baton Rouge: Louisiana State University Press, 1962), 181–82.

8. On the seizure of Paducah, see PG 2:190, 193, 196–97; OR 4:196–98; Bruce Catton, *Grant Moves South* (Boston: Little Brown, 1960), 48–50; and E. B. Long, "The Paducah Affair: Bloodless Action That Altered the Civil War in the Mississippi Valley," *Register of the Kentucky Historical Society* 70, no. 4 (1972): 253–76.

9. Woodworth, *Jefferson Davis and His Generals*, 52–53, 57–58; Jay Carlton Mullen, "The Turning of Columbus," *Register of the Kentucky Historical Society* 64 (1966): 217–18; Nathaniel Cheairs Hughes Jr., *The Battle of Belmont: Grant Strikes South* (Chapel Hill: University of North Carolina Press, 1991), 36–38. Thomas L. Connelly claimed that Columbus was not as forbidding as others have argued, calling it more of a trap than a bastion and asserting that the town provided "no additional security against a Union advance." This may be true in the abstract, but what mattered was that the Union high command, including Grant, believed the fortress was a substantial impediment to an advance downriver. See Connelly, *Army of the Heartland*, 54–55; Hughes, *The Battle of Belmont*, 37.

10. Hughes, *The Battle of Belmont*, 82–83; Mullen, "Turning of Columbus," 218; On Thompson and Hardee, see Jay Monaghan, *Swamp Fox of the Confederacy: The Life and Military Services of M. Jeff Thompson* (Tuscaloosa: University of Alabama Press, 1957); and Nathaniel Cheairs Hughes Jr., *General William J. Hardee, Old Reliable* (Baton Rouge: Louisiana State University Press, 1962).

11. OR 3:141–42; PG 2:151–52, 191, 203; see also Mullen, "Turning of Columbus," 218; PG 2:224–25; Catton, *Grant Moves South*, 60; Ulysses S. Grant, *Personal Memoirs of U. S. Grant*, 2 vols. (New York: Charles L. Webster, 1885), vol. 1, 269.

12. Catton, *Grant Moves South*, 39–40; OR 3:478.

13. Albert Castel, *General Sterling Price and the Civil War in the West* (Baton Rouge: Louisiana State University Press, 1968), 48–50; and Catton, *Grant Moves South*, 59; PG 2:224.

14. The term *secret service* was a Civil War euphemism for all intelligence enterprises, including espionage, scouting, counterintelligence, and criminal investigations. See Fishel, "Myths," 28; Record Group 393, pt. 1, entry 5502, boxes 13 and 14, National Archives, Washington DC (hereafter cited as RG).

15. For an excellent overview of information sources, see Peter Maslowski, "Military Intelligence Sources during the American Civil War: A Case Study," in *The Intelligence Revolution: A Historical Perspective*, ed. Lt. Col. Walter T. Hitchcock, USAF (Washington DC: Office of Air Force History, 1991), 39–70; see also Fishel, "Myths," 27–58.

16. PG 2:209–10, 224, 270. Maslowski, "Military Intelligence Sources," 41–47; RG 394, entry 2778.

17. PG 2:252, 292, 294; RG 393, entry 2770.

18. Foote assumed command of the western flotilla on September 6, 1861. U.S. War Department, *Official Records of the Union and Confederate Navies in the War of the Rebellion*, 30 vols. (Washington DC, 1894–1922), vol. 22, 307 (hereafter cited as OR Navy).

19. OR Navy 22:340, 349, 363, 373, 389–90; see also PG 2:292; Stanton, Berquist, and Bowers, *Civil War Reminiscences*, 89.

20. Maslowski, "Military Intelligence Sources," 49–50; Lew Wallace Collection, box 1, Indiana Historical Society, Indianapolis (hereafter cited as LWC).

21. For order-of-battle intelligence, see Lt. Col. Irving Heymont, *Combat Intelligence in Modern Warfare* (Harrisburg PA: Stackpole, 1960), 111–16. For Grant's early use of interrogations and order-of-battle intelligence, see A. L. Conger, *The Rise of U. S. Grant* (New York: Century, 1931), 234–35.

22. OR Navy 22:324–25; PG 2:225.

23. For a Confederate view of the importance of Paducah, see OR 3:189; PG 2:225.

24. OR 3:699; PG 2:210, 227–28.

25. OR 4:179–95; Woodworth, *Jefferson Davis and His Generals*, 30; Woodworth, "Indeterminate Quantities," 289–97; Parks, *General Leonidas Polk*, 181–85; OR 3:189; Wallace-Dickey Papers, box 2, Illinois State Historical Library, Springfield (hereafter cited as WDP).

26. Quoted in George Winston Smith and Charles Judah, *Chronicles of the Gringos: The U.S. Army in the Mexican War, 1846–1848* (Albuquerque: University

of New Mexico Press, 1968), 440; PG 2:22, 131; 3:10; Catton, *Grant Moves South*, 34; John Y. Simon, "Grant at Belmont," *Military Affairs* 45 (1981): 164.

27. PG 2:231–32, 235–36, 252–53, 258, 252.

28. PG 2:242. For an examination of the strategic turning movement, see Herman Hattaway and Archer Jones, *How the North Won: A Military History of the Civil War* (Urbana: University of Illinois Press, 1983), 14–17, passim; OR 3:478.

29. PG 2:262.

30. PG 2:216, 262–63, 282–83.

31. PG 2:269–70. "Mr. L." might refer to John Lellyett, a resident of Nashville and political crony of Andrew Johnson who spied for the Union army in Kentucky from 1861 to 1862. Leroy P. Graf and Ralph W. Haskins, eds., *The Papers of Andrew Johnson* (Knoxville: University of Tennessee Press, 1976), vol. 4, 63; see also PG 4:34–35; OR 4:405.

32. PG 2:269–70.

33. PG 2:273–74, 286–87.

34. OR 4:191; Hughes and Stonesifer, *Life and Wars of Gideon J. Pillow*, 195; Christopher Losson, *Tennessee's Forgotten Warriors: Frank Cheatham and His Confederate Division* (Knoxville: University of Tennessee Press, 1989), 33; OR 4:428, 191. For correspondence concerning Johnston and central Kentucky, see OR 4:193, 407–15.

35. Woodworth, *Jefferson Davis and His Generals*, 52–53; Parks, *General Leonidas Polk*, 187–88; OR 4:194; Connelly, *Army of the Heartland*, 64–68.

36. PG 2:300–301, 304.

37. PG 2:304, 314, 315–16.

38. Castel, *General Sterling Price*, 48–56.

39. Catton, *Grant Moves South*, 70; John C. Frémont, "In Command in Missouri," in *Battles and Leaders of the Civil War*, ed. Robert U. Johnson and Clarence C. Buel, 4 vols.(New York: Century, 1884–1889; reprint, New York: Castle Books, 1982), vol. 1, 286–87; Grant, *Memoirs*, 1:269–70; Andrew Rolle, *John Charles Frémont: Character as Destiny* (Norman: University of Oklahoma Press, 1991), 201–3.

40. OR 3:507; Simon, "Grant at Belmont," 162–63. Robert L. Turkoly-Joczik offered a more sympathetic rendering of the Pathfinder's tenure in Missouri. See "Frémont and the Western Department," *Missouri Historical Review* 82 (1988): 359–67.

41. PG, 2:311.

42. PG, 2:300; Simon, "Grant at Belmont," 162–63.

43. OR 2:507–508; PG 2:321; 3:4, 14.

44. PG 2:29–30; OR 3:510; PG 3:4, 17.

45. PG 3:18, 19, 23.

46. Brown passed through W. H. L. Wallace's command at Bird's Point. See WDP, box 2; see also RG 393, entry 5500; PG 3:19.

47. PG 3:25; LWC, box 1.

48. PG 3:24. The same dispatch contained a rumor that the Columbus garrison had been reinforced to forty-five thousand (a wild overestimate), which may have convinced Grant even more that Polk was preparing an impregnable defense.

49. Conger, *The Rise of U. S. Grant*, 79; OR 3:712.

50. Charles W. Wills, *Army Life of an Illinois Soldier* (Washington DC, 1906), 36; PG 3:12, 16.

51. OR 3:713, 714, 53:748; PG 3:33.

52. OR 3:224, 225–26.

53. PG 3:54, 56–57. For Thompson's version of Fredericktown, see Stanton, Berquist, and Bowers, *Civil War Reminiscences*, 106–17; PG 3:116.

54. OR 3:703, 4:444, 3:445; Hughes, *William J. Hardee*, 81–82.

55. OR 3:508; PG 2:322.

56. PG 3:43, 47, 54–55, 56–57; John F. Marszalek, *Sherman: A Soldier's Passion for Order* (New York: Free Press, 1993), 157–63.

57. PG 3:42–43.

58. PG 3:63–64. At about this time Grant dismissed another report of Confederates crossing to Belmont, claiming that they were only harvesting corn for Polk's commissary. See OR Navy 22:430 and PG 3:47.

59. PG 3:72. Smith also reported that several thousand troops had been transferred to Union City, Tennessee, and Feliciana, the location of Camp Beauregard (OR 3:510). Polk had 17,230 men at Columbus (OR 3:730).

60. PG 3:78; Catton, *Grant Moves South*, 60.

61. PG 3:25, 24, 30.

62. PG 3:18–19.

63. Jay Luvaas, "Napoleon and the Art of Command," *Parameters* 15 (1985): 35. Polk was responding to Johnston's order sending Pillow's five-thousand-man division to Clarksville. See OR 4:513.

64. PG 3:143–44; OR 3:300–301.

65. PG 3:144, 108–109, 111–12.

66. PG 3:114. For a description of Grant's preparations and his descent toward Belmont, see Hughes, *The Battle of Belmont*, 48–55, 78–84.

67. Catton, *Grant Moves South*, 75; Hughes, *The Battle of Belmont*, 71, 67–68, 74–77, 184; OR 3:306–8; Hughes and Stonesifer, *Life and Wars of Gideon J. Pillow*, 196–99.

68. Hughes, *The Battle of Belmont*, 91–188; Hughes and Stonesifer, *Life and Wars of Gideon J. Pillow*, 199–205; OR 3:306–8. Other treatments of the battle in-

clude James E. McGhee, "The Neophyte General: U. S. Grant and the Belmont Campaign," *Missouri Historical Review* 47 (1973): 465–83; and Henry I. Kurtz, "The Battle of Belmont," *Civil War Times Illustrated* 3 (1963): 18–24.

69. The Union suffered 120 killed, 383 wounded, and 104 missing of approximately 2,500 engaged, while the Confederate casualties were 105 killed, 419 wounded, and 117 missing out of nearly 5,000 engaged. Hughes, *The Battle of Belmont*, 184–85; Simon, "Grant at Belmont," 161; J. Cutler Andrews, *The North Reports the Civil War* (Pittsburgh: University of Pittsburgh Press, 1955), 119; Hughes, *The Battle of Belmont*, 207; Wills, *Army Life*, 43.

70. Augustus W. Alexander, *Grant as a Soldier* (St. Louis: Augustus W. Alexander, 1887), 41; Simon, "Grant at Belmont," 165–66; Kenneth P. Williams, *Lincoln Finds a General: A Military Study of the Civil War*, 5 vols. (New York: Macmillan, 1949–1958), vol. 3, 86; Hughes, *The Battle of Belmont*, 207.

71. PG 3:141.

72. PG 3:143–49.

73. PG 3:133.

74. PG 3:136–38.

75. PG 3:146; Hughes, *The Battle of Belmont*, 51; Simon, "Grant at Belmont," 165.

76. WDP, box 2; Franklin D. Nickell made this point in "Grant's Lieutenants in the West, 1861–1863" (Ph.D. diss., University of New Mexico, 1972), 293–94; Isabel Wallace, *Life and Letters of General W. H. L. Wallace* (Chicago: R. R. Donnelley, 1909), 141. William S. McFeely argued that Grant "had already made the decision to attack when he left Cairo" and that he had "set out to fight . . . not to demonstrate." *Grant: A Biography* (New York: W. W. Norton, 1981), 92.

77. On April 27, 1864, Rawlins wrote that "Colonel Bowers and myself finished yesterday General Grant's report of the battle of Belmont" and commented that "it places that engagement in its true light for transmittal to posterity, so far as could be known on our side." James Harrison Wilson, *The Life of John A. Rawlins* (New York: Neale, 1916), 425; see also Simon, "Grant at Belmont," 165; and Hughes, *The Battle of Belmont*, 46–47, 51–52.

78. Simon, "Grant at Belmont," 165; see also Simon's analysis of Grant's official report in PG 3:152.

79. PG 3:114.

80. PG 3:123–24; WDP, box 2.

81. PG 3:124. Other historians have supported this interpretation. See, in particular, Simon, "Grant at Belmont," 163–64; and Conger, *The Rise of U. S. Grant*, 372.

82. Wills, *Army Life*, 42–43.

83. This observation by G. F. R. Henderson is quoted in Williams, *Lincoln Finds a General*, 3:74.

84. PG 2:191; OR 3:478–79; PG 2:216; see also OR 3:484; Catton, *Grant Moves South*, 39–40; Frémont, "In Command in Missouri," 287.

85. Wilson, *John A. Rawlins*, 439.

86. Several Navy officers, including Foote and Porter, also pressured Grant to advance on Columbus. See OR Navy 22:396–97, 430.

87. Catton, *Grant Moves South*, 70–71; Simon, "Grant at Belmont," 165; Hughes, *The Battle of Belmont*, 53, 83; Conger, *The Rise of U. S. Grant*, 372. Union troops occupied Belmont in early September. See PG 2:178.

88. McGhee, "Neophyte General," 471; Catton, *Grant Moves South*, 74.

3 / War Crime or Justice? General George Pickett and the Mass Execution of Deserters in Civil War Kinston, North Carolina

DONALD E. COLLINS

During the early hours of February 2, 1864, fifty-three North Carolinians were captured by Confederate forces under the command of Maj. Gen. George E. Pickett. They were wearing the uniform of the United States Army and were caught in arms against their native state. Except for a few absentees, these men represented the entire roster of Company F, Second North Carolina Union Volunteer Infantry. Most were natives either of the county in which they were taken prisoner or of surrounding counties. Within four months of their capture, virtually all would be dead. Most fell victim to diseases acquired in Southern prisoner-of-war camps in Richmond, Virginia, and Andersonville, Georgia. Twenty-two, however, were publicly hanged in Kinston, North Carolina. Watching the executions were wives, neighbors, friends, and former comrades in arms in the Confederate army. The incident precipitated a controversy between Union and Confederate authorities that lasted two years and nearly brought down one of the South's most famous generals.

On the surface, the issues were simple. From the Federal viewpoint, the executed men were Union soldiers; once captured, they deserved to be treated as prisoners of war. President Abraham Lincoln made this a point when, on July 31, 1863, he ordered retaliation on "the enemy's prisoners in our possession." "It is . . . ordered, that for every soldier of the United States killed in violation of the laws of war, a rebel soldier shall be executed."[1] The reaction of Union authorities to the Kinston hangings was outrage and desire for revenge.

The Confederates argued that the men were simply deserters. Execution, therefore, was a legitimate punishment. In reality, however, the problem for the South was much more serious: how to stem the tide of desertion that swept, and depleted, Southern armies. From the early days of the war, officials had complained that Confederate forces were so weakened by desertions that "we are unable to reap the fruits of our victories and . . . invade the territory of the enemy." General Robert E. Lee, following his defeat at Antietam, complained to President Jefferson Davis that a large number of his troops never crossed into Maryland and that desertion and straggling deprived him of one-third of his effective force. He later wrote that he feared "nothing but the death penalty, uniformly, inexorably administered, will stop it."[2]

In February 1864 this widespread problem of Confederate commanders became a specific concern for George Pickett, whose campaign against New Bern, North Carolina, cast him into the midst of the thorny and tangled questions of how a general maintains his manpower against the constant hemorrhage of desertion. Where does military discipline end and atrocity begin? For Pickett the matter could never again be a mere academic or legal question. His application of Lee's suggested remedy for desertion brought him condemnation as a war criminal in 1865–1868 and criticism from some recent historians who attribute the mass executions to his alleged declining mental state following his ill-fated charge at Gettysburg and his subsequent fall from grace in the Army of Northern Virginia.[3]

A more reasonable explanation, carefully considering all of the circumstances, reveals that Pickett's actions were not those of a man in the throes of emotional disintegration but rather fit well with the picture of a rational but sorely tried commander wrestling with one of the fundamental problems of command: the maintenance of his army. In keeping with Confederate concerns over desertion in North Carolina—and Lee's expressed desires—Pickett intended to set an example that would stanch the flow of desertion.

Desertion was most appalling in North Carolina, and there the problem Pickett would face had been developing for some time. To understand Pickett's dilemma, and its ramifications for individual soldiers, it is necessary to understand the background of the 1864 Kinston hangings. North Carolina had the seemingly contradictory distinctions of providing both more soldiers to the Confederate army than any other state and of having more deserters from the army. Although North Carolinian disloyalty to the Confederacy was probably not much worse than in some other Southern states, it was publicly more pronounced. North Carolina was the last to secede and did so only after rejecting secession in a statewide vote of the people. Governor Zebulon Vance, who led the state through most of the war, was an outspoken critic of the Davis administration. And the *North Carolina Standard*, one of the state's leading newspapers, was so well known for its opposition to the Confederate war effort that North Carolina soldiers came to blame it for the growing number of desertions. Even the North Carolina Supreme Court gave aid and comfort to those desiring to avoid Confederate military service. Chief Justice Richmond M. Person was known to secure the release of virtually any conscript, deserter, or person accused of disloyalty who applied to him for a writ of habeas corpus.[4] Since desertion was not a crime in the state, citizens who shielded deserters felt safe from arrest for hiding them. Added to the problem, war-weary soldiers received volumes of letters from wives and family members urging them to come home—arguing that they "could desert with impunity." It was even said that they could "band together and defy the officers of the law" who came after them. As a result, large numbers were concealed from the army in many parts of the state.[5]

The Confederate congress debated the problem of desertion in North Carolina, and President Davis and Robert E. Lee, among others, expressed their deep concern. Governor Vance, despite his reputation for opposition to the Confederate government on many issues, became increasingly troubled over desertions by North Carolina soldiers. On January 28, 1863, he issued a proclamation that threatened trial and death for any deserter who did not return to duty by February 10.[6] Despite this, the state became an attractive refuge for deserters, who found natural havens in the swamps of eastern North Carolina and the mountains to the west. Deserters found aid and comfort from such secret Unionist organizations as the Heroes of America, which helped them to places of safety.

Unionists, men of questionable loyalty to either side, and deserters from the Confederate army began to find their way into the Union army soon after Federal forces occupied the northeastern coastal region of North Carolina early in the war. This influx appeared to confirm the widely held beliefs of Northern authorities in regard to the political leanings of citizens of the state. Commodore S. C. Rowan, writing from New Bern in March 1862, stated his firm conviction that "the hearts of the people of North Carolina are not with the rebels; the woods and swamps are full of refugees fleeing from the terror of [Confederate] conscription."[7]

Realizing the value of these men to the Union, Lt. Comdr. Charles W. Flusser and Colonel Rush C. Hawkins, commanders of the land and naval forces in the region, met with approximately 250 local residents in Plymouth and formed the First North Carolina Union Volunteer Infantry.[8] By January 1863, the regiment had increased to 534 men, and recruitment for the Second North Carolina Union Volunteers was initiated. Within another year, recruiters operating in the Union-occupied towns of Plymouth, Washington, Beaufort, Hatteras, and New Bern had raised fifteen companies made up of native eastern North Carolinians.[9]

From the very beginning, Northern military leaders realized the danger that North Carolinians in the Union army faced if captured by Southern soldiers. As a result, a conscious effort was made to protect these men from capture and punishment as traitors to the Confederacy. Flusser and Hawkins assured the recruits that "Southern men who . . . [fight] in the ranks of our army . . . [would] be looked upon as wards of the Government; and any outrage perpetrated upon them, or upon their families, would be severely punished."[10] A serious effort was made by Union leaders in the state to protect Unionists from capture and punishment as traitors by Confederate authorities. Hawkins would be haunted by guilt for decades after the war because of his inability to keep this promise.[11]

The First and Second North Carolina Union regiments were deliberately kept from combat situations and were used mostly in building and strengthening fortifications. Despite these precautions, Confederate assaults on New Bern, Plymouth, Washington, and other locales would result in the capture and/or death of a significant number in these regiments.

In addition to those truly loyal Unionist North Carolinians, men of lesser and more questionable motivations were also enticed into the Federal army. Recruiting broadsides addressed "To the Union Men" of the area appealed to those who simply wished to sit out the war in relative security or who wanted to remain near home and family. These were promised that their service would be as home guards who would "not be moved from the county, . . . nor . . . be called upon to march to any other part of the state, unless upon an occasion of emergency."[12]

North Carolina had its own version of the Federals' home guards. In 1861 the Confederate congress gave in to states' rights governors who appeared to be more concerned with their own states' defense than with presenting a united front against the common enemy. The Local Service Law of that year therefore authorized the recruitment of state troops for local defense. In North Carolina, the partisan rangers and railroad guard companies fell into this category. Service in such units was considered one of the most perfect ways to avoid conscription into the regular Confederate army. It was generally understood that by enlisting in local service organizations one avoided being removed from his home area to more active service and also escaped being sent to the battlefields of Virginia and other states. Rank-and-file Confederate soldiers had little respect for men who used local defense for the purpose of keeping out of danger, avoiding the draft, and remaining near their families.[13]

Half of the men of Company F, Second North Carolina Union Volunteer Infantry, began their military careers serving the Confederacy in one capacity or another. Most were members of Southern partisan ranger battalions or railroad guard units.[14] Upon enlistment, these men were promised orally, but not on paper, that they would spend their time within the general locality in which they joined.[15] Nethercutt's Battalion, to which the majority of the deserters to the Union army belonged, was headquartered in Trenton, in Jones County, North Carolina, a short distance from Kinston, where they would soon meet their fate. This unit had a reputation among Union troops in the region as "bush-wackers" who ignored "all the well known rules of legitimate warfare."[16]

Life in the partisan rangers was easygoing, with the men often enjoying the comforts of home while ostensibly serving the Southern cause. Described by one Confederate officer as "a rather free kind of troops," service was informal, consisting of going out for perhaps a week at a time on scouting and outpost duty. They had no regular camp, some men living at home with their families. Reports, though required, were seldom made by officers, who sympathized with their men. According to their commander, Major John H. Nethercutt, many were not in sympathy with the rebellion. Such men could not be counted upon to remain true to the service should their security be threatened.[17]

North Carolinians whose loyalty lay with the United States, or who at least felt no allegiance to the Confederacy, now had several options open to them. They could flee to relative safety behind Union lines; join the regular Federal army and fight for the preservation of the Union; enlist in a North Carolina Union regiment, where they could be close to their families, support them on army pay, and remain relatively safe from combat; or they could remain at home while giving the appearance of Confederate loyalty through service in partisan ranger and bridge guard units.

By the fall of 1863, events had taken place that would put an end to the easy life in such local service units and would be seen by these informal soldiers as a threat to the privileged position they enjoyed. Confederate losses at Gettysburg and Vicksburg, as well as the general downward course of the war, put a strain on Southern manpower. The questionable military value of local defense units did not go unnoticed by Confederate military and government authorities in the field and in Richmond.

In October 1863 the War Department in Richmond, on the recommendation of Brig. Gen. James G. Martin, ordered the creation of the Sixty-sixth Regiment, North Carolina State Troops. This would include those men in local service in eastern North Carolina who were of conscription age. Wright's and Nethercutt's battalions, including four railroad bridge guard and four partisan ranger companies, helped make up what Lieutenant John B. Neathery of the state adjutant general's office described as the "odds and ends not belonging to any other organizations."[18] All units assigned to the Sixty-sixth were ordered to rendezvous in Kinston in October and to move from there to Wilmington, pending removal to Virginia.

Confederate authorities realized that difficulties might arise from transferring men to general service who had been promised on enlistment that they would remain in the vicinity of their homes. To prevent disaffection, an attempt was therefore made to soothe feelings by offering the men a choice. They would be given the opportunity to go voluntarily with their units into the Sixty-sixth Regiment or be discharged and sent to conscription camps for assignment. The men affected by the order saw this, however, as simply "whipping the devil around the stump"; regardless of which path was taken, the results were the same: service in the Sixty-sixth.[19]

A substantial number actively opposed the order. A few successfully filed habeas corpus petitions to a sympathetic state supreme court and were discharged from the service. Many others simply fled to the woods or went home. This was particularly true in Nethercutt's Battalion, where officers and men expressed dissatisfaction with the consolidation order as a violation of their enlistment terms. Less than half showed up at the rendezvous site in Kinston. Major Nethercutt proposed that he and some other influential officers go to the men and attempt to persuade them to return. Maj. Gen. George E. Pickett, overall commander of the Department of North Carolina, took a similarly lenient approach in issuing a proclamation that promised there would be no punishment for any who voluntarily returned. As a result most returned, some coming in by squads.[20]

This hesitation to serve the Confederate cause resulted in a distrust of the Sixty-sixth North Carolina Regiment that took months to overcome. Guards whose loyalty was known to now Colonel Nethercutt were placed in camp to ensure against further desertions. Although the regiment as a whole later earned respect in the Confederate army through gallant service on some of the major battlefields of Virginia and North Carolina, the struggle for consolidation of the local defense organizations into more active Confederate service caused many men from such units to flee to the protection of the Union-occupied coastal region of North Carolina. Once there, they faced the same problems as other recently arrived Unionist North Carolina refugees. Many arrived with only the clothes on their backs. They needed employment to feed and care for their families, and the most readily available source of income was service in the Union army.[21]

They found overly aggressive Union army recruiters who were eager to take them into the service—few questions asked and few disabilities too severe to be overlooked. The commander of the Union's District of North Carolina, Maj. Gen. John J. Peck, found many of the recruiters to be an embarrassment. "Some of these officers . . . enlist all the men they can possibly persuade, without the slightest regard to their capacity, either mental or physical."[22]

Demanding special attention, Peck wrote, was the use of "virtual impressment and fraudulent enlistment," including the use of threats of violence against men who did not want to enlist. "Mere boys, children, some of them weak, puny, scrofulous, have been enlisted, passed by the surgeon, and mustered in by the mustering officer. And again, old men, eaten by disease or utterly incapacitated by old age and general infirmity, have been enlisted, fed, and accepted into the service as able-bodied soldiers."[23] In their eagerness to bring North Carolinians into Union service, recruiters even searched local jails and traveled to prisoner-of-war camps in Virginia and Maryland for Confederate prisoners willing to take the oath of allegiance.[24]

For several refugees these aggressive tactics proved fatal. Elijah Kellum, rejected as physically unfit for Confederate service, was recruited and accepted by the Second North Carolina Union Volunteers. In February, Confederate deserters David Jones and Joseph L. Haskett insisted in "deathbed" statements that they had been compelled to take the oaths of allegiance and enlist in the Second North Carolina. Amos Amyett (or Armyett), just moments before he was hanged for desertion by Confederate military authorities, stated that "I went to New Bern and [Union recruiters] told me if I did not go into their service I should be taken through their lines and shot. In this way I was frightened into it."[25]

Once in the army, North Carolina Unionists, derisively called "buffaloes" by Confederates, continued to face hardships. They were placed together in camps with hundreds of escaped slaves, where food and ammunition were short and where they went unpaid for months on end.[26] During November and December 1863 and January 1864 approximately sixty eastern North Carolinians, including the escapees from the Sixty-sixth North Carolina Regiment, made their way to recruiters in New Bern, Washington, and Beaufort and were placed in Company F, Second North Carolina Union Volunteers, stationed in Beaufort. They were promised enlistment bonuses of from one hundred to three hundred dollars, which circumstances would prevent all but a handful from ever collecting.[27]

Soon after the formation of Company F, its men were ordered to report to Colonel P. J. Claassen, commander of the Union outposts surrounding New Bern. On January 18, 1864, they were sent by General Peck to Beech Grove, an outpost about nine miles west of town in the vicinity of Batchelder's (also commonly called Bachelor's) Creek, where they joined fourteen men of the 132nd Regiment, New York Infantry. First Lt. Samuel Leith of the New York unit was in overall command. Described as a masked battery, the outpost was concealed in the forest and so constructed as to command the Neuse River. Within the blockhouse fort with its two steel rifled artillery pieces, the new recruits of the Second North Carolina probably felt safe from attack by their former comrades in the Confederate army.[28]

At about the same time that Company F took up its position at Beech Grove, General Lee was making plans in Virginia that would result in the capture of the outpost. Believing the time was right to retake New Bern from the enemy, Lee proposed to President Davis that an attack be made, with North Carolina brigadier general Robert F. Hoke in command. Davis approved the plan but placed Maj. Gen. Pickett over the better-qualified Hoke, since in his opinion an expedition of such proportions should be led by a man of higher rank.

On January 30, 1864, Pickett led a force of fourteen navy cutters and thirteen thousand men, divided into three columns, toward New Bern. The task of the central column, commanded by Pickett and Hoke, was to move down between the Trent and Neuse Rivers, surprise the Union troops on Batchelder's Creek, silence the guns in the star fort and batteries near the Neuse, and penetrate the town in that direction.[29]

Hoke's men advanced to within two miles of the Union outposts surrounding New Bern, where they camped without fires to maintain the element of surprise. At approximately 1:00 AM, they began their attack, stopped temporarily only by the removal of the bridge over Batchelder's Creek. The men of the Union outposts held for seven hours before making a hasty retreat, leaving behind everything but the clothes on their backs. To cut off the railroad into town, Hoke then moved his brigade six miles "with all possible speed."[30] He and Pickett then moved to within a mile of New

Bern, where they waited all day Tuesday for the assault that never came because General S. M. Barton's column on their right failed to carry out its assignment. Having failed in his campaign to retake New Bern, on Wednesday morning Pickett gave the order to withdraw toward Kinston.[31]

The fight at Batchelder's Creek, along with Hoke's rapid move toward New Bern on the morning of February 1, sealed the fate of the Unionist North Carolinians of Company F. Their outpost at Beech Grove was on the extreme right of the Union lines and a short distance east of Batchelder's Creek. Its concealed position, helped by the darkness of the night and a dense morning fog, not only hid it from the advancing Confederates of Hoke and Pickett but prevented communications with other Union troops. Attempts were made during the night to communicate with the outpost. One officer who volunteered to carry an order to them made it through Confederate lines during the night but lost his way in the swamp and was obliged to return. In the morning, fog prevented sending visual signals to the outpost, and Colonel Claassen sent a courier who was killed en route. The dispatch he was carrying fell into Confederate hands, providing them with the locations of the Union outposts, including, presumably, Beech Grove. A second messenger, 2d Lt. Arnold Zenette, died from a bullet wound to the head before reaching the outpost.[32]

The men at Beech Grove, meanwhile, were doomed by the poor judgment of their overly cautious commanding officer. Lieutenant Leith declined to take any action without hearing first from his superiors. Despite the desperate pleas of the North Carolinians to be allowed to lead the men of the outpost to safety along paths that, as natives of the county, they knew well, Leith would not permit his men to leave. He instead dispatched a request to New Bern for reinforcements and promised a fight to the last man unless relieved sooner. The message never reached its destination, as the courier was captured by the retreating Confederates under Pickett.[33]

The Confederate general, now aware of the hidden outpost, dispatched two regiments of Virginia infantry and two sections of artillery to take the Union position. Despite his boast to fight to the last man, Leith capitulated without a shot being fired. After raising the white flag, but before negotiations began, the Union commander warned the North Carolinians of the potential consequences of their capture and advised them to escape. Their flight was short lived, however, and all but a small number were captured by a scouting party from the Thirtieth Virginia Infantry Regiment.[34]

The North Carolinians, dressed in the new uniforms of Federal army recruits, were at first indistinguishable from other Union prisoners of war and were treated as such. As they were being prepared for transfer to Kinston, however, two were recognized by former comrades as deserters from their units. These men were immediately separated from the other prisoners and placed in the care of the provost guard.[35]

Pickett's army, weary from a hard march through rain and over muddy roads, camped for the night near Dover, North Carolina. Word soon spread that North Carolinians were included among the Union prisoners taken around New Bern, and curious soldiers came by to look them over. Lieutenant H. M. Whitehead and Sergeant Blunt King, of Company B, Tenth Regiment, North Carolina Artillery, recognized David Jones, a twenty-one-year-old native of Craven County, and Joseph L. Haskett, a twenty-six-year-old farmer from Carteret County, as deserters from their company.[36]

When General Pickett confronted the two men he was openly contemptuous and left no doubt about their fate. The previous day he had been overheard to say "that every God-damned man who didn't do his duty, or deserted, ought to be shot or hung." At about sunset, Pickett came out of his tent and confronted Jones and Haskett, who were standing near a campfire. He asked where they had been, and after listening to their reply angrily told them, "God damn you, I recon [sic] you will hardly ever go back there again, you damned rascals; I'll have you shot, and all other damned rascals who desert." Jones answered that he did "not care a damn whether they shot him then, or what they did with him." With that, Pickett ordered them away from his tent. He then told Generals Corse and Hoke, who were present during the confrontation with the two Confederates-turned-Yankee, that "we'll have to have a court-martial on these fellows pretty soon, and after some are shot the rest will stop deserting." Corse agreed, stating "the sooner the better."[37]

A court-martial board headed by Lt. Col. James R. Branch of Virginia and made up entirely of officers from Pickett's own state was organized immediately. Before it concluded its business, it would convene on three separate occasions in three different locations and hear the cases of twenty-seven of the Beech Grove captives, all charged with desertion from the Confederate army.[38] The remaining twenty-six prisoners from the Second North Carolina Union Regiment were regarded simply as prisoners of war and would be sent to Southern prison camps.

The court met that night while still in camp on the Dover road. Haskett and Jones admitted that they had deserted but insisted they had been forced by Union recruiters to take the oath of allegiance and enlist. Their claims disregarded, both were found guilty and sentenced to hang. The harshness of the sentence indicates the seriousness with which the Confederates viewed the crime of desertion to the enemy's army. Simple desertion was generally punished by a firing squad or some less extreme method. The execution was ordered to be carried out on February 5, 1864, in the presence of General Hoke's Brigade.[39] The swiftness of this and later executions so soon after the meetings of the court-martial board was in keeping with Pickett's announced intention of using their deaths as an example of the consequences of desertion. Speed was essential given President Davis's tendency to grant delays and pardons to Southern soldiers awaiting execution.[40]

It was not long before Confederate authorities learned the true number of deserters among the men taken at Beech Grove. As the identities of more men became known, some prisoners began turning upon others in the hope that cooperation might save their own lives. One man in particular stood out for his predilection to betray friend and country to protect himself. According to Walter Harrison, Pickett's inspector general, an unnamed sergeant among the Unionist captives used a copy of a company roster that he had in his possession to identify by name those deserters from the Confederate army that were in his unit. In the process, he caused the deaths of many of his comrades who otherwise might have gone undetected. His efforts at self-defense nevertheless failed. After testifying against his fellow Union soldiers, he himself became the last person court-martialed and sentenced to death.[41]

Upon arrival in Kinston on February 4, the prisoners were taken to the Lenoir County courthouse. There they were observed by curious townspeople, including the wife of prisoner Stephen Jones, who lived only a mile and a half from town. They were then removed to the dungeon of the Kinston jail to await court-martial and execution of their sentences. Conditions in the jail were harsh. Visitors reported that the prisoners slept on the floor and existed on a diet of one cracker a day. Those fortunate enough to have relatives and friends living nearby had their suffering relieved by gifts of extra food and quilts for bedding. Some visitors reported being turned away from the jail.[42]

As directed by the court, the execution of Haskett and Jones took place on Friday, February 5. The hangings, occurring so soon after the arrival of the Confederate expedition from New Bern, gave the appearance that there had been insufficient time for a trial and that the men had therefore not been granted this right. That morning, the two condemned men were visited in the jail by Reverend John Paris, chaplain of the Fifty-fourth North

Carolina Regiment, who was assigned to tend to their spiritual needs. He was a Confederate loyalist who had little sympathy for deserters. In his words, Haskett and Jones were both "illiterate" and the "most unfeeling and hardened men I have ever encountered."[43]

While Paris was attending to the two condemned men preparations were being made for their deaths. The rarity of execution by hanging left military authorities in the embarrassing position of having to search for rope as well as for a hangman. Both were found at the railroad depot, where Sergeant Blunt King was waiting with a shipment of pontoon boats from the New Bern expedition. King later confided to county jailer Isaiah Woods that he had volunteered his services to hang the two men whom he, ironically, had known previously as members of his own company in the Tenth North Carolina Artillery. He was later to deny this, telling Union investigators after the war that he acted against his will on orders from a Captain Adams of General Hoke's staff. Regardless of how his services were obtained, he was ordered to take rope from the pontoons and report to the execution site.[44]

When the time for the execution arrived, the men of Hoke's Brigade, including the Confederate regiment from which Haskett and Jones had deserted, formed a hollow square around the gallows. Beyond the square, a crowd of off-duty soldiers and civilians gathered. Although the proceedings were under the immediate direction of General Hoke, General Pickett was in attendance. Haskett and Jones were marched out to the gallows, which was located in a field within full view of the residents of Kinston. Captain Adams read the orders of the court-martial; then King and another soldier placed the nooses around the necks of the men and they were hanged. King was later observed cutting the buttons off the uniforms of the deceased men, perhaps for souvenirs.[45]

Pickett wasted little time in bringing more of the prisoners to justice. The court that had met the previous day on the Dover road reconvened immediately upon arrival in Kinston to hear the cases of five more of the Beech Grove captives. John L. Stanley, Lewis Bryan, Mitchell Busick, and William Irving, all deserters from Nethercutt's Battalion, and Amos Armyett of Whitford's Battalion were brought before the board, found guilty, and received the same sentence as Haskett and Jones. The date for carrying out the sentence was indefinite: "to be carried into effect, under the supervision of Brigadier General Hoke, and in the presence of his brigade, at such time and place as he may direct, in twenty-four hours after the publication of the sentence."[46]

There would be no leniency. Pickett had signed the execution order, and Hoke was determined to carry it out. This was revealed in the unsuccessful effort of Colonel Nethercutt to save the deserters from his battalion. Called from Wilmington to identify his men, he visited them in jail and then asked Hoke if anything could be done for them. The North Carolina general replied that he had orders to hang them, and he intended to do so.[47]

While Hoke's North Carolinians remained in Kinston, Pickett's Virginia brigades moved to Goldsboro, where the court-martial reconvened on February 11 for its third meeting. Ten more of Nethercutt's men—John J. Brock, William Haddock, Jesse James Summerlin, Andrew J. Brittain, Lewis Freeman, Calvin Hoffman, Stephen Jones, Lewis Taylor, William H. Daughtry, and John Freeman—as well as Joseph Brock, Charles Cuthrell, and William Jones of three other North Carolina units—were brought individually before the board.[48]

With so many men sitting before the Virginia officers for judgment, there was some activity on the prisoners' behalf by wives, relatives, and friends. This was generally ineffective. Bryan McCullen obtained an attorney to bring forward evidence in favor of his brother-in-law William Haddock, but the court would not admit him. According to McCullen, witnesses and counsel were also denied to other men.[49] There were others who sympathized with the prisoners. Some townspeople felt the sentences were too severe for the offense committed. A number of individuals, such as Kinston merchant Aaron Baer, who were suspected of pro-Union sympathies, chose not to visit the men in prison or to attend the executions out of fear that their attendance would bring retaliation by Confederate authorities.[50]

The meeting of the court-martial ended as the previous two had. No leniency was given. Thirteen sentences of death by hanging were handed down to be "carried into execution under the supervision of Brigadier General Hoke, in twenty-four hours after their publication, at such time and place as he may direct."[51] With eighteen men now under death sentence, General Hoke ordered that the five men convicted earlier would die on the gallows the next day, February 12, 1864. Orders were given to construct a new and bigger gallows capable of dealing with the increased number of condemned men.[52] With only twenty-four hours until the execution, Chaplain Paris visited the prisoners in their jail cell to attend to their spiritual needs. Each professed to be at peace with God, and two—John Stanley and William Irving—were baptized by the chaplain.

Having prepared themselves for eternity by making peace with their

God, the five condemned men marched to their deaths. At the gallows, a graying Armyett, the oldest of the prisoners at age forty-four, acted as spokesman for all. After professing that he "did wrong in volunteering" when he got to New Bern, the others agreed that they all felt the same way. Mitchell Busick added that he had joined only on threat of death by Union recruiters. The five ended with a joint statement to their former comrades in the North Carolina troops that they had "done wrong and regret it; and warn others not to follow our example." With that, Lieutenant John G. Justice, aide-de-camp on the staff of General Hoke, read the sentence, the nooses were placed over the necks of the condemned, and they were hanged.[53]

The thirteen remaining condemned men had four days to sit in the jail's dungeon to think about their deaths, which would take place on Monday, February 15. Chaplain Paris described the scene in a letter that appeared shortly afterward in the *North Carolina Presbyterian* and the *Wilmington Journal*: "I made my first visit to them as chaplain on Sunday morning. The scene beggars all description. Some of them were comparatively young men. But they made the fatal mistake. They had only twenty-four hours to live. . . . Here was a wife to say farewell to a husband forever. Here a mother to take the last look at her ruined son, and then a sister who had come to embrace for the last time the brother who had brought disgrace upon the very name she bore by his treason to his country."[54]

Last-minute appeals on behalf of the prisoners and their families were negatively, even harshly, received. Sheriff William Fields, who had the confidence of friends and relatives of the prisoners, went to military authorities in an unsuccessful plea for mercy for the men. Similarly, Celia Jane Brock failed in a final plea for her husband John. General Hoke's attitude toward such requests was demonstrated in a rather abrupt confrontation with Bryan McCullen, who had gone to see the general prior to the execution and asked for an order to retrieve the body of his brother-in-law John Haddock so he could bury it: "Hoke inquired if I wanted to bury him in the Yankee uniform? I replied that I did. Hoke then expressed surprise that so respectable a man as I would bury my brother in law in Yankee uniform. Capt. O. S. Dewey, the post quartermaster, who had kindly accompanied me, then interfered and obtained the order for me."[55]

The determination of Generals Pickett and Hoke to punish Confederate deserters was apparently resulting in a loss of morale among the officers and men of the brigade, who were called out to witness a total of approximately seventy executions in Kinston by either hanging or firing squad. The hangings in particular seemed to have touched a nerve. They "began and increased until they got to be frightful," according to Lieutenant Samuel Tate of the Sixth North Carolina. "It was sort of a general hanging down there. There were so many executions that I was considerably worried at having to take my men over so often."[56]

The morning of February 15 was given over to family visitation and religious rites for the condemned. The scene in the jail was described by Reverend Paris in his diary as truly moving. "The stress of [the] women and children was truly great." Catherine Summerlin, given only fifteen minutes to say farewell to her husband Jesse, was confronted by prisoner William Haddock, who asked her to give his clothes to his mother. Mrs. Summerlin reported that she had recently been harassed by a Colonel Baker, who took her horse and ordered soldiers to take provisions from her home. Eight of the condemned men were baptized in their cell by Paris, who had returned that morning with three other ministers. Two other prisoners, John and Joseph Brock, were taken to the Neuse River, where baptismal ceremonies were performed for them by Reverend George W. Camp, a civilian Baptist minister and Kinston merchant. After leading the men in prayer, Paris urged them to reveal the names of the "men who had seduced them to desert and go to the enemy." The names of five citizens of Jones County were given, which the chaplain wrote down to give to General Hoke for further action.[57]

The execution took place to the accompaniment of a military band in a field in back of the town. General Hoke, who was absent because of other duties, turned the ceremonies over to his staff officers. His brigade formed a square equidistant around the gallows, with onlookers outside. The thirteen condemned men marched through the soft sand of the old field to the scaffold, where they listened to a staff officer read the findings of the court-martial and the charges and specifications against them. Brigade chaplains offered public prayers in their behalf, after which the thirteen condemned men climbed the steps of the gallows and lined up in a row. They were given a last opportunity to make statements. If any were made, they went unrecorded. Ropes, ironically taken from a Confederate gunboat named the *Neuse*, were placed around their necks. At that instant, the wives of John Brock and Jesse Summerlin turned their eyes away, unable to watch their husbands die. The signal was given and the trapdoor dropped, sending the men into eternity. Brigade surgeons examined the bodies, confirmed their deaths, and the assembled troops were given orders to depart.[58]

The scenes that followed were bizarre. The hangman, a somewhat mysterious unidentified man, described as a tall, stout, dark-complected, cross- or squint-eyed man from Raleigh, extracted the "pay" for his day's work directly from the bodies of the dead men. Several people witnessed him cutting the buttons from uniforms and taking clothes, leaving some nude and others in their underwear. He later boasted that he "would do anything for money" and was well paid.[59] Some of the bodies were buried in a sandy grave at the foot of the gallows. Others were retrieved by their wives and relatives or by friends who volunteered their services. In some cases, widows lived within Union lines and were unable to make the journey to Confederate Kinston.

William Jones's widow complained later that "plenty would have been willing to have assisted me, but did not dare for fear of being called Unionist." She found her husband naked except for a pair of socks. Without a conveyance for his body, she returned home and sent her fifteen-year-old son and seventeen-year-old cousin. After a week, they found the body in a loft in the possession of a guard placed over it by a doctor. With his permission, they carried him home for burial. Sheriff Fields, a twelve-year veteran in the office, felt secure enough in his position to intercede for the deserters' families. At the widow's request, he removed Jesse Summerlin's body from the gallows and personally transported it twenty miles for a home burial.[60]

While the families were retrieving the bodies from the site of the mass execution, the court-martial board reconvened in Goldsboro on February 16 to consider the cases of the remaining six Beech Grove captives charged with desertion. There was, however, a noticeable lack of intensity in the proceedings. Gone was the seeming inevitability of the death sentence. One prisoner, William Clinton Cox, was found not guilty but remained a prisoner of war. The "extreme youth, . . . physical disability and mental imbecility" of Private Alexander McCoy resulted in simple confinement at hard labor. Two men, George Hawkins and Ruel Wetherington, were sentenced to be branded on their left hips with the letter *D* four inches in length. In addition, each was ordered to have a five-foot-long chain and twelve-pound ball attached to his left ankle and to work at hard labor on government projects for the duration of the war.[61]

Cox managed to avoid conviction as a result of testimony by Captain Guilford W. Cox, who had served with the prisoner in the Atlantic and North Carolina Bridge Guard Company. The captain used his position as provost marshal for Kinston to have himself summoned as a witness for the defense. The court accepted his argument that local service in a railroad guard company did not constitute Confederate service. Consequently, the prisoner was found not guilty of desertion. The court recommended, nevertheless, that he be turned over to civil authorities to be tried for treason. Two months later he died of fever in the Confederate prison camp in Andersonville, Georgia.[62] Ironically, Captain Cox deserted to the Union soon after saving his former comrade from the gallows.

Only two of the final six alleged deserters received the death penalty. The sentence for Elijah Kellum appears to have been undeserved. Court-martial records listed him not as a Confederate soldier but simply as an "enrolled Conscript in the Confederate service." According to W. S. Huggins of Kinston, Kellum was a young and illiterate farmer from adjoining Jones County who had "volunteered for one or two [Southern] companies; but none would receive him, he was so deformed and he had no constitution." He was, however, "to be sent to a conscript camp by some persons who wished to scare him; he hearing of it deserted to the Union lines." Despite this, conscription officer Captain Thomas Wilson testified to the contrary, and Kellum was sentenced to hang.[63]

The execution date for William Irving Hill, a deserter from Whitford's Battalion in the Confederate service, and Kellum was set for Monday, February 22, 1864. Like their now-deceased companions, they were to be hanged in Kinston in the presence of Hoke's Brigade. The setting was similar. On the day before and the morning of their deaths, they were visited by Reverend Paris, who baptized Kellum and led the two men in prayer. Although they claimed to be prepared for death, both protested that their execution was undeserved because they had been persuaded by others to desert.[64]

With the deaths of Kellum and Hill, the hangings ceased. None of the twenty-two deceased men had lived longer than ninety days after their ill-starred decision to enlist in the Union army. Most of the remaining thirty-one North Carolina Unionists captured at Beech Grove were no more fortunate than those who had died on the gallows. Three eventually received paroles; the fate of four others is unknown; and the final twenty-five prisoners lived a brief two months after their surrender. The suffering of the latter probably equaled that of their hanged comrades.

Since none of the surviving Beech Grove captives had deserted the Confederate army, they were accorded the status of prisoners of war. From Kinston they were taken to Goldsboro for transportation to a prisoner-of-war camp in Richmond, Virginia, arriving on February 11 and 12, 1864. Within days, some of the North Carolinians began reporting to the hospital suffering from fevers, bronchitis, debilitas, rubeola, diarrhea, and various other ailments. Confederate medical personnel, to the surprise of many, treated them with kindness and provided a proper diet. Owing to the breakdown of prisoner exchanges in 1863, however, Southern prisons became overcrowded, and Richmond's three prison hospitals overflowed to twice their intended capacity.[65] As a result, at least eleven of the North Carolinians died.

Beginning in mid-February 1864, an attempt to relieve the overcrowding was begun through prisoner shipments to the newly opened prison in Andersonville, Georgia. James Elliott, member of a fifty-man detail from the Fifty-sixth North Carolina assigned to accompany the prisoners to Georgia, reported that the men were "in a pitiable plight and infected with small-pox."[66] One prisoner from the Second North Carolina Union regiment died en route and was buried in Augusta, Georgia. The thirteen men captured at Beech Grove who arrived in Andersonville found sickness and death on an almost unbelievable scale because of the inadequacy of supplies and the Confederacy's increasing poverty. Of the thirteen North Carolinians to arrive at their destination, ten died within a month of the same illnesses that killed their comrades in Virginia. Three others were paroled and were spared the fate of their friends.[67]

There is little doubt that Generals Pickett and Hoke intended the mass executions to serve as a reminder to their own troops of the consequences of desertion and hoped that the harshness of the penalties and the firmness with which they were carried out would slow the flood tide of defections from the Confederate army. To drive this point home, they wasted little time in approving a sermon on the deserters' deaths for delivery to Hoke's entire brigade six days after the last execution, while the image of death was still fresh in their minds.

For more than an hour, Reverend Paris passionately extolled the virtues of patriotism and condemned the evils of desertion. Deserters were, according to Paris, no better than Judas Iscariot and Benedict Arnold. "If in this bloody war our country should be overrun," he argued, it would result largely from soldiers listening to defeatist elements at home. Discontent, he warned, was caused by so-called peace meetings composed of men "who talk more about their 'rights' than their duty and loyalty to their country" and by defeatists who claimed that "we are whipt!"; "it is useless to fight any longer!"; and "this is the rich man's war and the poor man's fight!" Certain newspapers had added to the fire, as did some clergymen preaching from the pulpit. These and letters from so-called friends at home, Paris warned, overcame some soldiers in the ranks, and "the young man of promise and of hope once, now becomes a deserter." Warning of the harsh consequences of a Union victory, Paris appealed to Confederate patriotism:

> Shall we then lay down our arms before we are overthrown? God forbid! Sons of Carolina, let your battle-cry be Onward! Onward! until victory shall crown the beautiful banner that floats over us today with such a peace as freemen only love, and brave men only can accept.[68]

Reactions to the mass executions ranged from fear to condemnation to approval. Within the Union-occupied eastern portion of the state, Colonel Edward Ripley reported utter demoralization in the ranks of the North Carolina Union regiments: "Indeed they are already looking to the swamps for the protection they have so far failed of getting from our Government. . . . I believe they will inevitably, in case of a fight, become panic-stricken and have a bad effect on the rest of this slim command."[69]

In Confederate Kinston, some local residents felt that the offense had not been sufficiently serious to warrant the severity of the punishment. This view resulted from the belief that Confederate authorities had broken their promise to the men of the local-service units that they would not be removed from the general area of their homes. Others expressed satisfaction with the penalties, wishing that such other "traitors" as peace activist William W. Holden had been hanged with them. Leonidas L. Polk, future state commissioner of agriculture and Populist Party leader, wrote that the "criminals" deserved to die, regretting only that he had had to watch.[70] Most Confederate and many Union soldiers felt that the traitors got their just desserts. One Northern soldier from the Twenty-fifth Massachusetts Infantry blamed the Federal government for allowing deserters from the enemy to serve against their former comrades.[71]

Official reaction to the deaths of the North Carolina Union soldiers was slow in coming from Federal military authorities. Maj. Gen. Peck, commander of the District of North Carolina, learned of the Kinston incident indirectly through correspondence involving the reported execution of a Negro Union soldier by Confederates during the New Bern campaign. He immediately corresponded with Pickett, his Confederate counterpart, at his Petersburg, Virginia, headquarters. Enclosed in Peck's letter was an order from President Lincoln mandating retaliation in such situations. "It is ordered," wrote the president, "that for every soldier of the United States killed in violation of the laws of war, a rebel soldier shall be executed." Peck informed Pickett that he intended to carry out the president's order unless the Southern general promised to bring the offenders to justice.[72]

Two days later, Peck learned for the first time that soldiers of the Second North Carolina Union Volunteers had been taken prisoner during the Confederate attack on New Bern. He quickly penned a second letter informing Pickett that in his "hasty retreat" from New Bern, he had taken prisoner fifty-three "loyal and true North Carolinians" in the service of the Union army. The names of these men were provided to ensure that they would be treated equally with other prisoners of war.[73]

Peck was unaware that seven men had already been hanged by the time he wrote the letter, and by the time it arrived in Pickett's headquarters thirteen more would be dead, with the final two awaiting execution. The slowness of the mail, which traveled by flag of truce boats and required an eight- to nine-day turnaround time, worked against any hopes of intervention. Peck's two letters, containing his threat of retaliation as well as what to Pickett would have been an irksome reference to the latter's "hasty retreat," placed additional roadblocks in the way of leniency toward the North Carolina Unionists. The Southern general gave his reply in two letters dated February 16 and 17. In regard to Union retaliation should the prisoners be executed, "I have merely to say that I have in my hands . . . some 450 officers and men of the United States army, and for every man you hang, I will hang ten of the United States army." Pickett then sarcastically thanked Peck for the list of the fifty-three men "which you so kindly furnished," since this would enable him to bring to justice any that had not yet been identified among the prisoners as Confederate deserters. Pickett then provided his Union counterpart with a list of twenty-two soldiers of the Second North Carolina Volunteers who had been tried, convicted, and executed for desertion from the Confederate army. The list erred in that, as of that date, Kellum and Hill were still alive. They would be hanged about the time Peck received the letter.[74]

With the deaths of the twenty-two prisoners, any further correspondence was pointless and served only to aggravate the situation. On February 20 Peck learned of the first executions from an article in the *Fayetteville Observer*. After informing his superiors of the situation, he wrote Pickett that he was holding two colonels, two lieutenant colonels, two majors, and two captains hostage in Fort Monroe for the safety of the remaining North Carolina captives. Pickett took the threat seriously and prepared for retaliatory executions should Peck carry out his threat. After informing his own superiors of the exchange of correspondence and the charges being made, Pickett requested that "the whole of the prisoners captured in this department be held at my disposal" in case the need arose for tit-for-tat executions.[75] The next day, he wrote Peck renewing his claim that the executed men were deserters from the Confederate army who had been "taken in arms against their colors." If, he added, the eight Confederate officers held hostage in Fort Monroe could be proven to have deserted from the Union army, Peck would be justified in their execution. "Otherwise, should you retaliate, you will simply be guilty of murder." Pickett repeated that his own threat of retaliation was still in effect.[76]

Frustrated at the stalemate and angered over the hanging of so many of his men, Peck concluded his correspondence with Pickett with a threat of retribution along with his side of the argument over the loyalty of the deceased captives from Beech Grove. "These men," he informed Pickett, "were ever loyal to the United States, and opposed secession" until forced into the service by the Confederacy's "merciless conscription." This might have "compelled the suspense of their true sentiments, but was powerless to destroy their love for the federal Union. . . . With tens of thousands . . . they seized the first opportunity to rush within my lines, and resume their former allegiance. . . . In view of their unswerving and unflagging loyalty, I cannot doubt that the government will take immediate steps to redress these outrages upon humanity." With this prediction of prosecution, Peck informed Pickett that "my duty has been performed, and the blood of these unfortunates will rest upon you and your associates."[77]

Peck had no intention of letting the matter drop. Copies of his correspondence with General Pickett were forwarded to Maj. Gen. Benjamin F. Butler, commander of the Department of Virginia and North Carolina in Fort Monroe, for further action. Butler fully accepted Peck's arguments and forwarded the correspondence to General Ulysses S. Grant with the suggestion that he contact Confederate authorities. Then, "upon their answer, such action may be taken as will sustain the dignity of the government, and give a promise to afford protection to its citizens."[78]

Grant disagreed with Butler's argument, as he had indicated in an earlier letter to Confederate general Joseph E. Johnston regarding Confederate deserters who had joined the Union army. "Of course," Grant had written, "I would claim no right to retaliate for the punishment of deserters who had actually been mustered into the Confederate Army and afterwards deserted and joined ours." He did not agree, however, to punishment for Union soldiers who had been conscripted but deserted before being sworn into the Confederate army.[79] Although Elijah Kellum fell into that category, this exception would never be seriously pursued by Union authorities.

In addition to disagreeing with Butler about Confederate deserters,

Grant was not inclined to prosecute Southern officers, many of whom he knew personally, for actions carried out under wartime conditions. This appears to have been particularly true in the case of Pickett, a former West Point associate with whom he had maintained a long friendship that would survive the war.[80] Following the war, Pickett learned that his friendship with General Grant notwithstanding he was among those excluded from pardon by President Andrew Johnson's proclamation of May 29, 1865. In an effort to remain peacefully at home with his family, he requested an exception in his case and signed an oath of allegiance. These were blocked, however, by Secretary of War Edwin M. Stanton who informed Johnston that Pickett was under investigation for the "unlawful hanging of . . . citizens of North Carolina."[81]

Pickett became greatly concerned when nothing came of his pardon application. Former Confederate president Davis had been sent to Fort Monroe in irons, a Federal grand jury was considering indictments of Lee and others in Norfolk, and President Andrew Johnson appeared determined to punish Southern leaders.[82] As a result, the Pickett family reluctantly agreed to go secretly into exile in Montreal, Canada, where they resided for a time under the alias of Edwards.[83] During his exile, he continued to campaign for assurances of safety from prosecution should he return home. Friends in the Union army, relatives, and Pickett himself wrote repeatedly to General Grant to intercede in his behalf with the president.[84]

Pickett had good reason to fear returning home. His role in ordering the execution of the twenty-two Second North Carolina Union Volunteer captives had created bitter enemies, particularly among their former officers and comrades in North Carolina. The apparent leader of the drive to bring Pickett to trial for war crimes was Captain W. H. Doherty, assistant quartermaster in New Bern. On September 13, 1865, he wrote the first of a series of requests to superiors in the army and government to bring to justice former Confederate generals Pickett and Hoke, "wicked and cruel men who have deliberately murdered . . . soldiers of the United States, when prisoners."[85] As a result, Secretary of War Stanton instructed Maj. Gen. Thomas H. Ruger, Peck's successor as commander of the Department of North Carolina, to appoint a board of inquiry to investigate. Doherty, the initiator of the investigation, was placed in charge of the three-officer board.

Between September 13 and November 14, 1865, the board held hearings in New Bern and Kinston in an effort to determine the identity of all those responsible for the alleged murders. Twenty-eight witnesses were called,

including widows of the deceased, former Confederate and Union soldiers, local officials, and citizens of the area who witnessed the hangings.
Perhaps the most damning testimony came from Confederate colonel John
H. Nethercutt, under whom thirteen of the deceased had served. From
him the board concluded that a number of the executed men had served in
the local defense service rather than in the regular Confederate army. They
could not, therefore, be guilty of desertion, the crime for which they had
been tried and hanged.[86]

On November 18, 1865, the board issued its final report. Responsibility
for the executions, it concluded, lay with the following individuals: General Pickett, who ordered the executions; General Hoke, who was in
charge of the hangings; the unidentified members of the court-martial
board, who sentenced the men; a Colonel Baker, who had "robbed and
persecuted their widows"; and the two voluntary hangmen, Blunt King
and the unknown executioner with the "cross or squint eye." Because these
men were "guilty of crimes too heinous to be excused by the United States
government, . . . there should be a military commission immediately appointed for [their] trial . . . to inflict upon [them] their just punishment."[87]

When the report reached Washington, Judge Advocate General Joseph
Holt, head of the Bureau of Military Justice in Washington, criticized the
board of inquiry for misinterpreting the testimony of witnesses and for
gathering insufficient evidence upon which action could be taken. According to Holt, the investigators had "misapprehended" Nethercutt's testimony regarding the status of the deceased men. "On the contrary," he
ruled, "the little evidence [produced] on that point . . . tends to show that
they were," in fact, deserters. He further criticized the board of inquiry for
not questioning a sufficient number of witnesses on this point:

> It is the opinion of this office . . . [that although] the blood of these
> murdered men should cry in vain from their dishonored graves for
> vengeance, it finds in the evidence submitted to it no grounds upon
> which personal charges could be established and sustained against the
> guilty parties.[88]

Holt forwarded the report to Secretary of War Stanton with the recommendation that the papers in the case be returned to the commanding general of the Department of North Carolina for further investigations. If a
new board should find sufficient evidence, a military commission should
then be appointed for the trial of the guilty parties.

Shortly after reopening the case for further evidence Holt found what he
believed to be the "smoking gun" necessary to convict Pickett of the Kin-

ston hangings. Holt informed Stanton that the former Southern general's letters of February 16 and 17, 1864, in which he curtly informed Union general Peck of the executions of the North Carolinians supplied evidence that was not available to the first board of inquiry. "Not only does the imperious and vaunting temper in which these letters . . . indicate his readiness to commit . . . any . . . atrocity, but his boastful admissions that he was in command at the time that the twenty-two men had been executed . . . all tend to show that he was in responsible command and furnish [the] evidence upon which it is believed charges can be sustained against him."[89]

Pickett's letters, Holt informed Stanton, should be sent to North Carolina to be included with any further evidence the "investigation now in progress" might turn up. As a preliminary step to a trial, Holt suggested that the former Confederate general should be arrested immediately and held for trial with any other guilty persons the new investigation might find evidence against.[90] Pickett, meanwhile, remained in hiding in Montreal, beyond the reach of Union authorities and safe from arrest.

The new board of inquiry was convened in Raleigh on January 23, 1866, under orders to find evidence bearing upon the circumstances of the "murders" and to identify those who could be held accountable. Hearings were conducted in Salisbury, Goldsboro, Kinston, New Bern, Halifax, Beaufort, and other localities. The investigators found it difficult, however, to obtain additional evidence. "Great distaste was quite generally exhibited by the witnesses to testify," they reported, "lest they might be considered by their friends in the light of informers." "Defective memories" seemed to be particularly prevalent.[91]

The second board of inquiry was nevertheless thorough in its search. Witnesses included former governor Zebulon Vance, ex-provisional governor William W. Holden, members of the state legislature, state supreme court judge William H. Battle, the secretary of state, and whoever they thought might possess pertinent information. The records of the state adjutant general's office were searched, muster rolls of the units to which the deceased men were said to have belonged were examined, and an attempt was made to locate records of the court-martial that had sentenced the men in question. Nothing, however, was found to implicate anyone other than General Pickett. Correspondence with the custodian of Confederate archives in Washington proved equally fruitless.

The only evidence found tended to bear out Pickett's contention that all the men captured and executed as a result of the New Bern expedition had previously enlisted in the Confederate army for either general or local service and were under the command of Confederate officers prior to enlistment in the United States Army. Consequently, men in those categories could legitimately be charged with desertion from Confederate service.

The board issued its conclusions on March 29, 1866, in Raleigh. While acknowledging the Confederacy's right to execute deserters in certain circumstances, it denied the right under other circumstances. In the board's opinion, men from Nethercutt's local-service battalion, members of bridge guard companies, and North Carolinians who fled to Union lines either before or after conscription could not be charged with desertion. In these cases, it was in agreement with the judge advocate general who argued that service in the Confederate military was itself a crime from which it was a person's duty to escape at the first opportunity. Having so fled and taken refuge in the United States service, the individuals in question were entitled to that country's protection and to its vengeance "for their shameful death."[92]

Regardless of this interpretation, the board regretfully reported on its inability, "after diligent search," to fix responsibility on anyone other than General Pickett. The evidence showed that his was the "prominent authority under whose direction everything connected with the murder of our soldiers took place." It did not contain sufficient grounds to sustain charges against any other individual.[93]

While the board of inquiry was investigating his case in North Carolina, General Pickett appealed to his friend General Grant to intercede in his behalf with President Johnson. In a letter dated March 12, 1866, and postmarked Washington DC, a repentant Pickett stated his case. Noting that the president had not acted upon his application for pardon and that "certain evil disposed persons are attempting to re-open the troubles of the past," he asked "if the time has not arrived for the Executive clemency to be extended in my case, . . . I merely wish some assurance, that I will not be disturbed in my endeavor to keep my family from Starvation, and that my parole . . . may protect me from the assaults of those persons desirous of still keeping up the War which has ended in my humble opinion forever."[94]

In response to Pickett's request, a parole was granted the same day. He was, according to the Union commander, "exempt from arrest by Military Authorities except [as] directed by the President of the United States, Secretary of War, or from these Hd. Qrs. so long as he observes the conditions of his parole."[95] Pickett was further exempted from the prohibition against travel and was given permission to travel about the United States.

Upon receipt of Pickett's request for clemency, General Grant for forwarded it to the president with his recommendation for approval written on the reverse side. Adding that "Gn. Pickett I know personally to be an honorable man," Grant asked assurances that the former Southern general would not be subject to a trial for offenses that, although harsh, were believed necessary if the Confederacy were to maintain its manpower. A trial, Grant argued, would only open up the question whether or not the government meant to keep the "contract entered into to secure the surrender of an armed enemy."[96]

The investigation appeared to be at a dead end. A House of Representatives resolution of April 16, 1866, requested information on the status of the case. Two days later, General Ruger reported from Raleigh that the investigation in North Carolina was still being delayed "owing to the difficulty of obtaining evidence of persons having knowledge of the facts."[97] Three months later, in July, Judge Advocate Holt recommended to the secretary of war that Pickett be arrested and put on trial before a military commission. On July 23, 1866, the House of Representatives passed another resolution requesting from President Johnson information relating to any application for pardon by Pickett as well as whether any further steps had been taken to bring him to justice since the adjournment of the board of inquiry in June 1866.[98]

President Johnson waited until December 11, 1866, to reply to the House of Representatives' resolution requesting information about Pickett's pardon and possible trial. Rather than providing direct responses to their inquiry, his answer to Congress came in the form of opinions given to him by the secretary of war, the attorney general, and the commander of the army. He left it up to the representatives of the lower house to read several documents: Pickett's letter arguing his case for clemency; a letter from Attorney General Henry Stanbery stating that no proceedings had been instituted against Pickett for "any offenses against the laws of war"; and a communication from Stanton that the expected decision of the Supreme Court in *Ex parte Milligan*, which dealt with the trial of individuals by military commission, made him hesitate to make a decision in the case.[99]

The Kinston incident was brought up in Congress again on July 18, 1867, when Grant appeared before the House Judiciary Committee, which was considering the impeachment of President Johnson. In response to his role in Pickett's application for a pardon, an irritated Grant testily replied, "You have no right to ask what my opinion is now."[100]

The case thus came to an inconclusive ending, with all sides apparently choosing to let the matter drop. In 1868, Ulysses S. Grant, having recently been elected president of the United States, was in a position to offer his Southern friend the office of marshal of the state of Virginia. Pickett declined the office and settled down to a life of relative obscurity in Richmond, Virginia. There he engaged in the insurance business until his death in Norfolk in 1875. His stature as a hero of the Confederacy had diminished to the extent that the story of his funeral was postponed for two days by the *Richmond Dispatch* in order to give full coverage to the unveiling of a statue of General Thomas J. "Stonewall" Jackson.[101]

The hanging of the men of Company F, Second North Carolina Union Infantry, was not easily forgotten. Several publications in both the North and South served as a reminder. *The Deserter's Daughter*, a novella written by Private William D. Herrington of the Third North Carolina (Confederate) Cavalry, appeared in 1864, shortly after the Kinston hangings. There is little doubt that it was based on the hanging of the men of the Second North Carolina Union Regiment.[102] Its popularity was such that a second printing in 1865 sold all but a few hundred copies. Less popular was the publication of Reverend John Paris's sermon on desertion to the assembled men of Hoke's Brigade. This was published in 1864 in Greensboro, North Carolina, in an effort to stem the desertion problem.

In 1886, Colonel James W. Savage, formerly of the Twelfth New York Cavalry, reminisced about the Unionists of North Carolina in a speech to an Omaha, Nebraska, audience. His speech and pamphlet-length publication *The Loyal Element of North Carolina during the War* presented one of the best descriptions in print of the capture of the North Carolinians at Beech Grove. A final work, published in 1897 but written in 1868, served as an attempt to keep the issue alive. Colonel Rush C. Hawkins, its author, had encouraged loyal North Carolinians to serve in the army and felt a sense of personal responsibility for the deaths of the men in Kinston. After the war he remained bitter against the Confederacy, Pickett, Hoke, and all involved in the deaths of the twenty-two men. The book expressed his contempt of Grant for his refusal to take part in bringing Pickett and Hoke to trial for war crimes.[103] With Hawkins's death and the confinement of these publications to the dusty shelves of rare book rooms and archives, the controversy surrounding the deaths of the men of Company F, Second North Carolina Union Volunteer Infantry, passed into the obscurity of history.

The question of guilt for the deaths of the twenty-two victims was never resolved. Did it lie with Pickett for ordering the executions or with the executed men themselves who unquestionably deserted one army for service in another or with Union military officials who failed to protect the men from Confederate vengeance? The most reasonable answer is that none were free of guilt, and all shared in the responsibility for their deaths.

Recent scholarship has suggested that Pickett used the Kinston deserters as scapegoats for "feelings of bitterness and . . .[a] sense of failure" that had been building within him since the Battle of Gettysburg.[104] Yet the facts in the Kinston incident can be given a different interpretation, one in which Pickett acted in keeping with the stated views of Robert E. Lee and other Confederate leaders that only significant and harsh punishment would stop the desertions then depleting Southern armies. The number of executions may be seen as an effort to set an example to deter further desertions and the swiftness in carrying out the order as an attempt to prevent President Davis from defeating the purpose with pardons and postponements. Pickett expressed his intention of using the executions to set an example immediately after the confrontation with Haskett and Jones in the camp on Dover road. The deserters were accorded military trials and executed according to standard military procedures. Chaplain Paris's sermon on desertion to the assembled troops lends further emphasis to the military nature of Pickett's reasoning. Other than the extreme nature of the example he set there is little reason to fault his actions in the affair.

The deserters themselves must bear some of the responsibility for their own executions. The circumstances surrounding their service in both armies lead to the conclusion that most felt loyalty to neither Union nor Confederacy. Their efforts to find safety in a war that was on their doorsteps led to relatively "safe" service in local-service units first for the South and, when this was threatened, in similar units for the North. As soldiers, they knew the consequences of their actions and met a fate that they understood.

Pickett's extreme action failed to stem the tide of desertion from the Confederate armies, even in Pickett's own division. By November of that year, one hundred men of Pickett's Division were in the guardhouse for desertion, and indications are that the majority of deserters were never apprehended. Pickett complained bitterly "that every man sentenced to be shot for desertion in his division for the past two months has been reprieved" by President Davis. Ultimately, the highest Confederate political authority proved to lack the stomach for the kind of wholesale executions that Pickett—and Lee—thought necessary to halt the exodus.[105]

In the end, the command problem that Pickett faced remained insoluble. The maintenance of an army of citizen-soldiers within a democratic society must of necessity rest to a large degree on the willingness of the great mass of the common people of that society to pay the price and support the cause—voluntarily. By use of a careful mix of inspiration—be it love of country, commander, or comrades—with the iron fist of military discipline the commander can at best hope to prolong somewhat the survival of the army that is his only bid for victory. The doing so is as much an art as any aspect of his task.

Notes

1. U.S. War Department, *The War of the Rebellion: A Compilation of the Official Records of the Union and Confederate Armies*, 128 vols. (Washington DC: Government Printing Office, 1881–1901), 1st ser., vol. 33, pp. 866–67 (hereafter cited as OR; all references are to series 1 unless otherwise noted).

2. OR 33:164, 168.

3. Edward G. Longacre, *Leader of the Charge: a Biography of General George E. Pickett* (Shippensburg PA: White Mane, 1995), 140–41; Lesley Jill Gordon, " 'Assumed a Darker Hue': Major-General George E. Pickett, C. S. A., May 1863-May 1864" (master's thesis, University of Georgia, 1991), 50.

4. Archie K. Davis, *Boy Colonel of the Confederacy* (Chapel Hill: University of North Carolina Press, 1985), 269.

5. Davis, *Boy Colonel of the Confederacy*, 234.

6. Davis, *Boy Colonel of the Confederacy*, 234, 268–69.

7. Richard Nelson Current, *Lincoln's Loyalists: Union Soldiers from the Confederacy* (Boston: Northeastern University Press, 1992), 64.

8. Rush C. Hawkins, *An Account of the Assassination of Loyal Citizens of North Carolina for Having Served the Union Army, Which Took Place at Kinston in the Months of February and March 1864* (New York: n.p., 1897), 8–11.

9. Current, *Lincoln's Loyalists*, 67; U.S. Archives, Compiled Service Records, NA-MC401, Muster Rolls of the Second North Carolina Union Infantry, microfilm copy, North Carolina State Archives, Raleigh, F.6.646P (hereafter cited as Second North Carolina Union Muster Rolls).

10. Hawkins, *Assassination of Loyal Citizens*, 8–11.

11. Hawkins, *Assassination of Loyal Citizens*, 4.

12. Michael K. Honey, "The War within the Confederacy: White Unionists of North Carolina," *Prologue: Journal of the National Archives* 18 (1986): 74.

13. U.S. Congress, House, *Murder of Union Soldiers in North Carolina*, 34th Cong., 2d sess., 1866, Ex. Doc. 98, serial 1263, 57, 62–63 (hereafter cited as *Murder of Union Soldiers*).

14. Confederate States of America, Headquarters [of Maj. Gen. George E. Pick-

ett], Department [of] North Carolina, General Order No. 6, Camp on Dover Road, February 3, 1864, Rare Book Collection, Z. Smith Reynolds Library, Wake Forest University (hereafter cited as Department of North Carolina Court-Martial Records).

15. *Murder of Union Soldiers,* 38.

16. J. Waldo Denny, *Wearing the Blue in the Twenty-fifth Mass. Volunteer Infantry, with Burnsides Coast Division, 18th Army Corps, and Army of the James* (Worcester MA: Putnam & Davis, 1879), 150–51.

17. *Murder of Union Soldiers,* 38–39, 66, 77.

18. *Murder of Union Soldiers,* 63.

19. *Murder of Union Soldiers,* 57, 63–64.

20. *Murder of Union Soldiers,* 57, 62, 66–67, 78, 85.

21. Honey, "War within the Confederacy," 88.

22. OR 33:870–71.

23. OR 33:870–71.

24. Ernest H. Wardell to Benjamin F. Butler, March 1, 1864, Ernest H. Wardell File, Second North Carolina Union Muster Rolls. For additional references to recruiting practices for the First and Second North Carolina Union regiments see Fred M. Mallison, "Okracoke and Portsmouth Islands in the Civil War" (master's thesis, East Carolina University, 1994), 55, 61–64, 66, 68–71.

25. *Murder of Union Soldiers,* 13.

26. Honey, "War within the Confederacy," 88. The term *buffalo* had several meanings. In this essay it is used to designate white North Carolinians who served in the First and Second North Carolina Union Volunteer regiments. A Unionist writing in October 1863 stated that "their uniforms make them appear so large that the people call them 'Buffaloes.' I think that they like to be called buffaloes. They go about in gangs like herds of buffaloes." See John G. Barrett, *The Civil War in North Carolina* (Chapel Hill: University of North Carolina Press, 1963), 174.

27. Second North Carolina Union Muster Rolls.

28. James W. Savage, *The Loyal Element of North Carolina during the War* (Omaha: n.p., 1886), 7–8; Walter Harrison, *Pickett's Men: A Fragment of War History* (New York: D. Van Nostrand, 1870), 24.

29. Barrett, *Civil War in North Carolina,* 203.

30. OR 33:62, 96.

31. Barrett, *Civil War in North Carolina,* 204–205; John Paris, *A Sermon: Preached before Brig. Gen. Hoke's Brigade, at Kinston, N.C., on the 28th of February, 1864* (Greensboro NC: A. W. Ingold, 1864), 4, John Paris Papers, Collection No. 575, in the Southern Historical Collection of the Manuscripts Department, University of North Carolina, Chapel Hill.

32. Savage, *Loyal Element in North Carolina*, 8; OR 33, 62–64.

33. Harrison, *Pickett's Men*, 114–15; Denny, *Wearing the Blue*, 248–49; A Line Officer in the Second North Carolina Union Volunteers, "Rebel Barbarities," in *The Rebellion Record: A Diary of American Events, with Documents, Narratives, Illustrative Incidents, Poetry, etc.*, ed. Frank Moore, 11 vols. (New York: G. P. Putnam, D. Van Nostrand, 1861–1868), vol. 8, 379–80 (hereafter cited as "Rebel Barbarities").

34. Harrison, *Pickett's Men*, 114–17; "Rebel Barbarities," 8:378–80.

35. Harrison, *Pickett's Men*, 116.

36. *Murder of Union Soldiers*, 80–81.

37. *Murder of Union Soldiers*, 80–81.

38. Department of North Carolina Court-Martial Records, 1–8. Most contemporary sources testified that the court-martial board was composed entirely of officers from Pickett's Virginia brigades. Pickett, however, in a letter to Ulysses S. Grant dated March 18, 1866, claimed that the board consisted of officers from Georgia, North Carolina, and Virginia. See John Y. Simon, ed., *The Papers of Ulysses S. Grant*, 20 vols. to date (Carbondale: Southern Illinois University Press, 1967–), vol. 16, 122 (hereafter cited as PG); *Murder of Union Soldiers*, 16, 78, 82.

39. Department of North Carolina Court-Martial Records, 1–2; *Murder of Union Soldiers*, 12, 70.

40. Dunbar Rowland, ed., *Jefferson Davis, Constitutionalist: His Letters, Papers, and Speeches*, 10 vols. (Jackson: Mississippi Department of Archives and History, 1923), vol. 6, 143, 188, 208, 326, 333–34. Although some of these occurred after the dates of the executions in Kinston, they nevertheless illustrate the concern of Lee and others of the Confederate command over Davis's actions.

41. Harrison, *Pickett's Men*, 117. An analysis of the muster rolls of Company F, Second North Carolina Union Volunteers, identifies only three sergeants taken prisoner at Beech Grove: Jesse Summerlin, Andrew J. Brittain, and William Clinton Cox. Summerlin and Brittain were the tenth and eleventh men tried and had served together in Nethercutt's battalion of partisan rangers. Both were hanged. Although Cox was not hanged, he was the last man tried. It is reasonable to assume that he is the person described by Harrison as betraying his fellow prisoners. He had not served with any of the other prisoners in the Confederate service and did not live near them before the war. The not-guilty verdict in his case may be looked on as a reward for cooperation as a witness against the other prisoners during the trials.

42. *Murder of Union Soldiers*, 19–20, 30, 35.

43. *Wilmington Journal*, April 28, 1864.

44. *Murder of Union Soldiers*, 33, 79–81.

45. *Murder of Union Soldiers*, 33–34, 36, 77, 79–80, 83; *Wilmington Journal*, April 28, 1864.

46. Department of North Carolina Court-Martial Records, 2–3.

47. *Murder of Union Soldiers*, 16, 41, 46.

48. Department of North Carolina Court-Martial Records, 3–6.

49. *Murder of Union Soldiers*, 16, 41, 46.

50. *Murder of Union Soldiers*, 41; Clifford C. Tyndall, "Lenoir County during the Civil War" (master's thesis, East Carolina University, 1981), 69–82.

51. Department of North Carolina Court-Martial Records, 6.

52. Leonidas L. Polk to "My Dear Sallie," February 13, 1864, Leonidas Lafayette Polk Papers, Collection No. 3708, in the Southern Historical Collection of the Manuscripts Department, University of North Carolina, Chapel Hill.

53. *Murder of Union Soldiers*, 13; "The Deserters Hung at Kinston, N.C.," *Wilmington Journal*, April 28, 1864.

54. *Murder of Union Soldiers*, 14.

55. *Murder of Union Soldiers*, 68–70.

56. *Murder of Union Soldiers*, 68–70.

57. John Paris Diary, February 15, 1864, John Paris Papers, Collection No. 575, in the Southern Historical Collection of the Manuscripts Department, University of North Carolina at Chapel Hill (hereafter cited as Paris Diary); *Murder of Union Soldiers*, 20, 28, 31; *Wilmington Journal*, April 28, 1864. Paris gave two conflicting occasions for when he learned the names of the persons guilty of encouraging desertion among Nethercutt's men: February 12, the morning the five men were hanged, and February 15, the morning the thirteen men were executed. The latter date, recorded at the time in his daily diary, should be accepted as correct.

58. *Murder of Union Soldiers*, 27–28, 31–32, 46, 69, 83.

59. *Murder of Union Soldiers*, 16–17, 28, 41.

60. *Murder of Union Soldiers*, 17, 28, 31, 42–43.

61. Department of North Carolina Court-Martial Records, 6–8. Second North Carolina Union Volunteer muster rolls show that McCoy died in a Confederate prison in Richmond, Virginia, on April 2, 1864. Hawkins was taken prisoner at Beech Grove and appears to have been a member of Company F, although his name is not listed on the unit's muster rolls. He was sent to prison in Richmond. Muster rolls show that Wetherington either escaped or was paroled and returned to duty in New Bern by September 1864.

62. *Murder of Union Soldiers*, 45; Second North Carolina Union Muster Rolls.

63. *Murder of Union Soldiers*, 40–41; Department of North Carolina Court-Martial Records, 6–7.

64. Paris Diary, February 21–22, 1864; *Wilmington Journal*, April 28, 1864.

65. H. H. Cunningham, *Doctors in Gray: The Confederate Medical Service* (Baton Rouge: Louisiana State University Press, 1958), 100, 102–3; Second North Carolina Union Volunteer Muster Rolls.

66. James Carson Elliott, *The Southern Soldier Boy* (Raleigh NC: Edwards & Broughton, 1907), 12–13.

67. Second North Carolina Union Volunteers Muster Rolls.

68. Paris, *A Sermon*, 8–11.

69. "Charles Henry Foster and the Unionists of Eastern North Carolina," *North Carolina Historical Review* 37, no. 3 (July 1960): 364–65.

70. Polk to "My Dear Sallie."

71. Denny, *Wearing the Blue*, 251.

72. OR 33:866–67.

73. OR 33:867.

74. OR 33:867–68.

75. *Murder of Union Soldiers*, 9.

76. OR 33:869–70.

77. *Murder of Union Soldiers*, 6–7.

78. *Murder of Union Soldiers*, 2–3.

79. Current, *Lincoln's Loyalists*, 121.

80. Longacre, *Leader of the Charge*, 20.

81. Hawkins, *Assassination of Loyal Citizens*, 34, 36.

82. Brooks D. Simpson, *Let Us Have Peace: Ulysses S. Grant and the Politics of War and Reconstruction* (Chapel Hill: University of North Carolina Press, 1991), 106–7.

83. Longacre, *Leader of the Charge*, 173–74.

84. PG 16:121, 17:221.

85. "The Case of G. E. Pickett," *New York Times*, December 12, 1866; Hawkins, *Assassination of Loyal Citizens*, 49–50. W. H. Doherty was a politically ambitious Northern educator. After five years as a senior professor at Antioch College in Ohio, he moved to North Carolina to assume the presidency of Graham College. When the war began, Doherty was serving as the principal of New Bern Academy. On April 12, 1862, he applied, apparently unsuccessfully, to President Lincoln for a position as judge of the United States District Court in North Carolina. Afterward, Doherty was made captain in the quartermaster corps in New Bern. No special reason is known for his intense interest in seeing Pickett prosecuted for war crimes. Memorial and Petition of W. H. Doherty for a Judgeship in North Carolina, New Bern Occupation Papers, Collection No. 1993, Southern Historical Collection of the Manuscripts Department, University of North Carolina, Chapel Hill.

86. *Murder of Union Soldiers*, 16, 48.

87. *Murder of Union Soldiers*, 15–17.

88. *Murder of Union Soldiers*, 47–49.

89. *Murder of Union Soldiers*, 53.

90. *Murder of Union Soldiers*, 53–54.

91. *Murder of Union Soldiers*, 55, 59–60.

92. *Murder of Union Soldiers*, 58–59.

93. *Murder of Union Soldiers*, 59.

94. PG 16:121–22.

95. PG 16:121–22.

96. PG 16:121–22.

97. *Murder of Union Soldiers*, 52.

98. *New York Times*, December 12, 1866; *Congressional Globe*, 39th Cong., 1st sess., 1866, 4047.

99. *New York Times*, December 12, 1866; James D. Richardson, comp., *A Compilation of the Messages and Papers of the Presidents, 1789–1897*, 10 vols. (Washington DC, 1897), vol. 6, 459–60.

100. PG 17:221.

101. *Richmond Dispatch*, October 26, 1875.

102. William D. Herrington, *The Captain's Bride: A Tale of the War; and The Deserter's Daughter*, ed. W. Keats Sparrow (Raleigh: Division of Archives and History, North Carolina Department of Cultural Resources, 1990), 11–12.

103. Hawkins, *Assassination of Loyal Citizens*, 45.

104. Longacre, *Leader of the Charge*, 140–41; Gordon, "Assumed a Darker Hue," 50.

105. OR 42, pt. 3, 1213.

4 / Engineering and Command: The Case of General William S. Rosecrans 1862 – 1863

PHILIP L. SHIMAN

Engineering is a crucial feature of military operations and an essential factor in military decision making. This was no less true in the 1860s than it is today. At the front, Civil War military engineers assisted the armies in marching and fighting. They conducted surveys and prepared maps to enable the leaders at all levels to formulate and execute their plans. They built, repaired, and maintained roads and bridges to allow the army to maneuver, and when necessary they destroyed or obstructed infrastructure to hinder the enemy's movements. They laid out and constructed fortifications to defend the army and essential posts, and they planned and supervised the construction of works intended to overcome the defenses of the enemy. No less important was their work behind the lines, sometimes far from the scene of the fighting. In the theater of war, the engineers' efforts were focused on securing and supported the armies' lines of communications, especially the railroads. They constructed and repaired tracks, bridges, culverts, and depots. They also built fortifications for the defense of the rail lines, especially the most vulnerable points, such as garrisoned posts, depots, and bridges.[1]

The maintenance and defense of the armies' communications was arguably the most important task of the Federal engineers and, indeed, the most formidable strategic problem faced by the Northern commanders. More than one campaign failed for logistical reasons, especially in the western theater. As the Federal armies penetrated into the Southern interior, their supply lines often stretched hundreds of miles through hostile territory. Communications based on rivers were generally secure enough as long as those rivers remained navigable, but when the armies left the security of the waterways they depended almost exclusively on long, thin rail lines that

were vulnerable to raids. Southern cavalry under Nathan Bedford Forrest, Jeb Stuart, and others and semiregular partisans such as those under John Mosby and John Hunt Morgan became expert at the lightning mounted raid that played havoc with Federal supplies. Southern guerrilla bands and even local residents could interrupt the flow of supplies by burning bridges, tearing up track, and attacking or derailing trains. Until they could defeat or at least neutralize these threats, Federal armies had much difficulty advancing into the Southern interior.

Because the United States Army had never fought a war on such a scale as this, and because many of these problems—such as those involving the railroads—were virtually unprecedented, there were few ready-made solutions. Army commanders and their engineer officers had to come up with their own. They struggled to do so while suffering under the handicap of inadequate resources in manpower and matériel, especially in the West. At the start of the war the army lacked sufficient equipment and well-trained engineer officers and men. At the time of the firing on Fort Sumter in 1861, the Corps of Engineers and Topographical Engineers together numbered ninety-three officers and one understrength company of soldiers. Within the first year of the war, the strength of the officer corps declined precipitously as men were lost to death, retirement, resignation, and the volunteer forces. Meanwhile, the only engineering equipment was a single, nearly worthless pontoon bridge train left over from the Mexican War. Although Congress did authorize a modest expansion of engineer personnel and expenditure of money for equipment, these resources were disproportionately assigned to the forces operating in Virginia, especially in the first two years of the war. The western commanders were left virtually on their own.[2]

The respective commanders dealt with this situation in different ways, finding and employing the resources that they did have available. Maj. Gen. William S. Rosecrans is an interesting case study in how this was done. In the fall of 1862, after eighteen months of war, Rosecrans's new command, the Army of the Cumberland, possessed little engineering matériel and only a rudimentary engineer organization, problems that had proved significant hindrances to its ability to conduct operations and achieve its assigned objectives. A year later, when Rosecrans was relieved of command following the defeat at Chickamauga, the Army of the Cumberland was well on its way to assembling the best-organized and best-equipped engineer department in the western theater, and perhaps of the war. This turnaround was the direct result of the personal attention and vigorous efforts of Rosecrans himself. Rosecrans's engineering reforms had a tremendous impact on the course of the war. They helped the North to seize and consolidate its hold on Middle Tennessee, providing a springboard for the final, fatal advances into the Southern heartland. Their influence would be felt even more during 1864, when the organizations created and trained by Rosecrans and his officers would play a major role in Maj. Gen. William T. Sherman's decisive success in the campaign for Atlanta.

That Rosecrans should have played a leading role in the development of engineer organization should be no surprise, given his own professional background. At the Military Academy—the leading engineering school in the country even as late as the 1860s—Rosecrans had been an excellent student, graduating fifth in this class in 1842, and had been accepted into the army's elite and exclusive Corps of Engineers. After a brief stint constructing seacoast fortifications at Hampton Roads in Virginia, he returned to West Point in 1843 to serve two tours as an assistant professor of engineering (and, for a year, of natural and experimental philosophy). In addition to teaching sections of cadets, assistant professors of engineering took part in an intensive study of engineering, strategy, and tactics under the supervision of the master himself, the legendary professor Dennis Hart Mahan. Upon leaving the academy for the second time, Rosecrans served for the next seven years on various engineering projects, including fortress construction and harbor improvement in Rhode Island, river and harbor surveys in Massachusetts, and work on the Washington Navy Yard. In 1854 he resigned from the service to seek his fortune in business.[3]

Upon the outbreak of the war, Rosecrans found himself much in demand by the government. He served briefly as engineer on the staff of Maj. Gen. George B. McClellan, then commanding the Union forces in Ohio. He turned down the offer of a position as chief engineer for the state of Ohio in favor of a field command in McClellan's army. He served with great distinction as a brigade commander in the triumphant campaign in West Virginia and then commanded the Department of West Virginia during the fall and winter of 1861–1862. The following spring he was awarded the command of a division in Maj. Gen. Henry Halleck's forces advancing upon Corinth, Mississippi, rising to commander of the Army of the Mississippi. On October 23, 1862, he assumed command of the Army of the Ohio, which he soon renamed the Army of the Cumberland.[4]

Few professional soldiers would think lightly of leading an army to battle without adequate engineering support, and Rosecrans was no exception. Like many of his fellow generals, he spent much of his wartime career begging for a greater share of resources. And, like the others, he usually begged in vain.[5] But Rosecrans was not one to give up easily when his requests were denied. If anything characterized the brilliant Ohioan, it was persistence and creativity, in equal measures. Denied the resources that he sought, he made do with what he had. As commander of the Army of the Mississippi in 1862, he created his own construction battalion, a corps of African-American pioneers under the command of a civil engineer. These pioneers rendered important service at the Battle of Corinth, building new fortifications for the tired army the night after the first day's fight—the first instance of African Americans serving as combat engineers in battle during the war.[6] Lacking adequate maps of the theater in which his army operated, Rosecrans organized his own corps of topographical engineers, consisting of officers detailed to every brigade and division headquarters. "Destitute of engineers or topographical engineers, groping our way through an unknown wooded and hostile country, we have been obliged to resort to every possible devices to obtain and diffuse information among commanders of troops," he told the War Department.[7]

As the newly appointed commander of the Army of the Cumberland, Rosecrans's task was to turn around the army's fortunes after its disappointing campaign of the previous summer. Under the command of Maj. Gen. Don Carlos Buell, the army had been detached from Halleck's mammoth army group at Corinth in June and sent east along the line of the Memphis & Charleston Railroad with the objective of seizing Chattanooga and opening communications with the Union sympathizers in East Tennessee. (A small force under Brig. Gen. Ormsby Mitchell was already occupying Middle Tennessee and menacing Chattanooga). Buell made slow but steady progress initially, and by August leading elements of his army were only twenty miles from Chattanooga.

But by then the advance had halted. Buell's troops were scattered across Middle Tennessee, engaged in either repairing the railroad or defending it against the raids of Confederate cavalry, partisans, and guerrillas. Buell struggled to cover the railroad and its garrison with wooden stockade fortifications to allow him to consolidate his scattered forces into a mobile army again, but he failed. Well-timed raids by Forrest and Morgan cut Buell's communications and paralyzed his army. Soon after, Confederate generals Edmund Kirby Smith and Braxton Bragg, acting in concert, bypassed the now-helpless Federal army and invaded Kentucky. Buell was forced to follow, and in a few days all of the Federal gains of the summer were lost. Bragg's Kentucky raid—for that is what his venture amounted to—was turned back at the Battle of Perryville, but the damage had been done: Middle Tennessee south of Nashville remained in Confederate hands. Rosecrans would have to begin the conquest anew.[8]

Rosecrans realized that much of Buell's failure had been attributable to the army's inadequate engineering organization and preparations. To begin with, the army lacked skilled engineer officers. There was but a single officer of the Corps of Engineers, Captain James St. Clair Morton, to take charge of all the army's engineering operations. Even as Buell was desperately trying to fortify his railroads to protect them from raids, he was forced to divert Morton to the essential task of fortifying the captured city of Nashville. The work on the stockade defenses for the railroad went slowly, in part because of the lack of experienced engineers to build them. "I have ordered time and again that the stockades be built and other defenses made," the frustrated Federal commander in Kentucky, Brig. Gen. Jeremiah Boyle, reported. "I will have to go in person to attend to it. . . . There is no man in Kentucky who knows how to do the work."[9]

Nor did the army have an adequate topographical staff to meet its needs. Buell had only one officer of the Corps of Topographical Engineers, Captain Nathaniel Michler, who with but a single assistant was responsible for providing the army with maps of Middle Tennessee and central Kentucky. Even as Michler struggled to perform this task, Buell reassigned him to prepare a map of the army's part in the recent operations at Corinth, thus removing the topographer from more pressing duties during the summer.[10]

The army also lacked an adequate force of trained engineer soldiers to perform the tasks requiring skilled labor, such as building bridges and framing the stockades. The only regularly organized engineers in the entire department was the understrength First Regiment of Michigan Engineers and Mechanics. This unit consisted to a large extent of skilled artisans and mechanics commanded by competent civil and railroad engineers. Buell used them for bridge repair and as pioneers for the army on the march.[11] Yet the First Michigan, numbering fewer than five hundred men in the summer of 1862, was too small to meet all the engineering needs of the army, and it had no experience with specifically military activities, such as the construction of fortifications or the assembling of pontoon brigades. Discipline was problematic in the First; the men had no military training or even arms and they refused to drill, believing that as engineers they should not be required to. Rosecrans's engineer staff was generally unimpressed with the First.[12]

Buell's engineers made only small-scale efforts to improvise labor organizations. Morton assembled a tiny force of two dozen civilian artisans to build the railroad stockades, but this makeshift construction crew was expensive—each man received three dollars per day, almost as much as a colonel of infantry—and, left leaderless by Morton's reassignment to the defenses of Nashville, it apparently disbanded.[13] Somewhat more successfully, Buell's superintendent of railroads, a civilian railroad engineer named John B. Anderson, hired a railroad crew numbering approximately ninety carpenters and laborers, who worked with a special construction train to repair the railroad bridges.[14]

Finally, Buell's army lacked essential facilities and equipment. The Topographical Office was small, poorly equipped, and unable to supply the army with the needed maps. The office produced only two copies of an important map of central Kentucky, one of which was sent to Washington, so the army largely marched blind during Bragg's raid.[15] Buell had also made no advance provision for the passage of rivers when he began his campaigns in the spring of 1862. During the march to join Grant at Pittsburg Landing in the early spring he was delayed for ten days restoring a bridge at the Duck River, which nearly kept him out of the Battle of Shiloh. When he later set out eastward from Corinth, he passed his army over the Tennessee River by ferry, a tedious procedure that delayed his movement. Faced with the need to cross the Tennessee again, Buell was forced to divert the First Michigan from railroad duty to construct pontoon boats. The unused boats were all destroyed on Buell's orders during the Federal withdrawal from Middle Tennessee.[16]

Rosecrans was determined to avoid all these pitfalls. By the fall of 1862 it was clear to him, and to everyone else, what had not been so clear back in the spring: the defeat of the Confederacy would require much more than simply marching southward and chasing off its armies. The Union had occupied nearly two-thirds of Tennessee in the spring with surprisingly little trouble but had been unable to hold much of the captured ground. To retake Middle Tennessee and hold it securely enough to advance further would require careful planning and preparation, to say nothing of rigorous execution. An army marching south from Nashville must overcome significant natural obstacles before reaching Chattanooga, including the Tennessee and other rivers and the barren Cumberland Plateau. Yet any delay occasioned by these obstacles could be fatal, as it was in the summer of 1862 when for weeks Chattanooga lay undefended but unassailed. "When we do move," he told his superiors, "I don't want to stop and tinker, and give the enemy time to get up expeditions against our lines of communications."

Rosecrans confidently expected to drive the Confederate army into head-long flight, and he wanted to be able to race forward to take advantage of the opportunities that presented themselves.[17]

Traversing the country and driving back the enemy was only the first problem for an invader, however; holding the captured territory and sustaining the army there indefinitely was quite another. "To advance in the face of these obstacles is not the only nor even the most important point of the problem," Rosecrans explained. "We must so advance as never to recede."[18] For supplies, the Federals would be almost entirely dependent on worn, rickety, single-tracked railroads and wooden bridges that were easily ruined by a retreating enemy. Even when restored, the railroads were exposed to attack by fast-moving cavalry and partisans and by the citizenry too. As Buell had discovered, securing the country could require an entire army in itself, an expense the Federals could ill afford. Rosecrans set out to solve these problems through careful planning, advance preparation, and a superior engineer organization.

Almost from the day he took command of the newly renamed Army of the Cumberland, Rosecrans energetically turned to the problem of revamping and preparing its engineering and topographical departments. He demanded additional officers from Washington—"The Army of the Potomac cannot possibly be as much in need of engineers as I am"—and even begged them from his fellow army commanders. Surprisingly, he got them. After little more than a month in command his engineering staff had doubled to four officers, with another added the following spring.[19]

Rosecrans also acted quickly to establish a new topographical organization modeled on the one he had devised and implemented in the Army of the Mississippi. On December 2, 1862, his headquarters ordered every brigade and division commander to detail an officer to topographical duty. (Later the order would apply to corps commanders as well, but at this time the army technically consisted of only one corps, the Fourteenth.) These officers were to gather data in the field on the roads, bridges, fords, and other significant military features and forward them to Michler at headquarters. The topographers also acted as advisors to their commanders regarding the geography and topography of the country and the activities of the enemy. Michler's office was responsible for compiling and publishing maps for distribution, by way of the topographers, back down to the line commanders. To do this, the office was gradually expanded to eleven assistants by March 1863.[20]

Rosecrans had more difficulty obtaining engineer troops to act as pioneers and pontoniers. Pioneers were soldiers or laborers assigned to perform mundane toolwork and tasks of immediate, tactical importance to the army, such as repairing roads, clearing obstructions, and building small bridges. Buell had originally used the First Michigan in this role, scattering the regiment among the various divisions of the army on the march to Nashville in the spring of 1862.[21] Rosecrans intended to apply the Michiganders exclusively to the railroad, the area of their expertise, to work beside Anderson's track-repair crew. He applied several times for Washington to send him pontoniers or engineer troops from Virginia or, at the very least, permission to raise his own; but his efforts were rebuffed. Because the highly skilled engineer soldiers were paid more than infantrymen, it literally required an act of Congress to raise them, and Congress showed no interest in raising additional regiments of volunteer engineers.[22]

No such authorization was required for an army commander to detail soldiers from the ranks as pioneers, however. On November 3, 1862, Rosecrans ordered each regiment in his army to detail twenty men, two from each company, for such duty. The men "will be selected with great care," he stipulated, "half laborers and half mechanics [i.e., artisans]." Each detachment was to be led by "the most intelligent and energetic lieutenant in the regiment, with the best knowledge of civil engineering." Rosecrans's order indicated that the pioneers would normally remain with the regiments unless called away for special duty. This may have been a deliberate falsehood intended to ensure that the regiments detailed their best men and not their dregs, as they tended to do for detached duty. If so, the deception worked. The colonels gladly complied, and one may easily imagine their surprise and distress when the pioneer details were soon whisked away to a camp of instruction near Nashville and consolidated permanently into a new organization, the Pioneer Brigade.[23]

Organizing the Pioneer Brigade was the task of the chief engineer, James St. Clair Morton. The thirty-three-year-old Morton was a flamboyant oddball such as was rarely found in the Corps of Engineers. He wore his blonde hair long and sported a bushy beard and was described by one observer as "a man of an eccentric disposition, but of much ability."[24] A reporter for the *Cincinnati Commercial* thought that "the mastery of his profession was not singular, but his mastery of all obstacles which obstruct his designs; the domineering confidence with which he assails difficulties in his path, and the success which invariably crowns his exertions are remarkable."[25]

Morton had made a name for himself before the war with his outspoken criticism of the engineer establishment. Upon his appointment as assistant professor of engineering at West Point in 1855, he publicly criticized Mahan in a report to the Board of Visitors, which landed him in front of a court of inquiry. He also condemned the use of masonry fortifications to defend the seacoast and published several tracts advocating the use of earthwork fortifications instead, a heresy to a corps whose prime mission was the construction of great forts of stone and brick. Morton's iconoclasm, outspoken individualism, and willingness to challenge engineer dogma won him many enemies in the army, but they no doubt endeared him to Rosecrans who shared these same traits.[26]

Like Rosecrans, Morton throughout the war was concerned with having an adequate force of skilled laborers for engineer service. Early in the conflict he formed the workers at his post at Fort Jefferson, off the Florida coast, into a makeshift company; later, as chief engineer of the Ninth Corps in 1864, he organized an engineer force for the corps by having a regiment detailed from each division for the duty.[27] In late 1862 and 1863, Morton applied his considerable organizing abilities to the Pioneer Brigade.

Morton formed the Pioneers into companies and battalions, corresponding with the organization of the army. Each company represented the men detailed from one brigade, and each battalion represented a corps. Initially, the Brigade consisted of three battalions, corresponding to the three corps of the army; later, a fourth battalion was added when the Reserve Corps joined the army. Officially, the Pioneer Brigade was merely a conglomeration of three thousand men representing different regiments, but Rosecrans and Morton treated it as if it were a single organization. Morton appointed a support staff, including an adjutant, commissary, and quartermaster. He also created a command structure for the organization, with its own acting majors and captains, although the officers' detail to the Pioneers was still officially comprised of lieutenants. Morton commanded the Brigade in person.[28]

The Pioneer Brigade was a curious hybrid creature, combining the functions and elements of traditional pioneers, engineers, and infantry. Morton and Rosecrans intended the Brigade to be a multipurpose organization. During mobile operations it would act as pioneers. When the campaign commenced, each battalion was to be assigned to accompany and support the corps from which the men had been drawn. One pioneer, Private Isaac Raub, described the duties of the Brigade: "we have to build Bridges where ever they are needed for the army to cross streems, some times we have to make rafts to float on the water where they are in a hurry and cant wait for

Bridges and some time we have to cut roads through the woods so as our . . . artillery and wagons can get through."[29]

However, when the army was encamped, or whenever circumstances dictated, the Pioneers could be massed to perform as engineer troops. With this objective in mind, Morton trained his men in special engineering duties, such as sapping, mining, and the construction of bridges and fortifications. In camp the men performed few of the tedious military chores such as scouting and picket duty, laboring instead on engineering tasks. "I like pioneering so far a good deal better than I do drilling," one new Pioneer, a carpenter, told his wife. "It comes same thing near what I used to work at when I was at home."[30] The men could not be paid as engineers, but they were allowed the extra pay authorized for fatigue duty, which was even more lucrative: those who worked with common tools earned twenty-five cents per day extra and those with mechanical tools earned forty cents.[31]

Morton, not unmindful of the prospects for achieving military glory, intended the Brigade to be a fighting command as well as an engineering organization. He ordered the officers to study the infantry drill and arranged for an artillery battery to be permanently attached to the command. As it turned out, the Brigade did little drilling, apparently on the explicit orders of Rosecrans who had plenty of work for the Pioneers to do.[32] Nonetheless, the Brigade's first and most celebrated action was a feat of combat, not engineering. On December 31, 1862, the first chaotic day of the Battle of Stones River, Rosecrans threw the Pioneers into a dangerous gap in the Union line, where they repulsed several Confederate charges. Rosecrans was so delighted by their performance that in his first message to Washington announcing the results of the battle, he singled out his chief engineer for praise and requested a brigadier general's appointment for him, which was quickly granted by a grateful War Department.[33]

For the construction of fortifications at the various major posts and depots in his control, Rosecrans relied extensively on hired engineers and laborers, especially African Americans. Although a law passed in July 1862 permitted the army to employ blacks as laborers, Buell, who followed the lenient "kid-glove" policy toward the South, had tried to restrict their use, especially runaway slaves. His chief engineer had fewer scruples. Morton's effort to requisition slaves from the local plantations failed. So during the crisis of the fall when an attack upon Union-held Nashville seemed likely, he rounded up hundreds of free African-American citizens as well as slaves and forcibly put them to work on the fortifications of Nashville.[34]

When Rosecrans assumed command of the army, he expanded the use of blacks at Nashville and other posts, such as Murfreesboro and Fort Donelson. The army conducted another impressment at Nashville in the summer of 1863 to round up laborers to build a railroad, but Rosecrans did not support that practice. In January 1863, Rosecrans tried to put the system on a more regular and equitable basis by establishing regulations concerning the hiring and employment of the laborers and promising them pay as employees of the engineer department. When the War Department was slow to authorize such payment, Rosecrans strongly pressed their case, arguing that "the necessity for paying them is, that from want, say, nine-tenths have deserted, and I think justly."[35] Later, he arranged for the recruitment of workers in the Eleventh and Twelfth Regiments of U.S. Colored Troops, in part to ensure their payment and in part to prevent their being enlisted into other regiments destined for combat duty. These two regiments remained on engineering duty on the railroads and fortifications.[36]

At Nashville, in addition to the freedmen, the army hired white foremen, skilled laborers, and civil engineers. By early November 1862, Morton was employing two officers, seven enlisted men, eighty-seven white civilians, and eighteen hundred African-American laborers "more or less," although the number of the latter declined to about seven hundred by the following spring. During the next two years the work of constructing the fortifications at Nashville—elaborate enclosed hilltop structures with deep ditches, stone scarps, and iron-faced artillery casemates—continued to be a major operation costing hundreds of thousands of dollars, an investment that paid handsomely when General John Bell Hood's Confederate army threatened the city late in 1864.[37]

Finally, Rosecrans devoted much attention to one of his primary concerns, the procurement of a pontoon train—he was always thinking about the Tennessee River. He asked Washington for a seven-hundred-foot bridge of iron or canvas pontoons, having heard that Buell's wooden boats (called bateaux) had leaked excessively. Whatever they were, he wanted them quickly. However, the engineer department had no experience with making iron pontoons; and canvas boats, Rosecrans was told, were unnecessarily complicated to make and to assemble in the field and were even more leaky and perishable than the wooden ones. Bateaux were the most reliable—Buell's had been made hastily with green lumber—and could be made the quickest, although that would still be six to eight weeks. Reluctantly, Rosecrans agreed to accept the wooden boats, which were manufactured in Cincinnati under engineer supervision.[38]

A company of Pioneers was specially drilled in the construction of pontoon bridges and assigned charge of the boats. Transportation for the bridge would remain a problem, however. Rosecrans could not procure sufficient wagons to transport all of the pontoons, so he arranged to have the rest shipped by rail to the river when needed. Much would depend on the Michigan Engineers and Anderson's work crew to open the railroad in time to bring up the boats when needed.[39]

Ever fussy and concerned with details—he did not delegate authority well—Rosecrans prepared his army carefully. During the fall of 1862, after assuming command Rosecrans devoted his efforts to reorganizing the army, including the engineer and topographical engineer departments, and gathering supplies. He also worked hard to secure the rail communications with the forward base at Nashville, which meant repairing the damaged tracks and bridges in southern Kentucky and northern Tennessee and building or repairing the stockade defenses of the road. In late December, Rosecrans marched on the Confederate army at Murfreesboro, and after a bloody, hard-fought battle at nearby Stones River he held the field, Bragg withdrawing southward toward Tullahoma.[40]

Rosecrans then paused for six months while preparing his army for the next advance toward Chattanooga. He was much criticized for the delay, both by his contemporaries and by later historians. The administration, anxious for a victory in the face of repeated defeats in Virginia and stalemate on the Mississippi, was particularly irritated by Rosecrans's seeming inaction and calls for additional resources.[41]

Yet the Army of the Cumberland was not entirely idle during this time. Morton continued the effort to render Nashville secure from attack and to construct stockade defenses along the newly won section of railroad to the new forward base at Murfreesboro. On the outskirts of the latter town, the chief engineer laid out and built a large fortified camp called Fortress Rosecrans, an impressive collection of mutually supporting lunettes and angled infantry curtains, with strong blockhouses and enclosed redoubts for interior defense. Inside this fortress, which straddled the Nashville & Chattanooga Railroad, Rosecrans established depots for the commissary, quartermaster, and ordnance departments. In addition to the fortifications, the Pioneers built warehouses, a sawmill, and other structures. One Pioneer wrote home in April, "the work is pushed on faster now than at any time yet. A sett [sic] of hands are working day and night in digging the foundation for a magazine." The fortress was designed to withstand a siege by an army as large as sixty thousand men. With this base and the larger one at

Nashville both well stocked and well secured, the army would be far less vulnerable to raids against its communications and therefore could be more confident and free in its movements.[42]

Meanwhile, Rosecrans was pushing forward the reorganization of the topographical department against the resistance of his chief topographical engineer. Michler opposed Rosecrans's unorthodox plan for the topographical corps, having little faith that such a decentralized system could be made to work. He noted that at Stones River most of the topographers had been diverted from their assigned duties by the line commanders they served, who tended to treat them as just additional staff officers. He also believed that the topographers, many of whom had no particular qualifications for the job, would require rigorous special training before achieving any proficiency in their duties. He wanted to gather a select few of the topographical officers and assign them to be his assistants at headquarters, where he could personally train them and supervise their activities. Rosecrans, who did not easily tolerate dissent, angrily rejected the idea, and he harassed his chief topographer mercilessly. Relations between them worsened until, under the ageless excuse of ill health, Michler finally obtained a transfer in May 1863. When Morton declared that he, too, could not organize a topographical corps from "the material within my reach," Rosecrans turned to Captain William E. Merrill of the Corps of Engineers.[43]

At age twenty-five, Merrill already had a distinguished war record by early 1863. The son of a Mexican War hero, Merrill had graduated first in his class at the Military Academy in 1859, and after a year on the fortifications of the Georgia and Florida seacoasts he returned to the Academy to teach engineering as one of Mahan's assistant professors. In July 1861, he joined Rosecrans's staff as assistant engineer and served in western Virginia. After only two months, the young and inexperienced officer conducted a reconnaissance without an escort and was captured. After five months as a prisoner, Merrill was posted to the Army of the Potomac and was wounded at the siege of Yorktown. He returned from his convalescence in time to serve with Maj. Gen. John Pope during his ill-fated campaign in central Virginia in the summer of 1863, which culminated in the crushing defeat at Second Bull Run. Merrill was subsequently transferred to Kentucky to help defend Newport and Covington during Bragg's raid. He built railroad defenses as chief engineer of the Army of Kentucky, and when that army joined the Army of the Cumberland as the Reserve Corps in March 1863 Merrill constructed more defenses in Tennessee.[44]

Merrill was one of the more remarkable officers of the Corps of Engineers, and indeed of the Union Army as a whole. Like his engineer colleagues, he was keenly ambitious, but unlike them his ambition was not for fame, glory, and a general's star—there were virtually no opportunities to obtain those in the engineer service of the army—but to make a contribution to the profession of military engineering. Merrill was unusually bright and thoughtful, and his agile mind was continually discovering innovative solutions to new problems regarding engineering technology and organization. It was the latter that particularly concerned him. Armies could no longer get by, he would warn the Engineer Bureau, "with no other means of assistance than the traditional equipment of an engineer officer in the first year of the war—a horse and an opera glass."[45] Unlike Michler and other regular army men who felt a professional disdain and even resentment toward the amateur soldiers and engineers, Merrill recognized that in order to win the war the North depended upon the talents and abilities that the civilians brought to the army. The challenge was to make use of those abilities and to improve them with effective organization and training. Only in this way could the army fully harness the available engineering manpower.[46]

It was with this faith in the volunteers, and a determination to make Rosecrans's plan work, that Merrill took charge of the topographical department of the Army of the Cumberland. He soon discovered that his department was in disarray. "I found the headquarters office almost destitute of assistants or means of doing work, and the engineers of the different commands utterly ignorant of what they were wanted for, and equally unsupplied with means of doing anything."[47] He started by bringing the topographical corps nearly up to full strength by ensuring the detail of officers, so that by July it numbered fifty men. He equipped them with small but accurate prismatic compasses and portable drafting kits, and he trained them carefully in their duties.[48] To aid their training, Merrill published detailed regulations that explained everything from the conduct of surveys to the colors, symbols, and scales to be used on the sketches.

Merrill devised an efficient process for collecting and transmitting the topographical data, which applied whether the army was in camp or on the march. Under his system, the corps topographers divided the area or route to be surveyed among the divisions, whose topographers further subdivided it among the brigades. The topographers were to investigate and survey the houses, roads, creeks, hills, and so on. The brigade topographers plotted and transmitted their information to the division topographers who compiled it and transmitted it to the corps topographers, who in their turn passed it up to the topographical office at army Headquarters. When the army occupied a county seat, the topographers were instructed to seize any maps available at the courthouse as well as those in the hands of the county surveyors—Merrill issued a list of the names and addresses of surveyors known to be living in Middle Tennessee. Merrill thus sought to achieve a smooth, steady, and orderly flow of topographical information back to headquarters.[49]

Merrill also adopted a device known as the "information maps." This was actually a method for data collection originally devised by Rosecrans for the Army of the Mississippi. Information maps were rough, spare sketch maps of the country adapted from the best information available, often a railroad or county land map. The Topographical Office prepared and issued them to the topographers, who were to correct and return them. Often the individual topographers were assigned a specific area to survey and correct. Upon receiving the new information, the office revised and reissued the maps as soon as possible. "From the method of construction it is impossible that they should be minutely accurate," Merrill observed, "but at the same time they are sufficiently so for military movements." This system did more than just provide maps for the army; it ensured that there was a constant two-way flow of information between headquarters and the field, and the field commanders always had access to the most current topographical information that Rosecrans himself possessed.[50]

The information map system depended on the ability of the Topographical Office to compile and publish maps in a timely manner. Merrill soon doubled its staff to twenty-four officers, enlisted men, and hired civilians, and he established new office procedures, such as keeping on hand reserve copies of all maps and requiring receipts for maps and other publications sent out.[51] Merrill also improved the office's printing facilities. Hitherto, the armies had reproduced maps in the field using the relatively new technique of photography. While very useful for many cartographic purposes, photography had significant shortcomings. Though faster than engraving each map, the reproduction of a large number of prints was slow and required adequate sunlight. The maps themselves tended to fade with use, and because the lenses used by the army were not very good the prints had some distortion on the edges, so adjacent map sections would not line up properly.[52] After performing his own study of the costs and benefits of several methods of map reproduction, Merrill procured lithographic presses. With this method, the image of the map was transferred to (or drawn directly upon) a flat specially prepared stone that was then inked and pressed onto paper. The resulting maps were clear, legible, and free from distortion, and they were printed quickly once the stone was prepared. Revisions could be made by drawing directly on the stone, or the stone could be washed clean for reuse.[53]

Lithographic printing was cheap and efficient, but the heavy stones and extensive preparation required by the process made it unsuitable for operation in the field. Perhaps at Rosecrans's suggestion, Merrill also adopted another new technique for reproducing maps, called the "quick map" or "black map." This technique was invented by a volunteer officer and experienced photographer, Captain William Margedant of the Tenth Ohio, while serving with Rosecrans in western Virginia in 1861.[54] The map to be copied was traced onto fine tracing cloth and set over a piece of special photographic paper. The result was a white map on a black background—hence the name "black map." As long as light was available, maps could be reproduced quickly. Changes were easily made by adding to or correcting the tracing and proceeding with new copies, which made it ideally suited to Rosecrans's "information map" system. The equipment was very portable, requiring only a small box and a few chemicals to fix the map. This made it possible to update and publish the "information maps" in the field while the army was on campaign and unable to have maps reproduced lithographically.[55] Although "sun-printing," as the technique was sometimes called, was not unknown at the time, Merrill had the wisdom to recognize its value and proper use.[56] This was an important and significant advance in topographical engineering.

Rosecrans's meticulous preparations paid ample dividends when his army finally began to move on June 23, 1863. In a two-week campaign of feints and maneuvers—and despite abysmal, rainy weather—Rosecrans forced Bragg to fall back from his heavily fortified base at Tullahoma to Chattanooga, thus abandoning all of Middle Tennessee to the Federals.[57] While the First Michigan and the civilian trackmen immediately set to work on the railroads, the Pioneers marched with the army to maintain the muddy roads. Some of the Pioneers were assigned to the various corps, as planned; others were given the miserable task of manhandling the heavy pontoon wagons, which were proving extremely unwieldy on the muddy Tennessee. Meanwhile, Merrill's Topographical Office published a steady stream of information maps showing the roads, houses, and rivers in the country through which the army was marching. Many of these maps included the note, "for all parts marked —?— information is wanted. All the Top[ographica]l Engineers are ordered to send such as soon as possible to these headquarters." Merrill also published maps of the key towns and their fortifications shortly after their capture.[58]

The campaign ended with the occupation of Tullahoma on July 7. Rosecrans paused again for six weeks to restore his supply line. This delay infuriated the administration, especially Secretary of War Edwin Stanton and General-in-Chief Halleck, who continually prodded Rosecrans to move. The prickly general was adamant, however, that the next advance would require further preparation. The army, he pointed out, was a long way from its base at Louisville and its depot at Nashville, and all supplies had to be brought up from these points by rail. Ahead lay "60 or 70 miles of barren mountain country, destitute of forage and subsistence, [and] traversed by a few difficult roads." After this was the Tennessee River, the line of which would likely be defended, perhaps by an entrenched enemy. Before the army could proceed, Rosecrans had, first, to reopen the railroad and to establish and defend new advanced depots and, second, to prepare for the crossing of the Tennessee.[59] It is doubtful that the administration had an accurate idea of the country through which Rosecrans was campaigning. Q.M. Gen. Montgomery Meigs, when later visiting the besieged army at Chattanooga after the defeat at Chickamauga, was surprised by the extreme difficulty of bringing up supplies. "Of the rugged nature of this region, I had no conception when I left Washington. I never traveled on such roads before."[60]

It was probably after watching the Pioneers struggling with the pontoons of the bridge train, and reflecting on the difficulty of repairing the railroad in time to bring up the boats left behind, that Rosecrans came up with a new idea for the bridge. The standard wooden bateaux he was using were appropriate for the well-paved highways of Western Europe but quite unsuited for the dirt tracks of Tennessee. They were large, awkward, and exceedingly difficult to maneuver on the rough, muddy roads that wound across the Cumberland Mountains. Furthermore, they required specialized wagons that were difficult to procure. The Russian-type "advanced guard" pontoons, consisting of a canvas cover stretched over a wooden frame, were lighter and could be disassembled for transport, but they nonetheless also required large special-purpose wagons.

Rosecrans's idea was to modify the Russian pontoon, separating the long side frames into two sections for transport. Upon arrival at the bridge site the sections could be joined together with a pin and the boats assembled as usual. This allowed the frames to be carried with their canvas covers in ordinary, common quartermaster wagons, which were easily obtained and because they used standard parts were easily repaired in the field. Rosecrans had his engineers make up a prototype that tested satisfactorily on the Duck River.[61] Alas, Rosecrans did not have the facilities to manufacture a complete set of boats, although, in his annoyance, he established his own engineer shops in Nashville so that in future his army could make its own equipment.[62] For the present he stayed with the bateaux, no doubt praying that the railroad would be completed in time.

The fate of the army that summer was in the hands of the engineers. Rosecrans assigned the Pioneers to assist the Michigan Engineers and the civilian crew to rebuild the bridges, which had all been burned by the Confederates in their retreat. By July 25, the railroad had been reopened as far as Bridgeport, on the Tennessee River. Rosecrans immediately began stockpiling supplies at Stevenson, his new forward supply depot, which, having also been burned by Bragg's men, was rebuilt by the Pioneers. By August 12, an important spur rail line was opened to Tracy City, although several more days were required to obtain a special engine that could run on that line. As soon as the spur was available for use, Rosecrans put his army in motion again.[63]

What would be called the Chickamauga campaign began on August 16. Through another series of skillful feints, Rosecrans convinced Bragg that he would cross the Tennessee upstream from Chattanooga when he really meant to cross downstream, near the railroad depots at Stevenson and Bridgeport from which his pontoon boats and supplies would be drawn. By the twenty-first his forces had arrived on the banks of the Tennessee. For the next ten days, the engineers worked feverishly to bring up the boats and prepare the crossing. The army crossed at four sites, commencing on the twenty-ninth; by September 4 it was entirely over, except for a corps observing Chattanooga from the north bank. At two of the sites, the troops and trains crossed on pontoon bridges; at the other two they were ferried across on rafts and flatboats. The ferries were operated and the bridges built by the Pioneers, with assistance from the infantry. As usual, Rosecrans micromanaged the operation, hustling the pontoons to the front, issuing detailed instructions for the construction of the bridges, and even personally selecting the exact sites where they were to be laid. With the exception of a break in the bridge at Caperton's Ferry, near Stevenson, the crossing was uneventful. His communications threatened, Bragg evacuated Chattanooga on September 6 and withdrew southward. Almost bloodlessly, Rosecrans had captured Middle Tennessee and Chattanooga.[64]

It was in the weeks following the crossing of the Tennessee that Rosecrans's campaign went awry. Admirably—for how many campaigns failed from a lack of such vigor?—Rosecrans raced ahead to press his advantage. Having convinced himself that Bragg was in headlong flight, Rosecrans incautiously scattered his army, with one corps lodged in Chattanooga and the others spread among the passes and valleys of the north Georgia mountains. Yet far from retreating in panic, Bragg's army was being reinforced, and Bragg was planning a counterstroke. His initial efforts misfired, but in a ferocious two-day battle along Chickamauga Creek on September 19 and 20, he succeeded in administering a severe defeat to the Army of the Cumberland, the larger portion of which fled—in the company of its dazed and demoralized commander—back to the safety of the defenses of Chattanooga. Rather than attempt a direct assault on the city, Bragg contented himself with besieging it. In October, Rosecrans, having lost the confidence of the administration, was replaced by a corps command, Maj. Gen. George H. Thomas. The Federals brought up reinforcements from Mississippi and Virginia; in November the combined Federal army, under the overall command of Maj. Gen. Ulysses S. Grant, decisively defeated Bragg's army and drove it back southward into Georgia. Federal control of Middle Tennessee would not be threatened for another year, and Chattanooga would remain in Union hands until the end of the war.[65]

Rosecrans's engineering organizations performed adequately if not always particularly well. Anderson's railroad construction corps, the First Michigan Engineers, and the Pioneers did succeed in opening the railroads and keeping the Army of the Cumberland in supply, but they were unable to do much more than that. The flimsy tracks of the Nashville & Chattanooga Railroad were badly worn from overuse and needed to be replaced, but Anderson's crew was too small and ill organized to do the job on the scale required. Anderson himself had the task of both running the roads and repairing them, and this he proved unable to do. Colonel William P. Innes of the First Michigan Engineers, a railroad engineer by profession, served as military superintendent of railroads for several months in lieu of Anderson during the late summer and fall of 1863, but he did little better. Under the pressure of the sustained Federal buildup around Chattanooga during the fall and winter of 1863–1864, the supply system nearly collapsed. Grant hastily assigned the Sixteenth Corps of the Army of the Tennessee, under Maj. Gen. Grenville Dodge (a railroad engineer) to open the badly wrecked Nashville & Decatur Railroad as an alternate supply route. The crisis finally eased only when a new specialized organization of the

Quartermaster Department, the U.S. Military Railroads, arrived from the East late that winter to rebuild and run the roads.[66]

Yet inadequate as Rosecrans's railroad organization was in the long run, it did what it had to do, which was to open the roads for supplies and pontoons and support the army during the rapid advance through Tennessee and the siege at Chattanooga. Furthermore, Rosecrans did make a lasting and important contribution to military railroad repair in the war: he initiated the practice of purchasing bridge trusses from Northern companies to replace those destroyed by the retreating Confederates. Truss bridges, resting on the original masonry piers, were far sturdier than the makeshift trestle structures hurriedly thrown up by the Pioneers and the Michigan Engineers, which were prone to collapse under the pressure of sudden freshets in the swift-running rivers and creeks of Middle and East Tennessee. As early as January 1863, the Cincinnati Bridge Company was building a railroad bridge for the army near Murfreesboro. In early September 1863 Rosecrans awarded a contract for a bridge over the Tennessee River at Bridgeport. By November, company representatives were at the front taking measurements of other sites requiring bridges. The companies manufactured the required bridge sections in Cincinnati and elsewhere and shipped them disassembled to the front for installation. The U.S. Military Railroads continued this practice, purchasing bridges for the railroads in East Tennessee and northern Georgia in 1864 and 1865.[67]

The Pioneer Brigade also had a mixed record. In addition to its work on the railroads and on the pontoon brigade over the Tennessee, the Pioneers provided good service during the siege of Chattanooga, digging fortifications and running a sawmill.[68] Yet discipline was generally poor in the brigade. They did little drilling, as has been noted, and at times there was much drunkenness. One Pioneer wrote home in January 1863, "We do not work hard. Our tools are dull, [none of us] are interested in taking care of them."[69] While the Pioneers performed well enough when concentrated for engineer work under Morton's watchful eye, they did particularly badly when scattered on pioneer duty with the army. During the march to Tullahoma during the summer of 1863 their behavior was a minor scandal. After one march two months later during the Chickamauga campaign, a division commander in the Twentieth Corps pointedly remarked, "I caught up with the Pioneer Brigade, and having a vivid recollection of having followed that brigade before, I decided upon trying another pass lying a little to the left."[70] Brig. Gen. William B. Hazen, a brigade commander in the

Twenty-first Corps, was more explicit in a complaint to headquarters. "I have . . . been thrown with a battalion of them on the march, and in camp, . . . and have no hesitation in pronouncing them a failure," Hazen wrote. "They were straggling along, no one having any particular charge of them, their tools never being unpacked, and whenever any work was to be done, a detail was always made from the regiments to do it."[71]

The bitterness of the army toward the Pioneer Brigade reflected in part the lingering resentment left over from the manner of its organization. "The whole pioneer concern [is] a stench in everybody's nostrils, and no one seems disposed to use them," Hazen noted in his complaint. "As it is now, the pioneers get no drill, very little control, no sympathy, but the contempt of everybody."[72] Justly or not, the army's ire at the Pioneers focused on Morton and made him the victim of one of Rosecrans's infamous outbursts. On June 28, Maj. Gen. Alexander McCook's Twentieth Corps had the misfortune of falling in behind the Pioneers and the pontoon train and was seriously delayed in its assigned march. McCook complained to Rosecrans that the Pioneers got in his way and provided no help when needed. Rosecrans sent for Morton and "abused him in a rough and violent tirade," Hazen later recalled. "The scene was humiliating. I have never been able to rid myself of the impression left upon me by the coarse and unjust language of General Rosecrans."[73]

The root of the problems of the Pioneer Brigade lay not in Morton's leadership but in the very structure of the organization. Each Pioneer was still a member of his own regiment, to which he looked—often in vain—for pay and promotion. It was especially difficult for him to obtain promotions because his services were rarely observed by his own regiment's officers and because the colonels did not want to waste a promotion on a soldier who was for all practical purposes permanently separated from his regiment. Furthermore, the Pioneer officers, whatever their "acting" rank and responsibilities in the Pioneer Brigade, were still paid only according to their official rank—as lieutenants. This situation naturally led to dissension and indiscipline.[74]

During nearly the entire period of Rosecrans's command, he and his engineer officers worked hard to convince the Engineer Bureau and Congress to transform the Pioneer Brigade into an official organization. Their efforts grew more insistent as the summer wore on and the Army of the Cumberland found itself with new railroads to repair and territory to protect. During the Chickamauga campaign, Merrill complained passionately of having a "brigade of 'Pioneers' who never pioneer" and declared that the army needed a proper regiment of trained engineer troops instead, which could be organized from the Pioneer Brigade. "We have now the means of doing everything that can be called for in the line of Engineering," he cajoled the chief engineer, Brig. Gen. Joseph Totten, "and all we ask from Washington is a little help in carrying through a necessary measure which we cannot effect of ourselves."[75]

After Chickamauga, as the army lay penned up in Chattanooga, Rosecrans begged to be sent some regular engineer troops from Virginia, or at least to be allowed to convert some of his infantry regiments to engineers under a law authorizing the formation of "veteran volunteer engineers." He did, in fact, assign several Ohio and Michigan regiments to temporary engineer duty to help build pontoon bridges, but at the time he was relieved from his command the War Department had still not acted on his requests.[76]

Although it suffered from similar organizational problems, the topographical department merited no such criticism. On the contrary, it fully proved its value. Throughout the Chickamauga campaign, Merrill's office continued to prepare and issue maps, not only for the army but for the reinforcements that came to its relief in the fall. By September, it was issuing 130 copies of each map edition, including one for every corps, division, and brigade commander and cavalry colonel.[77] The field commanders came to appreciate having the talented topographical officers on their staffs, and in their official reports relating their participation in the Battle of Chickamauga they often included Merrill's information maps and sketch maps prepared by their own topographers. Rosecrans himself greatly appreciated Merrill's efforts. In his official report of the Tullahoma campaign, he singled out Merrill for special praise, much as he had done for Morton after Stones River. Merrill's "successful collection and embodiment of topographical information," he wrote effusively, "rapidly printed by Captain Margedant's quick process, and distributed to corps and division commanders, has already contributed greatly to the ease and success of our movements over a country of difficult and hitherto unknown topography."[78]

The value of Rosecrans's engineer reforms should not be measured solely by their contributions to the campaigns of 1863 but also by their impact on subsequent operations. The institutions created by Rosecrans remained in place long after his departure from the army, and they achieved their full potential the following year under the effective leadership of Captain Merrill, who was appointed chief engineer in Morton's place permanently in January 1864. Thanks to Merrill's tireless efforts, the Army of the

Cumberland boasted the most efficient engineer and topographical engineer departments of any among Maj. Gen. William T. Sherman's three field armies—indeed, of any Federal army—and they rendered crucial service to Sherman during the campaign that captured Atlanta in September 1864.

The topographical corps was one of Sherman's main sources of tactical as well as topographical information. The topographers roamed to and beyond the front lines of the army, exploring the countryside and probing the positions of the enemy at great risk to themselves. The Topographical Office supplied Sherman's army with the great majority of its campaign and tactical maps. As the army was marching from its camps to the front in May, the office issued a mammoth map of northern Georgia, the primary campaign map used by Sherman and his generals. As the army pushed southward in unknown territory, the office continued to publish timely maps with the latest data, using the lithographic press of Margedant's "Quick Map" system. Merrill was quite justified in boasting that Sherman's army was the best supplied with maps of any during the war.[79]

Less apparent, but no less important, was the work of the Pioneer Brigade. During the first six months of 1864, Merrill kept the brigade back in Tennessee on engineering duty, save for a single company that had charge of Sherman's pontoon train at the front. The primary duty of the Pioneers was to build railroad defenses. Continuing Morton's efforts the year before, Merrill planned and constructed a system of small log fortifications scattered along the vast stretches of railroads captured by Rosecrans in 1863 and extended by Sherman in 1864. Merrill improved on Morton's design for the structures, adopting an enclosed blockhouse design with two thicknesses of logs in place of the open-roofed stockades built by Morton. These blockhouses were built to protect the bridges, the most vulnerable points of the railroads. The Pioneers performed the skilled labor required for framing the blockhouses, leaving the garrison to complete the work of adding a second layer of logs, covering the roof with dirt, and performing other such tasks requiring minimal skills. By the end of the war, 160 blockhouses dotted the countryside in Tennessee and Georgia along the key railroad lines. This defensive system helped neutralize the threat of cavalry and guerrilla attacks against Sherman's communications, and even the largest raids could effect only a temporary interruption in the flow of supplies to the front.[80]

The intense lobbying effort by Rosecrans and his engineers in 1863 finally paid off the following May when Congress authorized the reorganization of the Pioneer Brigade into an official engineer unit, the First U.S.

Veteran Volunteer Engineers. This was the first new engineering unit to be authorized in over two years. Merrill personally reorganized the regiment and commanded it as a Colonel of Volunteers; other officers were commissioned after being tested for their knowledge of engineering. By providing the Pioneer Brigade with a legal organization and command structure this act solved many of its discipline problems and finally eased the army's lingering resentment toward the Pioneers (who no longer had to be carried on the regimental books). Under Merrill's active management the regiment served well until the end of the war—at least no complaints were recorded against it. [81]

Another of Rosecrans's ideas that bore fruit in 1864 was the portable pontoon boat. Merrill found the prototype built by Rosecrans, and with the help of the Pioneers he improved on the design, making it lighter yet stronger. In place of the pins that held the sections together, Merrill substituted hinges, so that the side-frame sections folded instead of separating altogether. The resulting boat, which came to be known as the "Cumberland pontoon," was light enough to carry by hand, small enough to pack on a standard quartermaster wagon, and sturdy enough to support an army maneuvering in the field with its artillery and trains. Merrill had a bridge of such boats manufactured at the engineer shops in Nashville—another Rosecrans legacy—and sent it to the front, where, for the first two months of the Atlanta campaign, it was Sherman's only pontoon bridge. A year later, the train was deposited at the Engineer Depot in Washington, after having performed exemplary service in the long march through Georgia, the Carolinas, and Virginia. [82]

Modern perceptions of Rosecrans's campaigns in 1863 are inevitably influenced by the shadow cast by the disaster at Chickamauga. In the Civil War's pantheon of generals, Rosecrans is usually pictured as an argumentative, procrastinating loser who, like so many others, failed and gave way to the eventual victors, Grant, Sherman, Thomas, and Sheridan. This perception completely ignores what Rosecrans did accomplish strategically. Rosecrans succeeded in doing what his predecessor, Buell, had completely failed to do the previous year: seize and hold Chattanooga. He did so with such deceptive ease, in fact, that modern historians and even his contemporaries could overlook the difficulty of what he was attempting.

In some degree, most commanders faced the same sorts of engineering problems as Rosecrans: they had rivers to bridge, roads to build, railroads to repair and protect, fortifications to build, and countryside to map. Some

commanders solved these problems better than others. What made Rosecrans unusual was the extent to which he understood them and incorpo-
rated the solutions into his strategic thinking and planning. Rosecrans recognized that the challenge of traversing and occupying Middle Tennessee
was largely one of logistics and engineering. He learned from the experiences of those who failed before him, especially Buell. He had an accurate
sense of what needed to be done and how it should be done, and he devoted
much attention and energy to seeing that it would be done. He prepared
meticulously and, however slow he was to get started, avoided unnecessary delays once operations began. Rosecrans's passage of the Tennessee
was a superb operation by any standard.

Among the Federal commanders, only McClellan and Halleck approached Rosecrans's understanding of the uses and importance of engineering in warfare. Yet these generals were bound by traditional—that is
to say, European—conceptions of engineering organization and practice,
and they adapted their strategic thinking to match those conceptions.
Thus, McClellan conducted the operations against Yorktown like a classic
European siege, and one suspects that he would have much preferred to do
the same at Richmond rather than meet the Confederates in the open field.
Rosecrans, on the other hand, recognized that engineering was just one
tool in a commander's toolbox, albeit an important one. He struggled to
make his engineer organization meet the needs of his army and his strategy
and not the other way around.

Furthermore, in spite of his image as a commander who was always demanding more from Washington, Rosecrans was actually more self-reliant
than is usually realized, at least in the realm of engineering. When he found
himself unable to obtain the resources in manpower and equipment he
needed he worked to develop his own, adapting them to meet his needs according to his own innovative conceptions. The most notable example is
the topographical corps, which was entirely of his own design. Such a large
and decentralized organization, in which the topographers were appointed
by and attached to the subordinate headquarters of the army, was quite
novel and unprecedented in the American service. It was entirely opposed
to the traditional approach generally favored in the army, in which the topographical organization consisted of a small group of highly trained officers and assistants reporting directly to army headquarters—the approach
that Michler had advocated. So, too, was the "information map" system an
important and original development because it permitted a two-way flow
of information between army headquarters and the units in the field. Even

as army headquarters was gathering data and improving its own under-standing of the topography of the country it was providing the subordinate commanders with the latest information available. As sensible as this may sound, it was actually unusual in the Federal service, where information tended to flow upward but not downward—that is, when it flowed at all.

Rosecrans was also unusual in his search for innovative technological solutions to problems. His ready adoption of Margedant's Quick Map sys-tem is one example; his idea for a more portable bridge train, which eventu-ally became the Cumberland Pontoon, was another. The regular army's ap-proach to the development and acquisition of new technology was quite conservative in the nineteenth century. The use of balloons, which should have conferred a priceless intelligence advantage on the Federals, was aban-doned by the middle of the war because no one in the army quite knew what to do with them. The Ordnance Department resisted the adoption of the repeating rifle, and on more than one occasion Lincoln, who test-fired weapons himself, ordered their purchase over the objections of the chief of ordnance. (Quick to recognize their value, Rosecrans also requested re-peaters for his cavalry, and he even ordered some early machine guns for field testing.)[83] The Engineer Department was similarly suspicious of change and insisted on carefully subjecting new equipment to the most rig-orous scientific tests. This approach was not inherently bad—there were many worthless ideas being tossed about in this time of increasingly rapid technological change. But there were many good ideas also, which the army had inadequate means of evaluating. Rosecrans took matters into his own hands and made his Army of the Cumberland the most technologi-cally innovative of any during the war.

Finally, Rosecrans was unusual in that he institutionalized his innova-tions. In other armies, most notably the Army of the Tennessee under Grant, citizen-soldiers came up with innovative solutions to many prob-lems, but the ideas remained local or died altogether for lack of an institu-tional vehicle to perpetuate and spread them. In the Army of the Potomac, new ideas came and went with each command change, some commanders seeming determined to undo the contributions of those they replaced. Rosecrans established a foundation for the continuing development of his organizations and technology. Many of them—most notably the Pioneer Brigade, the Cumberland Pontoon, and the system of railroad defenses—were perfected long after Rosecrans's dismissal, part of a legacy of engi-neering innovation fully as important as his own exploits in 1863.

Notes

1. The literature on the engineers in the Civil War is thin, but see Dale E. Floyd, "Army Engineers in the Civil War," *Military Engineering and Technology: Papers Presented at the 1982 American Military Institute Annual Meeting* (Manhattan KS: MA/AH Publishing, 1984); O. E. Hunt, "Engineer Corps of the Federal Army," in *The Photographic History of the Civil War: Forts and Artillery*, ed. Francis T. Miller (N.p.: 1911; reprint, New York: Crown Books, 1957).

2. See Philip Shiman, "Engineering Sherman's March: Army Engineers and the Management of Modern War, 1862–1865" (Ph.D. diss., Duke University, 1991), 55–60. This article is adapted from that study.

3. George W. Cullum, *Biographical Register of the Officers and Graduates of the U.S. Military Academy from 1802 to 1867*, rev. ed., 3 vols. (New York: James Miller, 1879), vol. 2, 42; Thomas E. Griess, "Dennis Hart Mahan: West Point Professor and Advocate of Military Professionalism" (Ph.D. diss., Duke University, 1969), 161–63; William M. Lamers, *The Edge of Glory: A Biography of William S. Rosecrans, U. S. A.* (New York: Harcourt, Brace & World, 1961), 14–17.

4. Cullum, *Biographical Register* 2:42; Lamers, *The Edge of Glory*, 20–180; Rosecrans's testimony before the Joint Committee on the Conduct of the War, April 22, 1865, in U.S. Congress, Joint Committee on the Conduct of the War, report, *Rosecrans's Campaigns*, 38th Cong., 2d sess., 1865, 1 (hereafter cited as Rosecrans's Campaigns).

5. See, for example, Rosecrans to Totten, August[?] 1861, R701, Chief Engineer, Letters Received, Record Group 77, entry 18 (hereafter cited as Chief Engineer, Letters Received), National Archives; Rosecrans to Totten, October 19, 1861, R703, Chief Engineer, Letters Received; Rosecrans to Halleck, November 18, 1862, in U.S. War Department, *The War of the Rebellion: A Compilation of the Official Records of the Union and Confederate Armies*, 128 vols. (Washington DC: Government Printing Office, 1881–1901), 1st ser., vol. 20, pt. 2, p. 65 (hereafter cited as OR; all references are to series 1 unless otherwise noted); Rosecrans to Halleck, October 5, 1863, OR 30, pt. 4: 102.

6. Rosecrans, "The Battle of Corinth," in *Battles and Leaders of the Civil War*, ed. Robert U. Johnson and Clarence C. Buel, 4 vols.(New York: Century, 1884–1889; reprint, New York: Castle Books, 1982), vol. 2, p. 741; Rosecrans's testimony, April 22, 1865, "Rosecrans's Campaigns," 17; Lamers, *The Edge of Glory*, 133, 145.

7. Rosecrans to Edwin Stanton, October 22, 1862, OR 17, pt. 2: 286; Rosecrans's testimony, April 22, 1865, "Rosecrans's Campaigns," 17; Lamers, *The Edge of Glory*, 94–95.

8. For accounts of Buell's campaign see Kenneth P. Williams, *Lincoln Finds a General: A Military Study of the Civil War*, 5 vols. (New York: Macmillan, 1949–1958) 3:429–34, 437–38, 4:27–51; Herman Hattaway and Archer Jones, *How the North Won: A Military History of the Civil War* (Urbana: University of Illinois Press, 1983), 205–8, 214–19, 225, 231, 245–50, 257–61; Stephen D. Engle, "Don Carlos Buell: Military Philosophy and Command Problems in the West," *Civil War History* 41 (June 1995): 105–8.

9. Buell to Morton, August 6, 1862, OR 16, pt. 2: 268; Jeremiah Boyle to Buell, August 10, 1862, OR 16, pt. 2: 306.

10. Michler to Colonel Stephen Long, annual report, October 31, 1862, M74, Letters Received by the Topographical Bureau of the War Department, 1824–1865, Record Group 77, microcopy M506, roll 54, National Archives (hereafter cited as Topographical Bureau, Letters Received; all references are to Record Group 77, roll 54).

11. Don Carlos Buell, "East Tennessee and the Campaign for Perryville," *Battles and Leaders* 2:36; Charles Robert Sligh, *History of the Services of the First Regiment Michigan Engineers and Mechanics during the Civil War, 1861–1865* (Grand Rapids MI: White Print, 1921), 7–10; Francis F. McKinney, "The First Regiment of Michigan Engineers and Mechanics," *Michigan Alumnus Quarterly Review* 62 (1956): 140–44; OR 16, pt. 2: 247–48.

12. OR 16, pt. 2: 246–47; Isaac Roseberry Diary, entries of December 18 and 20, 1862, and March 9, April 9–12, and April 27, 1863, Emory University Library, Atlanta; William Merrill to Totten, September 1, 1863, M4425, Chief Engineer, Letters Received.

13. Morton to Totten, August 1, 1862, M4175, Chief Engineer, Letters Received.

14. John B. Anderson, testimony at Buell Court of Inquiry, January 12, 1863, OR 16, pt. 1: 297–98, 300.

15. Daniel D. Nettesheim, "Topographical Intelligence and the American Civil War" (master's thesis, U.S. Army Command and General Staff College, 1978), 50–51.

16. Buell, "Shiloh Reviewed," *Battles and Leaders*, 1:491; Alan C. Nevins, *The War for the Union*, vol. 2, *War Becomes Revolution* (New York: Charles Scribner's Sons, 1960), 80; Buell, "East Tennessee and the Campaign of Perryville," *Battles and Leaders*, 3:36; OR 16, pt. 1: 31, 32, 248, 486–87.

17. Rosecrans to Brig. Gen. George Cullum, November 26, 1862, OR 20, pt. 2: 98.

18. Rosecrans to Halleck, August 1, 1863, OR 23, pt. 2: 585.

19. Rosecrans to Halleck, November 18, 1862, and Rosecrans to Maj. Gen. Horatio G. Wright, December 4, 1862, OR 20, pt. 2: 65, 120; Rosecrans to Totten,

November 19, 1862, R807, Chief Engineer, Letters Received; General Order 42, Headquarters, Department of the Cumberland, December 22, 1862, OR 20, pt. 2: 215–16.

20. General Order 29, Headquarters, Fourteenth Corps, December 2, 1862, OR 20, pt. 2: 115; Michler to Major Israel Woodruff, March 29, 1863, M313, Topographical Bureau, Letters Received.

21. John Fitch, *Annals of the Army of the Cumberland* (Philadelphia: J. B. Lippincott, 1863), 192.

22. See Shiman, "Engineering Sherman's March," 73–75.

23. General Order 3, Headquarters, Fourteenth Corps, November 3, 1863, OR 20, pt. 2: 6–7.

24. Theodore Lyman, *With Grant and Meade from the Wilderness to Appomattox*, ed. George R. Agassiz (Boston: Atlantic Monthly, 1922; reprint, Lincoln: University of Nebraska Press, 1994), 167.

25. W[illiam] D. [Bickham], *Rosecrans's Campaign with the Fourteenth Army Corps, or the Army of the Cumberland* (Cincinnati: Moore, Wilstach, Keys, 1863), 81–82.

26. Griess, "Dennis Hart Mahan," 268–80; Edward Hagerman, *The American Civil War and the Origins of Modern Warfare: Ideas, Organization, and Field Command* (Bloomington: Indiana University Press, 1988), 23–24; Morton, *Letter to the Hon. John B. Floyd, Secretary of War* (Washington DC: W. A. Harris, 1858); Morton, *Memoir on the Dangers and Defenses of New York City* (Washington DC: W. A. Harris, 1858); and Morton, *Memoir on American Fortification* (Washington DC: W. A. Harris, 1859). See also Cullum, *Biographical Register*, 2:437.

27. Morton to Totten, September 5, 1861, M3978, and Morton to General Richard Delafield, June 9, 1864, M4731, Chief Engineer, Letters Received.

28. Morton, *Memorial of the Commander of the Pioneer Brigade to Major-General Rosecrans, Commanding the Army of the Cumberland*, copy enclosed in Morton to Totten, February 16, 1863, M4251, Chief Engineer, Letters Received; Fitch, *Annals*, 184–86.

29. Isaac P. I. Raub to Mary Jane Raub, May 10, 1863, Isaac P. I. Raub Letters, Nesbitt-Raub Family Collection, U.S. Army Military History Institute, Carlisle Barracks, Pennsylvania. See also Fitch, *Annals*, 187–88.

30. Morton, Report of Operations for November 1863, enclosed in Morton to Totten, December 8, 1864, Chief Engineer, Letters Received; Isaac Raub to Mary Jane Raub, May 10 and 14, 1863, Raub Letters, U.S. Army Military History Institute, Carlisle Barracks, Pennsylvania.

31. Raub to Mary Jane Raub, May 20, 1863, Raub Letters, U.S. Army Military History Institute, Carlisle Barracks, Pennsylvania.

32. General Order 31, Headquarters, Pioneer Brigade, April 11, 1863, General and Special Orders and Circulars Issued by the Pioneer Brigade, Record Group 391–1, entry 816, National Archives; Lt. Col. Arthur Ducat to Colonel 3M, May 6, 1863, D345 DC1863, Department of the Cumberland, Letters Received, Record Group 391–1, entry 4724, National Archives; Isaac Raub to Mary Jane Raub, May 10 and August 21, 1863, Raub Letters, U.S. Army Military History Institute, Carlisle Barracks, Pennsylvania; Garret Larew Diary (typescript), various entries, Larew-Phisterer Family Papers, U.S. Army Military History Institute, Carlisle Barracks, Pennsylvania.

33. Henry V. Freeman, "Some Battle Recollections of Stone's River," in Illinois Commandery of the Military Order of the Loyal Legion of the United States, *Military Essays and Recollections*, vol. 3 (Chicago: Dial Press, 1899), 234–39; Morton, official report, January 5, 1863, OR 20, pt. 1: 243–35; Rosecrans to Stanton, January 5, 1863, OR 20, pt. 1: 186; Stanton to Rosecrans, January 7, 1863, OR 20, pt. 1: 306; Rosecrans, official report, February 12, 1863, OR 20, pt. 1: 197–98.

34. Bobby L. Lovett, "Nashville's Fort Negley: A Symbol of Blacks' Involvement with the Union Army," *Tennessee Historical Quarterly* 41 (spring 1982): 3–9; Fitch, *Annals*, 619–20, 632–33. One tactic was to surround a church on Sunday and drive all able-bodied adults, men and women, to fortifications; Fitch, *Annals*, 619–20; Peter Maslowski, *Treason Must Be Made Odious: Military Occupation and Wartime Reconstruction in Nashville, Tennessee, 1862–1865* (Milwood NY: KTO Press, 1978), 100.

35. Maslowski, *Treason*, 100; General Order 6, Headquarters, Department of the Cumberland, January 27, 1863, and General Order 172, Headquarters, Department of the Cumberland, July 23, 1863, Department of the Cumberland, General Orders, Record Group 393–1, entry 942, vol. 2, National Archives; Rosecrans, endorsement on Morton to Major J. D. Kurtz, April 29, 1863, OR 23, pt. 2: 290–91. The failure to pay the workers became something of a scandal. Morton, who was ordered to pay them in the fall of 1863, was preoccupied with more pressing duties and was unwilling or unable to do so (and the government failed to provide sufficient funds). Lieutenant George Burroughs, who inherited the task from Morton as supervising engineer for Nashville, botched it so badly that his activities became a target of a government inquiry. See Burroughs to the Board of Commissioners for Contraband Refugees, July 31, 1864, no. 824, and Burroughs, testimony before the Refugee Commission, August 1864[?], no. 1165, box 2, Burroughs Retained Papers, Record Group 77, entry 281, National Archives; U.S. Congress, Senate, *Report of the Commissioners of Investigation of Colored Refugees in Kentucky, Tennessee, and Alabama*, 38th Cong., 2d sess., 1865, Ex. Doc. 28, 12–15.

36. General Order 173, Headquarters, Department of the Cumberland, July 23,

1863, Record Group 393–1, entry 942, National Archives; Maslowski, *Treason*, 106, Lovett, "Fort Negley," 16.

37. Morton to Major William Slidell, November 4, 1862, unentered letter, Department of the Cumberland, Letters Received, Record Group 393–1, entry 4724, National Archives; George Burroughs to the Board of Commissioners for Contraband Refugees, July 31, 1864, no. 824, box 2, Burroughs Retained Papers, Record Group 77, entry 281, National Archives; Lovett, "Fort Negley," 9–22. For the employment of black laborers at Chattanooga in late 1863 and 1864 see C. Stuart McGehee, "Military Origins of the New South: The Army of the Cumberland and Chattanooga's Freedmen," *Civil War History* 34 (December 1988): 326–27.

38. OR 20, pt. 2: 83, 94, 97, 98, 102, 120, 133–134.

39. Major Frank S. Bond to Lieutenant George Burroughs, August 17, 1863, OR 30, pt. 3: 56; C. Goddard to Maj. Gen. James Negley, August 20, 1863, OR 30, pt. 3: 85–86.

40. Williams, *Lincoln Finds a General*, 4:222–85; Hattaway and Jones, *How the North Won*, 318–23; Peter Cozzens, *No Better Place to Die: The Battle of Stones River* (Urbana: University of Illinois Press, 1990).

41. Williams, *Lincoln Finds a General*, 5:139–67; T. Harry Williams, *Lincoln and His Generals* (New York: Random House, 1952), 247–51.

42. Brig. Gen. Zealous B. Tower to Maj. Gen. George H. Thomas, April 28, 1865, OR 49, pt. 2: 502–503; James St. Clair Morton, *Memoir Explaining the Situation and Defense of Fortress Rosecrans* (Fortress Rosecrans TN: Pioneer Press, 1863), copy enclosed in Morton to Totten, June 24, 1863, M4345, Chief Engineer, Letters Received; Isaac Longnecker to J. F. Lenz, April 15, 1863, Isaac Longnecker Letters, Fulton-Lenz Papers, Civil War Times Illustrated Collection, U.S. Army Military History Institute, Carlisle Barracks, Pennsylvania.

43. Michler to C. Goddard, January 19, 1863, Nathaniel Michler Letterbook, United States Military Academy Library, West Point, New York; Michler to Woodruff, March 29, 1863, M313, Topographical Bureau, Letters Received; Morton to Totten, 11 May 1863, M4305, Chief Engineer, Letters Received; General Order 124, Headquarters, Department of the Cumberland, May 31, 1863, OR 23, pt. 2: 376–77.

44. Cullum, *Biographical Register*, 2:714; Margaret E. Merrill, "William E. Merrill," *Professional Memoirs of the Corps of Engineers* 9 (Nov.–Dec. 1917): 639–42.

45. Merrill to Totten, September 1, 1863, M445, Chief Engineer, Letters Received.

46. Merrill has been almost entirely ignored by scholarship on the Civil War, but see Shiman, "Engineering Sherman's March," 137–41, 155–59, 162–63, 338–48, 510–41.

47. Merrill to Garfield, September 28, 1863, OR 30, pt. 3: 912.

48. Merrill to Totten, July 5, 1863, M498, Topographical Bureau, Letters Received.

49. General Order 124, Headquarters, Department of the Cumberland, May 31, 1863, printed copy enclosed in Morton to Totten, June 7, 1863, M4325, Record Group 77, Chief Engineer, Letters Received; "Circular to Corps, Division, and Brigade Topographers," Topographical Engineer Office, Department of the Cumberland, June 23, 1863, copy enclosed in Merrill to Totten, July 5, 1863, M498, Topographical Bureau, Letters Received.

50. Rosecrans's testimony, April 22, 1865, "Rosecrans's Campaigns," 17; "Information Maps," Engineer Circular 3, Topographical Engineer Office, Headquarters, Department of the Cumberland, August 12, 1863, enclosed in Merrill to the Topographical Bureau, August 22, 1863, M724, Topographical Bureau, Letters Received.

51. Merrill, official report and returns for June 1863, enclosed in Morton to Totten, July 28, 1863, M596, Topographical Bureau, Letters Received; Merrill to Totten, August 11, 1863, M676, Topographical Bureau, Letters Received.

52. William Merrill, "Block-Houses, Etc.: The Engineer Service in the Army of the Cumberland," in Thomas B. Van Horne, *History of the Army of the Cumberland*, 2 vols. (Cincinnati: Robert Clarke, 1885), 2:456.

53. Merrill, undated memorandum, M110, series 1863, Department of the Cumberland, Letters Received, National Archives, Record Group 393–1, entry 4724; James Mercur, "Lithographic and Photolithographic Works," no. 31. Paper presented to the Essayons Club, 1874, in *Printed Papers of the Essayons Club* (N.p.: Battalion Press, n.d.), 1–3.

54. Margedant served as head of the Topographical Engineer Office in 1864, after Merrill's promotion to chief engineer.

55. Merrill to Totten, July 8, 1863, M4354, Chief Engineer, Letters Received,; Merrill, "Block-Houses, Etc.," 2:456–57.

56. Merlin E. Sumner, ed., *The Diary of Cyrus B. Comstock* (Dayton OH: Morningside Press, 1987), 249.

57. Williams, *Lincoln Finds a General*, 5:202–38; Hattaway and Jones, *How the North Won*, 402–4.

58. Copies of these maps can be found in the OR, vol. *Atlas*, plates 34 and 35.

59. Rosecrans to Halleck, August 1, 1863, OR 23, pt. 2: 585–86; Morton to Totten, July 9, 1863, M4351, Chief Engineer, Letters Received.

60. Meigs to Stanton, September 27, 1863, OR 30, pt. 1: 891.

61. William P. Loughlin, "Detached Service," in *History of the Ninety-sixth Regiment, Illinois Volunteer Infantry*, ed. Charles Addison Partridge (Chicago: Brown, Pettibone, 1887), 630; James R. Willett, *Rambling Recollections of a Mili-*

tary Engineer (Chicago: Illinois Commandery, Military Order of the Loyal Legion of the United States, 1888), 9–10; Merrill, "Block-Houses, Etc.," 2:454.

62. Captain George Burroughs to Major John Barlow, May 8, 1865, no. 869, Burroughs's Retained Papers, box 2, Record Group 77, entry 281, National Archives.

63. Morton, official report, July 10, 1863, OR 23, pt. 1: 581; Colonel William P. Innes, official report, July 13, 1863, OR 23, pt. 1: 582–85; Rosecrans, official report, October –, 1863, OR 30, pt. 1: 50; Isaac Raub to Mary Jane Raub, August 16, 1863, Raub Letters, U.S. Army Military History Institute, Carlisle Barracks, Pennsylvania.

64. Williams, *Lincoln Finds a General*, 5:239–44; Peter Cozzens, *This Terrible Sound: The Battle of Chickamauga* (Urbana: University of Illinois Press, 1992), 39–45; Rosecrans, official report, October –, 1863, OR 30, pt. 1: 52; Maj. Gen. Alexander McCook, official report, October 2, 1863, OR 30, pt. 1: 485; Brig. Gen. Charles Cruft, official report, September 28, 1864, OR 30, pt. 1: 726; Isaac Raub to Mary Jane Raub Letters, U.S. Army Military History Institute, Carlisle Barracks, Pennsylvania.

65. Williams, *Lincoln Finds a General*, 5:244–69; Cozzens, *This Terrible Sound*, 46ff.

66. William F. Smith to Grant, December 15, 1863, OR 31, pt. 2: 414; Thomas to Grant, January 14, 1864, OR 32, pt. 2: 88–89; Ulysses S. Grant, *Personal Memoirs of U. S. Grant*, 2 vols. (New York: Charles L. Webster, 1885) vol. 2, pp. 46–48; Thomas Weber, *The Northern Railroads in the Civil War* (New York: King's Crown Press [Columbia University], 1952), 180–91.

67. Isaac Roseberry Diary, entry of January 9, 1863, Emory University; Rosecrans to James Guthrie, September 2, 1863, OR 30, pt. 2: 297; Brig. Gen. Charles Cruft to Maj. Gen. Joseph J. Reynolds, November 2, 1863, OR 31, pt. 3: 18; Anderson to Grant, November 4, 1863, OR 31, pt. 3: 38–39, 65; Colonel William W. Wright, official report, April 24, 1866, OR, 3d ser., 5:933–71.

68. Itinerary of the Pioneer Brigade, August–September 1863, OR 30, pt. 1: 928–29.

69. Isaac Longnecker to J. F. Lenz, January 13, 1863, Longnecker Letters, U.S. Army Military History Institute, Carlisle Barracks, Pennsylvania.

70. Brig. Gen. R. W. Johnson to Lt. Col. George P. Thruston, August 22, 1863, OR 30, pt. 1: 115.

71. Hazen to Garfield, July 22, 1863, as quoted in William B. Hazen, *A Narrative of Military Service* (Boston: Ticknor, 1885), 407–408.

72. Hazen, *Narrative*, 406–9.

73. McCook to Garfield, July 10, 1863, OR 23, pt. 1: 467; Hazen, *Narrative*, 408. Hazen and others thought that this humiliation was directly responsible for

Morton's death the next spring in Virginia by causing him to expose himself rashly to enemy fire.

74. Morton to Totten, February 16, 1863, M4251, Chief Engineer, Letters Received.

75. Merrill to Totten, August 30, 1863 (M4424), September 1, 1863 (M4425), Chief Engineer, Letters Received. See also Shiman, "Engineering Sherman's March," 159–63.

76. OR 30, pt. 4: 102, 207, 244, 307, 361, 415, 435; General William F. Smith to General Reynolds, November 5, 1863, vol. 106, Records of the Chief Engineer, Department of the Cumberland, Record Group 393, National Archives.

77. Merrill to Totten, September 3, 1864, M842, Topographical Bureau, Letters Received; Garfield to Merrill, October 3, 1863, OR 30, pt. 4: 59; Nettesheim, "Topographical Intelligence," 69–72.

78. Rosecrans, official report, July 24, 1863, OR 23, pt. 1: 409; testimony of Lieutenant Nathan D. Ingraham at court of inquiry, February 15, 1864, OR 30, pt. 1: 1035; Captain William B. Gaw to Thomas, August 20, 1863, OR 30, pt. 3: 84–85; Maj. Gen. Philip Sheridan to Colonel Bernard Laiboldt, July 28, 1863, OR 52, pt. 1: 420; Merrill to Totten, September 3, 1863, M842, Topographical Bureau, Letters Received. Maps by various topographers can be found scattered throughout OR 30, pt. 1.

79. Ambrose Bierce, "George Thurston," in *The Collected Works of Ambrose Bierce* (New York: Neale, 1909–1912), vol. 2, 210–11; Ambrose Bierce, "The Crime at Pickett's Mill," in *Collected Works*, 1:286; Merrill, "Block-Houses, Etc.," 2:457–58; Shiman, "Engineering Sherman's March," 361–85.

80. Merrill, "Block-Houses, Etc.," 2:439–54; Leland R. Johnson, "Civil War Railroad Defenses in Tennessee," *Tennessee Valley Historical Review* 2 (summer 1972): 20–26; Shiman, "Engineering Sherman's March," 506–41.

81. Morton to Totten, February 16 (M4251), March 16 (M4267), June 6 (M4323), 1863, Chief Engineer, Letters Received; Merrill to Totten, May 10, 1863 (M4308); August 30, 1863(M4424); September 1, 1863 (M4425); Chief Engineer, Letters Received; OR 30, pt. 3: 213; pt. 4: 102, 207, 244, 307, 361, 415, 435; "An Act to Organize a Regiment of Veteran Volunteers," approved May 20, 1864, *Statutes at Large*, vol. 13, 80.

82. Merrill, "Block-Houses, Etc.," 2:454–56.

83. F. Stansbury Haydon, *Aeronautics in the Union and Confederate Armies* (Baltimore: Johns Hopkins University Press, 1941); Robert V. Bruce, *Lincoln and the Tools of War* (Indianapolis: Bobbs-Merrill, 1956; reprint, Urbana: University of Illinois Press, 1989).

5 / T. J. Jackson and the Value of "The Right Sort of Man"

WILLIAM J. MILLER

By March 1944, Commander Arleigh A. Burke had earned a reputation as an aggressive and inspired commander of warships. Six months earlier, with his Destroyer Squadron 23, he had successfully interdicted Japanese supply operations near Bougainville and New Ireland in the southwest Pacific, marking himself as a naval officer with a bright future. In that third month of 1944 Burke was ordered to join the staff of Vice Adm. Marc A. Mitscher, commander of Fast Carrier Task Force 58, and the appointment pleased neither man.

Immersed in the largest naval conflict in history, Chief of Naval Operations Admiral Ernest King struggled to coordinate the more traditional aspects of his war machine—surface and amphibious operations—with the new and dominant factor of naval air power. King decreed that every aviator admiral must have a nonaviator chief of staff and every admiral with a nonaviation surface warfare background must have an aviator as chief of staff. Mitscher, who wore wings but had significant experience in surface command, objected in vain and reluctantly added the destroyerman to his staff. "Admiral Mitscher certainly did not want me," recalled Burke. "He didn't want anything to do with me. He had made up his mind, I think, that he was going to bypass me [and] the chief of staff job he was going to do himself."

Burke, of course, was an extraordinary officer—a mere eleven years after reporting to Mitscher, Burke became chief of naval operations—and he soon made himself invaluable to Mitscher. The two served well together, and Burke developed an intense admiration for his boss: "If I ever loved any man," he wrote years later, "it was Admiral Mitscher."[1]

Such "arranged marriages" of commander and staff do not always end happily, precisely because the men involved are not always of the caliber of Burke and Mitscher. Armies and navies the world over have relied principally upon seniority, politics, or sometimes ill-advised policies, like King's perhaps, to determine who obtained promotions and staff billets. The result has been pairings that at worst have led to poorly conducted operations and at best to lost potential to the commander. Such a pernicious emphasis on professional attainments persists despite the lessons of history that fairly shout that it is not a man's training alone that makes him a good officer and commander but how he interprets and applies that training. Character, spiritual condition, and principles determine how and to what effect people will apply their knowledge.

Among history's successful generals, few have demonstrated a better grasp of the crucial influence that character has on military affairs than Thomas J. "Stonewall" Jackson. The Confederate general valued the dedication, selflessness, and trustworthiness of both field and staff officers more than he did their professional learning and prowess. Jackson recognized that such men gave their commanders the flexibility and opportunities that lead to success, and so he sought to fill both his staff and his brigades with what he called "the right sort of man." Jackson's topographical engineer, Jedediah Hotchkiss, serves as a model of Jackson's ideal officer, and his performance in the 1862 Valley campaign illustrates the great value that a man of moral strength can have to a commander. Hotchkiss was merely one among many men of "the right sort" with which Jackson sought to fill his command structure, but his example offers the best validation of Jackson's philosophy of emphasizing moral matters ahead of professional ones when selecting and promoting subordinates.

Jackson took pains to select only exceptional men for duty at headquarters, and the resulting staff was a galaxy of extraordinarily bright—perhaps even brilliant—men of culture and accomplishment. At various times during the war Jackson's official family included three doctors of divinity or theology, at least eleven holders of master's degrees or above, a former congressman and diplomat, and at least four attorneys and nine educators, five of whom had held professorships or chairs. All the more impressive is the extreme youth of the staff. Several were in their twenties; in fact, at least three defy categorization by profession because they too young—boys in their early twenties fresh out of college.[2]

The intellectual and professional attainments of the men at Jackson's headquarters did not by itself make them, collectively, an exceptional staff. No commander would deny that intelligence was necessary in a staff officer, but each general weighs other soldierly qualifications differently, some valuing military training above all else, for example, others rating the officer's field or experience most highly. Jackson gave due weight to all these factors but looked for more. "Whilst I highly prize Military education," he told an acquaintance, "yet something more is required to make a man a general."[3] And he would say the same about staff officers. "My desire is to get a staff specially qualified for their specific duties," he declared, immediately offering a qualification: "But if a person desires office in these times, the best thing for him to do is to pitch into service somewhere, and work with such energy, skill, and success as to impress those around him with the conviction that such are his merits that he must be advanced, or the interests of the service must suffer. . . . My desire is to make merit the basis of my recommendations."[4]

Jackson's desire for a meritocracy at his headquarters and within his command in general produced friction. Just as there were those who would rise through merit, there were those who would fail, and the laggards, which included men of experience and attainment, sometimes puzzled over Jackson's definition of merit. In his own mind, however, it was plain: "I know one general officer who is so incompetent for his position, as to be unable to take proper care of his command in ordinary campaign duty.— What can be expected of such an officer in battle? The trouble in the case that I refer to, results from want of Military information, judgment, nerve and force of character. Merit should be the only basis of promotion."[5]

Jackson did not subscribe to the notion that any man of attainment, civilian or military, would be the right man in the right job no matter what that job was. The fate of battles and campaigns rested not solely on divine providence nor merely on arms and intellect but also on the character of the combatants, so Jackson subscribed fully to one of Napoleon's more enduring maxims: "In war the moral is to the material as three to one."

The Corsican's dictum might find fewer adherents among moderns, influenced as they are by the extraordinary advances in technological warfare in the last half of the twentieth century, but countless military men—of Napoleon's century up to the present—have affirmed the emperor's prescience. Prussian theorist Carl von Clausewitz wrote that his widely studied treatise *On War*, dealt with matters "composed in equal parts of physical and moral causes and effects. One might say that the physical seem little more than the wooden hilt, while the moral factors are the precious metal, the real weapon, the finely honed blade."[6]

Moral factors, like love, hate, courage, fear, and all other concepts at the essence of humanity, are difficult to describe precisely, one reason that the *Oxford English Dictionary* devotes three-and-one-half pages to *moral* and its derivatives. In one sense, things moral are directly related to ethics—to the conformity to goodness and rightness in actions and volitions, to habits in life with regard to right and wrong conduct. In another sense, however, things moral deal with questions not of conduct but character. Moral conduct is only an indication of moral composition or character. In times of peace, we may be more concerned with morality in the sense of conduct, but in times of crisis, wars and disasters, for example, we care less for civility and more for the strength of character that lies at the heart of it. This is what Napoleon and Clausewitz meant when they referred to the importance of the "the moral" in war—courage, confidence, hope, determination, zeal, and a willingness to submit to discipline.[7] And this, too, was what Jackson sought in the men with him.

By the time of his participation in the Civil War, Jackson was a devout Presbyterian, a sect in which strains of the moral teachings of Stoic philosophers and their emphasis on character and conduct were prominent. Throughout his adult life, a concern with internal matters—character, duty, obligation, sincerity, gratitude—was the defining aspect of Jackson's personality. He endeavored to live an efficient and useful life by living a godly life. Before the war, he explained to friends in Lexington, Virginia, where he taught at the Virginia Military Institute, "I never raise a glass of water to my lips without a moment's asking of God's blessing. I never seal a letter without putting a word of prayer under the seal. I never take a letter from the post without a brief sending of my thoughts heavenward. I never change my classes in the section room without a minute's petition on the cadets who go out and those who come in. . . . The habit has become as fixed almost as breathing."[8] Given its importance in his own life, it was unavoidable that "the moral" would play a significant part in Jackson's generalship.

On a hot Sunday, August 17, 1862, Jackson and a few members of his staff rode to preaching in Culpeper County, Virginia. During the ride, Jackson remarked: "The right sort of man is one always striving to do his duty and never satisfied if anything can be done better."[9] Jackson's topographical engineer, Jedediah Hotchkiss, deemed the pronouncement worthy of record in his journal, and indeed it was, for the concept of "the right sort of man" lies at the very heart of Jackson, as a general and as a man.

Duty is the operative word in Jackson's definition of the right sort of man, just as it is the word most used by historians and biographers to explain Jackson's exceptional motivation. Duty is an abstract concept, however, and knowing what connotations the word carries for modern readers does not ensure that we know what the word meant for Jackson and his compeers in the nineteenth century. Modern readers are, perhaps, more inclined to think of duty in terms of an obligation, a responsibility, or a burden. Jackson may have seen it that way, but his concept of duty was probably deeper.

Recognizing a duty is acknowledgment that we are merely a part of something larger than ourselves—not isolated entities at the center of our own universes but functioning parts of a larger whole to which we must contribute. Duty, therefore, is a willing suppression of selfhood. When one embraces duty, he or she is declaring voluntary subservience so that he or she may serve some higher purpose. Service, the sacrifice of personal motives for the good of others, is the essence of duty. This vision of oneself as a servant of others lies at the heart of Christianity, and Jackson's writings and those of the people who knew him clearly reveal that he entertained this vision of himself. Jackson, then, saw duty not as a burden but as an opportunity for service. The right sort of man is at bottom a man committed to service not self.

So, Jackson sought selfless men—men who would serve others before themselves, who would willingly forego rest and food whenever the good of others required it and who would not be content to leave a job unfinished. Jackson found several such men: Alexander Swift "Sandie" Pendleton, Dr. Hunter Holmes McGuire, Quartermaster John Harman, Commissary of Subsistence Wells J. Hawks, and topographical engineer Jed Hotchkiss, all of whom would become part of the handful of men most responsible for the success of Jackson's Valley campaign.

Hotchkiss, like Jackson, was a self-made man. Each had left a modest, if not impoverished, home to make his own way in the world. Jackson, an orphan, left his Virginia home to attend West Point. He earned respectable class rank through determined hard work and a reputation for courage in the Mexican War. He entered the Civil War as a country professor of modest means. Hotchkiss did not have the advantage of a public college education. He left his father's home in New York at the age of seventeen and walked southward. In the summer of 1847, he entered Virginia's Shenandoah Valley with nothing but the clothes he carried, a few books, and an almost desperate desire to learn. Hotchkiss was a serious, studious, devout young man who found work as a tutor in the upper Shenandoah Valley. He gained the respect of his neighbors, some of whom built a private school,

Mossy Creek Academy, and installed Hotchkiss as principal at age twenty-one. Throughout the 1850s, Hotchkiss studied on his own, teaching himself the principles of surveying, engineering, and cartography. He made a reputation in the valley as an educator and earned a seat on the board of visitors of Washington College in Lexington. When the war came, Hotchkiss was in Churchville, Virginia, running his own school, Loch Willow Academy. Though a native New Yorker and a Unionist by inclination, he scarcely hesitated before throwing his lot with the state of Virginia. Like most residents of the valley, he loathed the idea of dissolving the Union but could not abide Abraham Lincoln's calling for troops in April 1861 to suppress "the rebellion" of Southern states.

Hotchkiss entered the war in June 1861 as a teamster, driving supplies over the mountains to Confederate troops in western Virginia. Not until March 1862 did he, his extraordinary knowledge of the valley, and his gifts as a cartographer come to the attention of General Jackson. The general summoned Hotchkiss to headquarters for what amounted to a brief Jacksonian soliloquy. He inquired about Hotchkiss's experience in the army, about his surveying and mapping, then came to the point: "I want you to make me a map of the Valley, from Harpers Ferry to Lexington, showing all the points of offence and defence in those places. Mr. Pendleton will give you orders for whatever outfit you want. Good morning, Sir."[10] Thus the interview closed, according to Hotchkiss, and the topographer joined Jackson's headquarters.

Hotchkiss later felt that Jackson had chosen that time to engage his services because of his actions during the retreat from Kernstown. The little battalion to which Hotchkiss belonged had not been engaged in the fight but had been close enough to the battlefield to be caught in the undertow of chaos and panic during the withdrawal. Near Tom's Brook the men grew restive as the stream of bloody soldiers and broken regiments flowed from the north. Hotchkiss remained calm and reassured the men that all would be well, and the militiamen stood their ground as ordered. General Jackson had been an interested observer of Hotchkiss's self-possession.[11] Two days later Hotchkiss was hired.[12]

The rise of Hotchkiss from teamster to staff officer strikingly illustrates Jackson's idea of how the right sort of man must rise to prominence. Let him "pitch into service somewhere, and work with such energy, skill, and success as to impress those around him . . . that he must be advanced, or the interests of the service must suffer."[13] Jackson's spring campaign in the valley, in which Hotchkiss was to play such a critical part, was an act of desperation. Maj. Gen. George B. McClellan and his enormous Army of the Potomac bore down on the Confederate capital of Richmond in eastern Virginia that spring, and few were those—North or South—who could see so much as a glimmer of hope in the Confederacy's future. The Confederate triumvirate of President Jefferson Davis and Generals Joseph E. Johnston and Robert E. Lee had not united in one plan to stop the Federals, but they all understood that if the North concentrated all of its manpower and resources in Virginia on taking Richmond, the city and perhaps the Confederacy were lost. Johnston and, to a greater extent, Lee thought that they could avoid a Federal concentration at Richmond if Jackson could keep the twenty thousand or more Federals in the valley busy enough that Washington would not consider shifting them to reinforce McClellan. Jackson was eager to try, but the task was not a small one.

After the Battle of Kernstown in late March 1862, Jackson could count perhaps twenty-five hundred men in his valley army. Within a month, he would increase his force to about six thousand soldiers, but many of the recruits were not only untrained but unarmed. With this small body of men, Jackson was to deter the twenty-five thousand Federals in or moving into the valley. The Confederate force in the valley would grow to about seventeen thousand, but Jackson was always outnumbered in the region. He held a numerical advantage at only one place that May and June, and that was at each place he attacked. That Jackson was able to concentrate his forces so consistently at the point of contact with the enemy owed much to his vigor and to Jed Hotchkiss's knowledge of the valley.

The Shenandoah Valley is about 140 miles long and from 12 to 24 miles wide, bounded on the northwest by North Mountain of the Allegheny range and on the southeast by the Blue Ridge. For about 50 miles near its middle, the valley is split by a huge mass of sandstone called Massanutten Mountain. The long ridgelike mountain towers one thousand to seventeen hundred feet above the valley floor and splits the Shenandoah River into two forks. The North Fork flows northward on the west side of Massanutten, and the South Fork, the larger stream, flows on the east. The presence of the river, numerous tributaries, and a relatively few good roads over fewer gaps in the mountains made movement in the valley complicated. It was Hotchkiss's task to simplify Jackson's ability to move in the valley, and because of his familiarity with the region and its residents, many of whom were old friends or acquaintances who could answer specific questions about roads and rivers, Hotchkiss was uniquely equipped to perform the duties Jackson asked of him. "I was thoroughly familiar with every portion of it," he wrote after the war, "from having walked and ridden over nearly every road in it, and gone along the crests of its mountain ridges during the dozen years or more preceding the Valley campaign. . . . My knowledge of the Valley was such that I could from memory make a sketch of almost any portion of it, showing its detailed topography, and I may be pardoned for saying that my facilities for reproducing topographical details from memory was such that instead of asking me to make a map Jackson acquired the habit of 'please strike me off a map' as though it were a mechanical process."[14] It is unlikely that any other man had the combination of knowledge and work ethic that Hotchkiss brought to the task.

Jackson put his new asset to work immediately. Hotchkiss spent late March and early April sketching terrain and evaluating military positions in the vicinity of Edinburg, Mount Jackson, and Rude's Hill. Not until mid-April did Jackson attempt to develop Hotchkiss's full potential as a staff officer.

The general moved his command southward from its camps at Rude's Hill to Harrisonburg then westward to the Elk River Valley below Swift Run Gap in the Blue Ridge Mountains. To make the position secure from Federal incursion, Jackson would need to destroy three bridges over the South Fork of the Shenandoah River. Bridge burning was normally a job for cavalry, but Jackson had reason to question the effectiveness of his mounted arm. Colonel Turner Ashby commanded somewhere between twenty-one and twenty-six companies of cavalry—so poor were Ashby's administrative skills that the precise size of his command cannot be determined.[15] Ashby was very brave, seemingly fearless in the almost daily skirmishes he fought with Federals trying to probe Jackson's position, but the cavalier was slovenly when it came to disciplining his command. "When Ashby's men are with him," observed Hotchkiss, "they behave gallantly, but when they are away they lack the inspiration of his presence, and being undisciplined they often fail to do any good."[16] On April 16, Ashby's slack discipline cost him more than fifty troopers, an entire company, when the men were captured sleeping in a church. They had posted neither pickets nor sentries. A day later, Federals surprised Ashby and drove his command out of Mount Jackson, forcing him to relinquish a crucial highway bridge and compelling Jackson to abandon his position at Rude's Hill. It is no wonder, then, that Jackson had lost a large measure of confidence in his cavalry. He would send cavalry to burn the South Fork bridges, but he would send a suitable supervisor as well. The assignment went to Hotchkiss.

Hotchkiss led 150 of Ashby's cavalrymen northward to destroy the bridges. The column rode about ten miles to the first bridge, and there Hotchkiss left a detachment with orders to take up the planking on the bridge and prepare to fire it. He then went on the remaining six miles to the second bridge, stopping just short and sending a scout. The cavalrymen under Jordan began growing restive. Hotchkiss already knew that Ashby enforced little discipline in his command, but he was disgusted to see that many of the troopers with him that day, including the commander, were drunk.

The scout returned to say no Federals were in sight, and Hotchkiss sent an officer and three men to burn the bridge. He ordered the rest of the cavalry to feed their horses in preparation for the ride back to the first bridge. Minutes later, all was chaos.

> The men went forward to burn the bridge and had put hay in the mouth of it and set it on fire, when a column of the enemy appeared and fired a volley and their dragoons charged, a messenger at once reported that they were coming, and I ordered the men to their horses and told [Captain Macon] Jordan to front his men—and I went forward to reconnoiter, when Jordan followed me instead of attending to his men, and the enemy came charging up and firing when our men broke at once, except some 3 or 4, and a perfect stampede of them took place, the enemy pursuing for 3 miles, every attempt to rally [Jordan's men] was unavailing, some actually throwing away their guns, many their coats, blankets &c, &c—I never saw a more disgraceful affair.[17]

Hotchkiss gave up trying to rally the fugitives and went on to ensure that the men at the first bridge completed their work of destruction, which they did. He then returned to headquarters and made his report. Hotchkiss was embarrassed by the incident, not for himself, but for Jordan and his troopers—"all owing no doubt to the state of intoxication of some of the men, and to the want of discipline."[18] Did Hotchkiss deserve to share culpability for the failure of the mission? Had he, for example, shown poor judgment in permitting a portion of the riders to rest and feed their horses before the work was done? Hotchkiss apparently felt no guilt, and Jackson was content to let the onus of blame rest on Ashby. A few days later, Jackson broke up Ashby's command and sent Hotchkiss on another independent mission.

In the last week of April, Jackson contemplated an offensive movement against an isolated Federal force of Maj. Gen. John C. Frémont's command in the Allegheny Mountains west of the valley. His plan was to move secretly around the Federals at Harrisonburg, doing what he could to mislead them of his intentions, join with Brig. Gen. Edward Johnson's 3,000 men, thereby increasing the size of his total force by 50 percent, then strike into the mountains toward the Federals. As he prepared for the movement, Jackson needed information about Johnson's force and the terrain on the west side of the valley, so he sent Hotchkiss. For several days, Hotchkiss rode about western Augusta County, consulting with Johnson, scouting Union positions, and making sketches. At the end of the first week in May, Jackson arrived with his army. Now commanding an army of 9,000, Jackson moved westward into the mountains toward Frémont. His men were ready for a fight. "Started this morning for Buffalo Gap and the Shenandoah Mountains," wrote one officer in his diary, "to give the enemy a taste of Jackson."[19]

The march was swift, and on May 8 as the army neared the town of McDowell, where the vanguard of Frémont's force lay encamped, Jackson detailed Hotchkiss to lead the advance. He moved forward with skirmishers up the winding mountain roads, over which he had driven as a teamster less than a year before. At each turn in the road, Hotchkiss stopped to ensure the way was clear of Federals. He would then turn and wave his handkerchief as a signal to Jackson, who would lead the van of the main column forward. The slow, cautious process continued to the summit of Bull Pasture Mountain.[20]

On the crest, Jackson asked Hotchkiss for information about the valley before them, at the bottom of which lay McDowell, occupied by a Federal brigade under Brig. Gen. Robert C. Schenck. Having spent time at McDowell the previous summer, and having made good use of that time by scouting and surveying the region, Hotchkiss could respond to Jackson's request quickly and fully. He took the general to a "projecting ledge of rocks on the right-hand side of the road from which the enemy's position was visible and pointed out to him the details of the locality." To help illustrate his descriptions, Hotchkiss sketched out a map for Jackson on the spot.[21]

Jackson decided that because the afternoon was well advanced the artillery should be moved up during the night to support an attack in the morning. He directed Hotchkiss to find a road by which artillery could be brought up. The Federals, declining to wait for Jackson to attack them in the morning, had stealthily climbed the mountain and attacked Jackson's infantry. The Battle of McDowell was short and confused, fought as it was near the end of the day in thick woods and on steep slopes. The Federals withdrew in the darkness, and Jackson prepared to resume the fight at daylight, but sunrise on May 9 showed that there would be no fighting that day. The Federals had retired from the mountain and abandoned McDowell. Jackson gave his men a day of rest and then set his army off in pursuit of the outnumbered Schenck, chasing him deeper into the mountains.

Jackson decided that even if his pursuit was swift the prey could still escape. He needed to hem Schenck in, and he called upon Hotchkiss to do it. "Sometime during the afternoon of the 10th," remembered Hotchkiss,

> I should say between three and four p.m., while we were waiting developments in front, the General beckoned to me then turned and rode back along the road by which we had advanced, I following him, until we reached a wood road that turned into the woods to our left. We rode up that a little ways when he turned and addressed me, emphasizing his words, shaking his long index finger towards me, and said, in his quick, rapid way: "General Banks is in Harrisonburg, Gen. Frémont is at Franklin, there is a good road between them. Gen. Frémont ought to march to Gen. Banks, but I don't think he will do it, I want the road between them and Dry River Gap blockaded by daylight tomorrow morning so he cannot do this. Please take a squad of couriers and ride back to Churchville, by way of McDowell, and take Capt. Sterrett's company of cavalry, which you will find near Churchville and go and blockade Dry River Gap. Send me back a messenger every hour telling me where you are and what you have done."

Hotchkiss asked if Sergeant S. Howell Brown might accompany him. Jackson assented, and Hotchkiss set off at once, trailing a long string of couriers behind him.

The incident is remarkable for several reasons. It shows how serious Jackson was about maintaining secrecy. He took Hotchkiss away from the staff, away from the marching column and into the woods where no one, not even friendly ears, could hear the assignment. If secrecy was so crucial, presumably Jackson did not tell any other members of the staff where Hotchkiss was even after he had left. No one at headquarters knew what Hotchkiss was up to, nor anything about the river gaps, except Jackson.

The importance of the mission, in Jackson's mind, is indicated by the requirement that Hotchkiss report every hour. Jackson had to know the status of Hotchkiss's mission to know how he was to deal with Schenck and Frémont. If Hotchkiss failed and Frémont slipped out through one of the gaps into the valley to join Banks, Jackson would be trapped in the mountains and vastly outnumbered by the combined Federals. The assignment also showed Jackson's supreme confidence in his topographical engineer.

After a ride of about fifty miles, Hotchkiss's party reached Churchville near midnight. He found the local cavalry company—about 60 men—and after feeding his horse and himself led the advance northeastward toward Dry River Gap. Before dawn, the riders approached the town of Rawley Springs at the eastern end of the gap. Hotchkiss sent pickets out to the east toward Harrisonburg only twelve miles away, where much of the Federal army lay in ignorance of Jackson's movements, and sent the rest of the party up into the gap. Just at daylight, Hotchkiss stopped, left one detachment with the horses, and set the rest of the men to felling trees and rolling rocks into the road. Within a few hours, the work was complete; the gap was closed. The men then moved southward to the North River Gap and blocked it with boulders and felled trees. His work done, Hotchkiss rested his mount. The topographer had ridden well over one hundred miles in perhaps eighteen hours.

Meanwhile, Jackson's pursuit of Schenck was frustrated when the retreating Federals set fire to the woods by the road. The billowing smoke and flying ash slowed the Confederates to a standstill, and according to one of his staff Jackson declared that the smoke was "the most adroit expedient to which a retreating army could resort to embarrass pursuit and that it entailed upon him all the disadvantages of a night attack."[22] Though Jackson would have liked to strike Schenck again, he was satisfied that these Federals would be no more trouble, fleeing deep into the mountains as they were with no open route by which they could join their friends at Harrisonburg. Jackson had, for the time being at least, put Frémont out of the game. The Southerners about-faced and marched out of the mountains and once again to the valley, where Jackson met with Maj. Gen. Richard S. Ewell, whose eight thousand men Richmond had placed at Jackson's disposal. The valley army now numbered seventeen thousand men, and Jackson was determined to use his command to defeat and disperse the Federals in the valley.

The Federals at Harrisonburg under Maj. Gen. Nathaniel P. Banks had cooperated with Jackson's plan by remaining quiet while the Confederates disposed of Frémont, and now Banks was even withdrawing down the valley toward Winchester. After a brief consultation, Jackson and Ewell decided to pursue and, if possible, attack Banks.[23]

On May 23, Jackson's combined force, now numbering about seventeen thousand, attacked a portion of Banks's force at Front Royal, at the northern end of the Page Valley. The Confederates drove the Federals back in confusion and two days later defeated the Northerners at the Battle of

Second Winchester. Banks's command fled northward in chaos, through Winchester and on to the Potomac River and the safety of the Maryland shore.

As Banks crossed the Potomac, Jackson allowed most of his weary army two days of rest around Winchester. On the third day, the general moved off in pursuit of Banks, a movement that might have been interpreted as an attempt to follow the beaten and confused Federals into Maryland. This, of course, is how he hoped the Federals would see his advance, but he had no intention of crossing the Potomac. He sent one brigade—his old brigade, which now shared his nickname of "Stonewall"—in advance of the main column. General Charles Sidney Winder, commanding the Stonewall Brigade, marched all the way to the river to ensure that Banks crossed.

The victory at Winchester could scarcely have been more complete. Jackson's loss in killed, wounded, and missing in the fights at Front Royal and Winchester did not exceed four hundred, while Federal losses in prisoners alone came to more than three thousand. Hotchkiss had been active in consummating the victories at Front Royal and Winchester, as had other members of Jackson's staff, particularly Quartermaster John Harman and Wells Hawks, Jackson's commissary of subsistence. The two had the agreeable though difficult task of removing tons of captured Federal commissary stores from Winchester, Martinsburg, and Harpers Ferry. More than 33,000 pounds of bacon, 2,609 pounds of sugar, 504 bushels of salt, 103 head of cattle, and an amazing 80 tons of hard bread came into Hawks's hands. He immediately began issuing rations from this small mountain of stores and making preparations to move the rest to storehouses. Harman worked with Wells to move the precious stores southward, but, in Jackson's words, the captures were "so large in quantity that much of it had to be abandoned for want of necessary means of transportation. Major Harman . . . had but one week within which to remove it, and, although his efforts were characterized by his usual energy, promptitude, and judgment, all conveyances that within that short period could be hired or impressed were inadequate to the work."[24]

Despite the ringing triumph for the Confederates, the Federals were not ready to relinquish their designs on the valley, and the campaign took a dramatic turn. On May 29, Jackson received news that two strong Federal columns were moving on his rear. Maj. Gen. Irvin McDowell was marching westward toward Front Royal with thirty thousand men, more than twice what Jackson commanded. General Frémont, who had been thrashing about in the mountains since Jackson's May 8 victory at McDowell, had been ordered into action by President Lincoln himself and was now approaching Strasburg from the west with his fifteen thousand or more. Frémont had had a long march out of the mountains, for the most direct routes back into the valley were still blocked, thanks to the efficiency of Hotchkiss and his workers three weeks earlier. In addition to McDowell and Frémont, a strong Federal force was forming across the river at Harpers Ferry.

Jackson acted quickly to slide out of the three-sided box, but he would need to buy some time to move all of his widely scattered troops to safety. He set his army in motion back to Winchester and thence on to Strasburg. The Stonewall Brigade remained at Halltown, near Harpers Ferry, through May 30. He recalled it and hoped to wait for it to join him, if possible, but he needed time. At least one subordinate disappointed him. Colonel Zephanier Turner Conner, commander of the Twelfth Georgia, which garrisoned Front Royal at the end of May 1862, abandoned his post when he learned of the approach of ten thousand Federals from the east. According to Hotchkiss, Conner informed Jackson that he had to withdraw because of the overwhelming numbers and that "unless immediately succored all is lost." Jackson called Conner to headquarters and asked him three questions: "Colonel, how many men did you have killed, sir?" "None," Conner replied. "How many wounded?" "None, Sir," said Conner. "Do you call that much of a fight?" Jackson had Conner cashiered out of the army.[25]

To guide the Stonewall Brigade to safety, Jackson again called upon Hotchkiss. "I want you to go to Charles Town and bring up the first brigade," Jackson told Hotchkiss. "I will stay in Winchester until you get here if I can, but if I cannot, and the enemy gets here first, you must bring it around through the mountains."[26] Hotchkiss said he understood and departed immediately. "I rode rapidly and reached Charles Town . . . quite early in the morning," he recalled, "and at once found Gen. Winder, who commanded the Stonewall Brigade . . . and gave him Gen. Jackson's orders." Winder immediately put his troops on the road for what would turn out to be one of the more memorable marches of perhaps the best marching brigade of the Civil War. And it was a brutal march. The rain fell in sheets, and the roads turned to mud. After long hours on the road, each minute filled with anxiety about whether he was leading the brigade to safety or into the waiting arms of overwhelming numbers of Federals, Hotchkiss led the column through Winchester at about dusk. They continued on through town in the gathering darkness with orders to reach Jackson at Strasburg that night. But the men in the ranks had nearly reached the limit of their endurance. One officer present recalled that "by this time our men were straggling fearfully." Four regiments of the brigade had marched that day thirty-four or thirty-five miles, through mud and rain, and the Second Regiment had marched continuously, under worse conditions (for no rations had been issued to them for at least two days) from Loudoun Heights, which fact made the march about five miles more than the other regiments marched.[27] It was about 10 PM when Winder decided his men could go no further that night.[28] Hotchkiss, too, was worn out and slept in the hay of a stall in a stable beside his horse.[29]

In the morning, June 1, Winder and Hotchkiss led the advance southward again toward Strasburg. The weary Stonewall Brigade could have no rest, however, for Jackson had his entire army on the road to elude the slowly closing jaws of McDowell and Frémont. The Confederates moved hastily on to Mount Jackson, Ashby's cavalry acting as a rear guard. Jackson and his entire command had escaped. The valley army continued southward, skirmishing with the Federals for more than fifty miles in the days that followed.

Hotchkiss would play an important role in the remaining week of the campaign, scouting Federal positions from the top of Massanutten Mountain and, at the Battle of Port Republic, guiding Brig. Gen. Richard Taylor's Louisiana brigade to the flank of the key Federal artillery position on the field, contributing substantially to the Confederate victory. But such tasks might be considered as within the realm of his duties as topographical engineer. It was through his extratopographical duties in extreme circumstances—especially at Dry River Gap and in retrieving the Stonewall Brigade from Charlestown—that Hotchkiss had made his greatest contributions to Jackson's successful campaign. It was in these missions as well that Hotchkiss both illustrated and validated Jackson's theory of the value of the right sort of man. Hotchkiss was reluctant to admit defeat in any enterprise. He was not satisfied until his duty had been done, and he pushed himself physically to accomplish the task at hand well and promptly. Wherever he went, therefore, Hotchkiss became the proverbial right man in the right place at the right time.

Others, too, proved Jackson's theory but in reverse. Colonel Conner showed that the wrong man in the wrong place would fail, and that failure might lead to catastrophe. Conner's capitulation to circumstances at Front Royal opened the door to disaster, which Jackson averted only through the excellent work of staff members like Harman and Hawks and the exceptional performances of Hotchkiss, General Winder, and the men of the Stonewall Brigade. Ashby, too, and his poorly disciplined men sometimes failed at the critical moment. The cavalry chief, in general, performed outstanding service for Jackson that spring, a fact Jackson acknowledged, but the commanding general also felt his cavalry chief's performance left much to be desired. The disorganized and slovenly state of Ashby's command caused Jackson unnecessary concern, at times limited his strategic options, and on the night of May 24–25 south of Winchester cost Jackson a victory. All this was ample proof, in Jackson's mind, that Ashby was not "the right sort of man," for he was satisfied despite the fact that conditions in his command could obviously have been arranged better.[30] In writing of Ashby to an acquaintance, Jackson was typically blunt: "I would regard it as a calamity to see him promoted."[31]

Jackson's principle of "the right sort of man" was at the heart of his success as a general. For all his "genius," a difficult quality to define, Jackson unquestionably owed much of his success, perhaps all of it, to force of character. Perhaps the leading modern historian of Jackson's campaigns has declared that "the salient military characteristic of Jackson . . . was an extraordinary clenched-jawed determination—a determination beyond that possessed by anybody else on either side. He won because he would not lose."[32] Jackson's writings reveal an intensely introspective man guided by a very few narrow principles. He would do right in all circumstances no matter what it cost him. He would do the will of God, subjugating his own desires and comfort to the good of others. He would do his duty every waking moment.

In searching for subordinate officers, whether they be brigade commanders or staff members, if Jackson was not looking for a reflected image of himself he was at least looking for men who shared his principal commitment, namely, a determination to do what was right. It is revealing that the nearest Jackson ever came to uttering a boast was when he spoke of his staff. In December 1862, he told a friend that he had "the best and most efficient staff in the army." He spoke of the special characteristics of each member of his staff, of their qualifications for the respective duties, and of the manner in which they discharged them. He especially commended Hawks, Harman, and Pendleton, as well as Hotchkiss, of whom he said: "his skill in acquiring and communicating a knowledge of the topography of the country was very remarkable, surpassing that of any one he had ever known; he also commented on his unceasing diligence and energy in discharging the duties of his office and in the execution of difficult duties entrusted to him."[33]

The relationship between a commander and his subordinates is not merely an affiliation between a supervisor and an assemblage of competent-but-interchangeable technicians and managers but a complex human relationship in which a leader and his nearest followers mesh on personal and professional levels to drive toward a common goal. Jackson understood that a good man, even one of modest professional attainments, would almost always make a good officer—one to be relied upon in every event—whereas a man wanting in character, no matter how talented or brilliant, might fail at the critical moment. From the outset, the general made it his policy to subject subordinate officers to strict scrutiny and to hold them to a high standard of performance. He could not always decide who commanded his regiments, brigades, and divisions, but he did have control of who served at headquarters, and the result was a staff of remarkable strength and facility. It is possible, if unlikely, that other generals of the Civil War possessed a staff of greater collective intelligence or talent but doubtful that any commander of an army in the field possessed a staff more effective than Jackson's or one that provided their chief with more freedom to improvise while on campaign. Jackson earned a prominent place among history's generals not solely because of his strategic brilliance but because he understood the importance of the tools with which he would work and took care to ensure they were of high quality. Jackson was one of those enlightened leaders who understands that courage matters more than knowledge, that determination means more than talent, and that self-sacrifice achieves more than ambition.

Notes

1. Arleigh A. Burke, "Spruance, Mitscher, and Task Force 58," in *Carrier Warfare in the Pacific*, ed. E. T. Woolridge (Washington DC: Smithsonian Institution Press, 1993), 156–57, 167.

2. Jedediah Hotchkiss Papers, Library of Congress Manuscript Division, Washington DC, microfilm reel 39, frame 370 ff (hereafter cited as Hotchkiss Papers).

3. Jackson to William Porcher Miles, Strasburg, March 5 [15?], 1862, William Porcher Miles Papers, Southern Historical Collection, University of North Carolina, Chapel Hill (hereafter cited as Miles Papers). Quoted in Frank E. Vandiver, *Mighty Stonewall* (New York: McGraw-Hill, 1957), 213.

4. Quoted in G. F. R. Henderson, *Stonewall Jackson and the American Civil War* (New York: Longmans, Green, 1943), 136. See also R. L. Dabney, *Life and*

Campaigns of Lieut. Gen. Thomas J. Jackson (Boston: Blelock, 1865; reprint, Harrisonburg va: Sprinkle Publications, 1983), 250.

5. Jackson to William Porcher Miles, Strasburg, March 5 [15?], 1862, Miles Papers. Also quoted in Vandiver, *Mighty Stonewall*, 213.

6. Karl von Clausewitz, *On War*, ed. and trans. Michael Howard and Peter Paret (Princeton: Princeton University Press, 1976), 184–85.

7. One may carry the point one step further and say "moral" in the sense of courage, confidence, hope, and the like is distinct from the concept of morale, which refers to the condition of a person or a body of troops. Morale is a measure of their spirit whereas "the moral" is the spirit *and* the character.

8. Roy Bird Cook, *The Family and Early Life of Stonewall Jackson* (Charleston wv: n.p., 1948), 131–32.

9. Hotchkiss Journal, August 17, 1862, Hotchkiss Papers (hereafter cited as Journal, by date). Much of Hotchkiss's journal writings have been published as *Make Me a Map of the Valley*, ed. Archie McDonald (Dallas: Southern Methodist University Press, 1973).

10. Journal, March 26, 1862.

11. Journal, March 24, 1862.

12. Hotchkiss, *Make Me a Map*, 11.

13. Quoted in Henderson, *Stonewall Jackson and the American Civil War*, 136. See also Dabney, *Life and Campaigns*, 250.

14. Letter from Jed Hotchkiss to William L. Chase, March 28, 1892, general correspondence folder on General T. J. Jackson, Hotchkiss Papers.

15. James I. Robertson Jr., *Stonewall Jackson: The Man, the Soldier, the Legend* (New York: Simon & Schuster, 1997), 361.

16. Letter to his wife, April 20, 1862, Hotchkiss Papers, reel 4, frame 738.

17. Letter to his wife, April 20, 1862, Hotchkiss Papers, reel 4, frame 737.

18. Letter to his wife, April 20, 1862, Hotchkiss Papers, reel 4, frame 737.

19. Diary of Lieutenant John W. Mauk, Company K, Tenth Virginia Infantry, reprinted in Harry M. Strickler, *A Short History of Page County Virginia* (N.p.: n.d.), 177.

20. Hotchkiss Journal, May 8, 1862.

21. Hotchkiss Journal, May 8, 1862.

22. William Allan and Jedediah Hotchkiss, *History of the Campaign of Gen. T. J. (Stonewall) Jackson in the Shenandoah Valley of Virginia* (Philadelphia: J. B. Lippincott, 1880; reprint, Dayton oh: Morningside Bookshop, 1987), 80.

23. Allan and Hotchkiss, *Jackson in the Shenandoah*, 80.

24. U.S. War Department, *The War of the Rebellion: A Compilation of the Offi-*

cial Records of the Union and Confederate Armies, 128 vols. (Washington DC: Government Printing Office, 1881–1901), 1st ser., vol. 12, pt. 1, pp. 708, 720–21. Wells J. Hawks was forty-seven in 1861 and in less-than-robust health. A coachmaker with no military experience, he had served in the Virginia state legislature and as mayor of Charlestown, Virginia, but was beyond military age when the war came so was excused from entering the army. He enlisted in the Second Virginia, one of the regiments in what would become the Stonewall Brigade. In October of 1861, Jackson, apparently having satisfied himself of Hawks's mettle, brought him to headquarters as major and chief commissary of subsistence. Hawks brought his son as a courier, aged 13. See Hotchkiss Papers, reel 39, frame 366.

25. Hotchkiss Journal, May 30, 1862. See also Hotchkiss, *Make Me a Map*, 50, and Robert K. Krick, *Lee's Colonels* (Dayton OH, 1991), 97–98.

26. Hotchkiss Journal, May 31, 1862.

27. Hotchkiss Papers, reel 49, frame 180 ff.

28. Hotchkiss Papers, reel 49, frame 180 ff.

29. Letter to S. J. C. Moore, September 8, 1896, Hotchkiss Papers, reel 34, frame 212.

30. On the night of May 24–25, 1862, Ashby's men stopped to plunder abandoned Federal wagons. The cavalry command in effect disintegrated just when Jackson needed it most—when in pursuit of a panic-stricken foe. Jackson relieved Ashby of command for dereliction of duty but restored him a week later. Hotchkiss to Holmes Conrad, September 8, 1896, Hotchkiss Papers, reel 34, frame 211.

31. Jackson to Alexander Boteler, May 6, 1862, quoted in Robertson, *Stonewall Jackson*, 371.

32. Robert K. Krick, interview by William Miller, in "A Touch of Genius in the Valley: A Conversation with Robert K. Krick," *Civil War*, no. 56 (April 1996): 8–19.

33. Jackson is quoted by Reverend Beverly Tucker Lacy, Hotchkiss Papers, reel 39, frame 282.

6 / Ulysses S. Grant and the
Problems of Command in 1864

BROOKS D. SIMPSON

Many historians view the elevation of Ulysses S. Grant to the position of general in chief of the United States Army as a critical step in securing the triumph of the Union in the American Civil War. Appraisals of his performance in the campaigns of 1864, however, range from lavish praise to contentious criticism. Historians have looked at Grant's relationship with Lincoln, his management of grand strategy, his approach toward the Virginia theater of operations, and his supervision of operations against Robert E. Lee's Army of Northern Virginia. Rarely, however, have they examined Grant's performance in these four related areas systematically, demonstrating how these levels of command interacted, or explored the constraints upon Grant's freedom of action. It is worth examining once more the situation Grant faced as he assumed overall command in order to offer an informed assessment of his performance. In so doing, one must remember the constraints under which he operated and that served to restrict his alternatives; one must also keep distinct the various levels of command just enumerated as well as the interplay between these levels of command.

In *Lincoln and His Generals* (1952), T. Harry Williams offered what still stands as the classic assessment of Abraham Lincoln's performance as commander in chief of the Union military effort. A major feature of this work was Williams's interpretation of the relationship between Lincoln and his final general in chief. Previous scholarship had suggested that Lincoln left Grant alone and gave him a "free hand" to conduct operations as he saw fit. Williams countered that Lincoln "approved of Grant's strategy and let the general execute it because Grant conformed his plans to Lincoln's own strategic ideas." Williams's Lincoln was always in charge, kept a close eye on Grant, and often corrected Grant's initial impulses, thus demonstrating that he was a better "natural strategist" than any of his generals, including Grant.[1]

Williams's account of the Lincoln-Grant relationship has won wide acceptance among scholars. Yet there is another way to view the relationship, particularly as it bore upon military matters during the campaigns, political and military, of 1864. Lincoln turned down Grant's initial campaign proposals, which stressed maneuver and striking at Confederate logistics, and insisted upon a direct confrontation with Lee. Grant readily acceded but found that while the president sought a decisive and relatively bloodless victory on the battlefield to reinforce the administration's chances of victory in the fall elections, these same political concerns meant that generals of suspect military ability but great political influence would command armies in the spring campaign. Three of these generals—Nathaniel Banks, Benjamin Butler, and Franz Sigel—failed at critical junctures, disrupting Grant's plans and contributing to the politically demoralizing bloodshed in Virginia. So did the declining fighting effectiveness of the Army of the Potomac as a result of expiring enlistments and an influx of conscripts and inexperienced soldiers as well as that army's well-known hesitation to act aggressively.

Grant's early months in Virginia educated him about the shortcomings of his subordinates and the command problems he faced. But his efforts to overhaul his subordinates in the summer of 1864 fizzled as politics once more intervened. Only Grant's patience, persistence, and the eventual success of other campaigns under his overall supervision secured the results on the battlefield necessary to guarantee Lincoln's reelection. The campaigns of 1864—on the battlefield and at the ballot box—were intricately intertwined. It was Grant's understanding and acceptance of political constraints, not Lincoln's military skill, that proved crucial to victory on both fronts. While Lincoln showed flashes of military insight, what made this command team work was Grant's grasp of the political concerns of his civilian superior.[2]

If the Lincoln-Grant relationship deserves reassessment, so too does Grant's handling of command problems. For the general in chief found his subordinates particularly troublesome, especially in the Army of the Potomac. His relationship with George G. Meade, that army's commander, proved an awkward one for both men, for Meade had to operate with Grant looking over his shoulder. Meade's handling of his army often reflected his frustration and irate temper. In Washington, Henry W. Halleck played the part of frustrated strategist to the fullest, often injecting himself into command decisions instead of acting as a conduit for communications between Grant and other armies and between Grant and the administration. Nor was Grant entirely blameless. His initial assessments of Butler, William F. Smith, and William B. Franklin proved seriously flawed: both Butler and Smith would fail Grant at critical junctures. While due allowance can be made for Grant's unfamiliarity with his subordinates at the outset of the campaign, this excuse cannot be offered for his failure to oversee with more care the operations around Petersburg, especially the Battle of the Crater. In the end, Grant triumphed because he had managed to nullify Lee's ability to take the initiative, allowing his commanders elsewhere to deliver the blows that guaranteed Lincoln's reelection.

Grant probably realized that he would not have total control over military planning before he became lieutenant general. In January 1864, Halleck, then still general in chief, had asked him for his ideas on grand strategy. Grant offered his ideas in two lengthy letters. In the West he mapped out a two-pronged offensive against Atlanta from Chattanooga and Mobile, arguing that the Confederates would be caught in the closing vise of two Union armies. In the East he called for an invasion of North Carolina, designed to rip up rail lines, free slaves, and encourage that state's peace movement; the invading column would look to the land to supply much of its needs. Robert E. Lee might well have to abandon Virginia to protect his supply lines.

Grant's plan, standing in stark contrast to characterizations of Grant as a mindless plodder and butcher, was bold, imaginative, and achievable. It took a broad view of the eastern theater, nullifying Lee's advantageous position in Virginia. It promised a war of maneuver and decision, not a slugfest of attrition. But Lincoln and Halleck rejected it. Halleck, misunderstanding the plan's thrust, told Grant that Lee's army remained the primary objective, to be met and defeated in open battle in Virginia. To reduce the Army of the Potomac to mere parity with Lee's Army of Northern Virginia in order to secure forces for the North Carolina operation was deemed too risky.[3]

Grant's plan of attack against Atlanta also required revision. Lincoln, determined to bring more of Louisiana under Union control to bolster his efforts to reconstruct the state, wanted Nathaniel Banks to lead an expedition up the Red River to Shreveport. James H. Wilson, one of Grant's former staff officers, observed from Washington that "there is a somewhat feverish anxiety on the part of the Government to bring back or reorganize the state governments in the conquered territory with as little delay as possible." Such an expedition, Lincoln believed, would also gather cotton for the Union and serve as a show of force against the French in Mexico. Banks, whose chief qualification for wearing a major general's shoulder straps was his political standing in Massachusetts, had been placed in charge of reconstructing Louisiana by the president. But Lincoln had faith in Banks not only in his capacity as a representative of the administration's Reconstruction policy but also as a general. Perhaps the president knew something that had escaped others about Banks's military ability.[4]

Although Grant's efforts to offer advice went unheeded, this setback did not damage his chances at becoming general in chief. Lincoln, in fact, seemed more concerned about whether Grant had a strategy to take the White House than about his possible plans to defeat the Confederacy. It would make no sense for the president to promote the fortunes of a possible rival in an election year. This helps to explain why the administration, according to Lincoln's private secretaries, "exercised no influence in the matter, neither helping nor hindering" the passage of a bill reestablishing the rank of lieutenant general. Only after news of Grant's lack of interest in the presidency reached Lincoln's ears did he decide that Grant was indeed the man for the job of general in chief. Grant traveled to Washington in March 1864 to accept his commission as lieutenant general.[5]

The new general in chief soon found that there were strings attached to his new position. He had come to Washington believing that he would be allowed to make his headquarters where he pleased. He refused to command from the capital; Halleck as chief of staff would facilitate communications between Grant and his subordinates as well as between Grant, Stanton, and Lincoln. Initially, Grant thought he might move from army to army as needed. However, Lincoln expected him to take the field against Lee; before long, Grant came to agree, because, as he later observed, "no one else could, probably, resist the pressure that would be brought to bear upon him to desist from his own plans and pursue others." He had already had a taste of such pressure from Lincoln himself in their first private meeting. The president described a plan of campaign that he had once offered Ambrose Burnside—that of flanking Lee by landing an army between two rivers along the Virginia coast and advancing westward to meet the Army of Northern Virginia. Grant listened politely, said nothing, and ignored the suggestion—an improvement, at least, upon the probable reaction of George B. McClellan. But such conversations made it clear to him that "here was the point for the commanding general to be."[6]

In such circumstances, Grant changed his mind about the appointment of subordinates. At first, he had contemplated replacing George G. Meade as commander of the Army of the Potomac. If he was to accompany that army, however, there would be no reason to remove Meade, an inclination reinforced by the favorable impression Meade made on Grant at their first meeting in March. Grant also came away from his visit with the Army of the Potomac believing that it was unlikely the army could carry out the North Carolina operation with any success. There was something about the army that disturbed him. As Grant did not know the abilities of the generals and men he was to command, a cautious, sure approach would reduce the risk of failure. For Grant was impressed, as he told his old colleagues in the West when he returned for a final visit, with "the necessity of closing the war with this campaign."[7]

Several weeks later Grant journeyed down to Fort Monroe to meet Benjamin F. Butler—another one of Lincoln's political generals, elevated to command to please Radical Republicans and some Democrats. It would be unfair to Lincoln to say that he imposed Butler upon Grant, for initially Grant liked Butler, in large part because he and Butler thought alike about what Butler's Army of the James should do in the coming campaign. Grant's initial assessment of Butler proved a serious mistake, especially his belief that Butler possessed enough initiative and insight to handle matters largely without supervision. He assigned William F. Smith, once a candidate for Meade's position, to a corps command under Butler in order to provide him with a proficient subordinate. Grant had been impressed by Smith's performance during the Chattanooga campaign, especially in setting forth the plan whereby Union forces reopened supply lines to the city. Whether Smith would be a capable combat commander was another question. His previous experience leading troops in the Army of the Potomac, especially at Fredericksburg, suggested that he hesitated at crucial moments; moreover, he was disputatious by nature. Left to his own devices, Butler, whose experience as a combat commander was quite limited, demonstrated in the months to come that he did not warrant Grant's confidence. Neither did Smith.

If Grant came away from his encounters with Meade and Butler favorably impressed, the same cannot be said for his sentiments toward Franz Sigel and Banks. Sigel had secured command of the Department of West Virginia because Lincoln believed that he could attract German-American voters to support the Republican Party. To remove him without cause would be politically counterproductive, although Grant became annoyed when Sigel, bypassing regulation channels of communication, telegraphed a West Virginia congressman to see to it that two Pennsylvania regiments were assigned to his command. Grant openly worried about Banks, fearing that he would soak up reinforcements sent to him on loan from Sherman's army. He was not alone in his concerns. "It seems but little better than murder to give important commands to such men as Banks, Butler, McClernand, Sigel, and Lew Wallace," Halleck declared, "and yet it seems impossible to prevent it."[8] As it could not be prevented, Grant accepted it.

By April, Grant had developed a plan in accordance with the guidelines set forth by the administration. In the West, Sherman was to move out against Joe Johnston and Atlanta; Grant still hoped that Banks could wrap up his operations in Louisiana to launch an offensive against Mobile, but he observed the administration's priorities. In the East, Grant sought to apply some of the guiding principles in his original plan to the constraints under which he operated. While Meade moved directly against Lee's army south of the Rapidan-Rappahannock River network, Sigel would advance south through the Shenandoah Valley, denying it to the Confederates as a source of supply and as an avenue of invasion while compelling Lee to detail a force to oppose him. Two other forces in his department would move against rail links in southwest Virginia. Butler and the Army of the James would move by water to Bermuda Hundred, located halfway between Richmond and Petersburg, and from there threaten Lee's supply lines and the Confederate capital itself. Lee, if all went well, would be trapped. Unable to counterattack by moving north through the Shenandoah, and afraid for the security of his capital and his supplies, Lee would be forced to come out and fight on terrain of Grant's choosing or flee to the security of the Richmond defenses. Indeed, Grant sought to engage Lee as quickly as possible in order to pin him away from Richmond, thus allowing Butler greater freedom of movement against the small Rebel forces confronting him. This is what he preferred to do, for, as he later commented, it was better to fight Lee outside of the Richmond fortifications than in them. If Lee turned to attack Butler, Grant would pursue him and come up against the rear of the Army of Northern Virginia. Lincoln grasped at once how Butler and Sigel would contribute to the campaign: "Those not skinning can hold a leg."[9]

One must remember what was being asked of Grant in 1864. The argument that he had unlimited resources with which to defeat Lee and the Confederacy is nonsense. As J. F. C. Fuller once argued, Grant's "problem was not merely one of winning the war in the most economical way, but of crushing the rebellion in the shortest possible time."[10] He had to accomplish this task under serious constraints. His ambitious initial plans had been curtailed under administration pressure. What emerged was a military plan tailored to meet political exigencies. The timetable set by the electoral process put pressure on Grant to seek success on the battlefield as soon as possible. He would have to achieve this result with subordinates in key positions who owed their rank to their political clout, not their military skill. To remove these men would damage the administration politically; to retain them in command to appease political constituencies might well lead to military setbacks, thus prolonging the campaign, reducing the prospects of a quick victory, and increasing the number of casualties suffered—all results that would hurt the administration. Williams was undoubtedly correct when he insisted that Grant did not exercise a free hand in planning his campaign in 1864. Lincoln exercised an ultimate veto over these plans. What he overlooked was the fact that Lincoln's influence was rooted at least as much in political as in military concerns. That Grant enjoyed as much leeway as he had was due in large part to his own awareness of the constraints he had to observe. What the general made of these constraints is unrecorded, although in previous campaigns he had accepted the reality of political considerations and worked within them. As Lincoln himself appreciatively noted, Grant "doesn't ask me to do impossibilities for him, and he's the first general I've had that didn't."[11]

What happened to Nathaniel Banks served as a clear reminder of what Lincoln meant by "impossibilities." After a promising beginning, Banks's advance toward Shreveport was halted by a Confederate attack at Sabine Crossroads on April 8. Another column advancing south from Arkansas was forced to turn back due to logistical difficulties, and before long the Red River began to fall, almost stranding a naval flotilla. Grant, frustrated at Banks's failure—and the indefinite postponement of the Mobile operation—requested his removal. Halleck explained that Banks's strong political connections would make it difficult for Lincoln to accede to Grant's request, and if Banks was removed Lincoln's plans for Reconstruction in Louisiana would suffer a setback. Eventually, Banks was restricted to Reconstruction, while Edward R. S. Canby took over field operations. Not for months to come would there be an effort to take Mobile.[12]

Undeterred, Grant set his plan in motion on May 4, 1864. He accompanied Meade and the Army of the Potomac against Lee. The campaign that followed is one of the most misunderstood in the history of the Civil War, in part because many scholars have underestimated the impact of politics on the conduct of operations. Most accounts focus on the main confrontation between Grant and Lee, giving short shrift to the roles assigned Sigel and Butler. Yet these two offensives played an integral role in Grant's conception of the Virginia campaign. Had Sigel and especially Butler succeeded in their assignments, the course of events would have been significantly altered. That Grant's offensive against Lee turned into pitched assaults alternating with flanking marches was not his original intent, and it is wrong to say that Grant actually sought a war of annihilation. He certainly did not foresee the events of the next forty days. Rather, he accepted them as consequences of the failure of Butler and Sigel to execute their assignments.[13]

And fail they did. Sigel's hesitant advance up the Shenandoah Valley met with disaster on May 15 at New Market, where an inferior Confederate force drove the Federals from the field. "He will do nothing but run," Halleck told Grant. "He never did anything else." Butler, unable to handle the discretion Grant left in his hands, failed to exploit his initial success at seizing Bermuda Hundred, preferring to squabble with his equally contentious subordinates rather than move on Richmond or Petersburg. Thus, Grant's efforts to pin Lee down at the Wilderness and Spotsylvania in a series of bloody clashes went for naught.

Moreover, Grant was having his own difficulties with the Army of the Potomac, let alone Lee. As he later put it, "I was new to the army, did not have it in hand and did not know what I could do with the generals or men." Meade proved hot tempered and chafed at Grant's presence, believing (rightly, to some extent) that it impinged on his own ability to command. That Grant's intervention often was necessary did not lessen Meade's irritation. Nor did the four infantry corps commanders fare well. Winfield Scott Hancock's health deteriorated during the campaign, due in part to the lingering aftereffects of his Gettysburg wound; Gouverneur Warren proved a complaining and uncooperative corps commander; John Sedgwick's death at Spotsylvania elevated Horatio Wright into a position to which he was unaccustomed; and Ambrose Burnside, despite flashes of capable leadership, rarely rose above mediocrity and often fell below it. Grant struggled to push the army onward: his presence ensured that it would not move backward.[14]

The fighting quality of the Army of the Potomac was not what it once was. Many men were contemplating the end of three years in uniform with a determination not to be cheated by death. Reports from several sources make clear that many of the soldiers reported wounded were but slightly so and had taken advantage of their injury to fall back from the front lines. The new recruits that arrived were either inexperienced combat soldiers, including regiments of heavy artillery armed as infantry and an entire division of African-American soldiers, or they were conscripts, most deemed worthless as soldiers by veterans and Grant alike. Weeks of continuous fighting wore out soldiers who had previously rested for weeks after major engagements. If the Army of Northern Virginia showed signs of collapse, so did the Army of the Potomac. Grant's commitment to press on relentlessly against the foe, with assault following upon assault, wore down his men even as it ate away at Lee's strength. Thus, when the Confederates seemed at the point of collapse, weary Yankee regiments could not seize the opportunities their previous sacrifices had done so much to create.[15]

Grant became so preoccupied with these problems that he was unable to exercise sufficient control over Sigel and Butler to salvage his original design. Thus thwarted, he relied upon one of his major strengths as a commander—the ability to improvise in response to circumstances—and decided to exercise the option he had long considered of joining Butler opposite Richmond and Petersburg. Lee raced to block the Union advance, and on June 1 the two armies clashed at Cold Harbor. Grant, laboring under the belief that just one more assault would crack Lee's supposedly demoralized forces, ordered an assault on June 2, but delays forced him to postpone it twenty-four hours. Sensitive to Meade's protests that he was interfering too much in the operations of the Army of the Potomac, Grant left the details of the planning to Meade. These decisions contributed to a disaster of the first order on June 3. Lee took advantage of the delay to perfect his entrenchments; Meade failed to reconnoiter the terrain and the enemy's position and did not attempt to coordinate the assault columns of the different corps. The result was predictable: Lee's men drove back the Federals with ease, inflicting heavy casualties within a matter of hours. What had happened was not the logical culmination of a month of endless pounding but an improvised response to what appeared to be a golden opportunity—and one with disastrous consequences.

At first, headquarters did not realize the magnitude of the setback. "The battle ended without any decided results, we repulsing all attacks of the enemy and they doing the same," Meade observed the day after the battle, adding that he thought that both sides suffered roughly equal losses. "I had immediate and entire command on the field all day," he added. In light of what had just happened, this was nothing to brag about. Grant later admitted "that there had been a butchery at Cold Harbor, but that he had said nothing about it because it could do no good."[16]

Cold Harbor was a bloody mistake: Grant admitted as much in later years. But its actual impact on the campaign was more problematic. Grant had no intention of giving up his plan of campaign. Convinced that additional assaults would be costly, if not futile, he tried one more time to sever Lee's supply line by swinging south across the James River and toward Petersburg in mid-June. He concealed the full extent of his move so well that Lee was not sure of his opponent's intentions for several days. But once more Grant fell short of achieving victory. The lead assault column, under William F. Smith, overran Petersburg's outer defenses on June 15, but Smith, convinced that he faced much heavier opposition than he in fact did, failed to press his advantage. Reinforcements under Winfield Scott Hancock arrived late because of confused and delayed orders, but Smith halted them too. On June 16 Grant urged a renewed effort, but assaults that evening and the next two days fell apart owing to hesitation and squabbling among subordinates. Meade grew so exasperated that he ordered his corps commanders to attack on their own since his efforts at planning a coordinated assault had proved futile. Grant, who had been supervising the crossing of the James (and keeping an eye on Butler) could not be in two places at once. He reluctantly resigned himself to siege operations.[17]

These failures proved critical to Grant's overall plan. He realized that immediate success on the battlefield was essential to inspire a war-weary North. Indeed, without some major military victories, a restive Northern public might well reject Lincoln's reelection bid. "People seem discouraged, weary, and faint-hearted," noted one New Yorker. "They ask plaintively, 'Why don't Grant and Sherman do something?'" The cost of such a campaign would be heavy casualties, a price Northern voters would be willing to pay only in case of an overwhelming triumph quickly obtained— an unlikely result. And Lincoln was worried about casualties, a concern he expressed to Grant.[18] Decisions made for political reasons in the spring of 1864 thus ultimately proved counterproductive, for the results damaged the prospects for political victory by hampering military operations.

Grant's operations had, as of the summer of 1864, failed to achieve the objective of securing Lincoln's reelection. Northern voters, unable to see the military advantages secured at Richmond and Atlanta, believed victory was still far off. With "intense anxiety," Lincoln hurried down to Grant's headquarters; Grant reassured him that the campaign was not yet over. Lee was now pinned against Richmond. He had predicted that if the campaign came down to a siege, the Confederate capital was doomed. At last Grant got his way in one matter: David Hunter displaced Sigel. Staff officer Horace Porter noted that Grant "has to get rid of political generals, by degrees, after demonstrating by their failures that they are not fitted for command."[19] Yet Hunter also ultimately failed to clear the valley, although for a few days it looked as if he would do so. Lee sent Jubal Early west to check Hunter; this done, Early headed north, intent on throwing a scare into the Lincoln administration in thinly garrisoned Washington. Such a blow, Lee knew, would shake Northern morale and might force Grant either to abandon the siege or launch a hasty attack.

News of Early's offensive only added to Grant's ongoing woes. In late June, he confronted a series of crises in command assignments. Once more, political and military interests were interwoven. Dissatisfied with Meade's performance at Cold Harbor and Petersburg, Grant discovered that Meade's high-strung temper and snappish personality had caused rifts with his subordinates. Butler and Smith had become irreconcilable enemies, disrupting the operations of the Army of the James. Butler's handling of his offensive against Richmond had revealed his shortcomings as a field commander, and before long Grant would learn that Smith had also failed to measure up to his expectations. These problems were soon compounded in the aftermath of Early's dash toward Washington, when disunity among area commanders in Maryland, Virginia, and the District of Columbia allowed Early to slip back south unmolested. Someone had to coordinate military operations in the Washington area with the goal of destroying Early's force and taking the Shenandoah Valley out of the war. If Grant failed to resolve these three crises in command, he would not be able to continue pressing against Lee.[20]

Once more, Grant's original inclinations on how to resolve these problems were modified by political considerations. He first addressed the command problems in the Army of the James, accepting Halleck's proposal that Butler be relegated to department command while Smith would exercise command in the field. If Butler refused to accept a desk job, Smith would likely have to go. But an order drafted by Halleck designed to implement this decision proved flawed, and Butler, hinting that if not satisfied he would exercise his political leverage against the Lincoln administration, put a halt to any effort to shelve him in the rear. Grant realized that unless he was willing to remove or transfer Butler—actions that would not have received the support of the Lincoln administration—he was stuck with him. Meanwhile, Smith's willingness to criticize Butler and Meade became so pronounced that Grant felt he had no alternative but to remove him—and he had learned enough about Smith to reassess his earlier high estimate of his ability. When Smith confronted Grant about his displacement, Grant, after offering several flimsy pretenses, finally told Smith, "You talk too much."[21]

It was important for Lincoln that Butler be kept happy. He had distanced himself from the entire incident, with good reason. The president had just accepted the resignation of Treasury Secretary Salmon P. Chase, a favorite among many Radicals, and had decided not to sign the Wade-Davis Bill, which embodied the notions of many congressional Republicans about Reconstruction. These acts sparked criticism of the administration. Indeed, several Republicans were actively contemplating a call for a second presidential nomination. Perhaps Lincoln could be induced to step aside; if not, perhaps Radical dissidents could rally behind another man. In these circumstances, to offend Benjamin Butler could prove very dangerous to Abraham Lincoln's chances of reelection.[22]

Butler's retention created other difficulties. If Grant had to leave the Petersburg front for any reason, Butler, by virtue of his seniority in rank, would command both his army and the Army of the Potomac. Yet Lincoln, anxious to dispose of Early, wanted Grant to do just that in early July, calling on his general in chief to take charge of matters around Washington—just as matters with Butler and Smith reached their climax. After initially indicating his willingness to comply, Grant changed his mind, informing Lincoln that "it would have a bad effect for me to leave here." Instead, he considered naming Meade to command the forces around Washington. Such a move would allow the grumpy commander to escape Grant's direct oversight of his movements, and it might bring peace to the high command of the Army of the Potomac. Grant also contemplated placing William B. Franklin in charge, having previously thought of him as a possible field commander for the Army of the James. Franklin had been Grant's classmate at West Point, and William F. Smith had often spoken highly of him, but Franklin's previous experience revealed a mixed record: at Fredericksburg his ineptitude contributed to Union defeat there. Why Grant remained confident in his abilities is unclear, although Franklin had doubtless taken advantage of a recent visit to City Point to press his claims for a command. On July 25 Grant shared his ideas with Lincoln in a letter that his own chief of staff, John A. Rawlins, carried to Washington. "Many reasons might be assigned for the change here suggested," he told the president, "some of which I would not care to commit to paper but would not hesitate to give verbally."[23]

Lincoln, taking the hint, asked to meet with Grant. The meeting was delayed until the end of July, for Grant had high hopes of cracking the Petersburg siege by a series of blows above and below the James River. Once more, Union forces blew a chance for victory when they failed to exploit a breech in the Confederate lines east of Petersburg created by the explosion of a mine on July 30. Friction and poor judgment among Grant's subordinates contributed to the result: as one of Grant's staff officers observed, "there were screws loose somewhere and the machine would not work." Ambrose Burnside, who promoted the idea of the mine, found Meade churlish and uncooperative. Just before the assault, Meade instructed Burnside not to employ his division of African-American soldiers in the opening assault wave, although these men, the only fresh soldiers in the entire army, had been training for weeks for the assault. Burnside then let his other division commanders draw straws to see who would lead the attack, and this uninspired decision proved disastrous when fate decreed that James Ledlie, a poor excuse for a major general but a great drinker, would spearhead the charge. As Ledlie drank in a rear area, his men botched their attack, and before long the rest of Burnside's command succeeding in arriving just in time to be part of the repulse—one that cost Burnside his command. Nor did Grant particularly distinguish himself. He supported Meade's decision not to employ Burnside's African-American division, and he failed to exercise direct supervision over the entire operation, although by now he should have known the implications of leaving matters to Meade and Burnside. "Such opportunity for carrying fortifications I have never seen and do not expect again to have," he sadly remarked; yet he could not shake a share of the responsibility for what happened.[24]

Grant and Lincoln met the day after the setback. The president pronounced Franklin unacceptable for the Washington command (or any other). He was far more receptive to Meade's appointment, but he told Grant that to transfer Meade at this time would look as if he had been removed for poor battlefield performance. But Lincoln agreed with Grant's desire to create a new command position uniting under one head the forces around Washington. Perhaps, the president mused, George B. McClellan might be induced to take the field once more—a move that would remove him from contention for the Democratic presidential nomination. Nothing came of this discussion, and perhaps Lincoln wanted to do nothing more than bring it up. As he returned to Washington, however, news arrived at Grant's headquarters that Early had once more crossed the Potomac River. It was time to do something about the command situation around Washington before disaster struck.[25]

Grant finally decided that Phil Sheridan was the man to bring Early to bay. At first, he tried to replicate the command situation he had proposed for Butler, allowing Hunter to retain nominal department command while Sheridan headed the forces in the field, "with instructions to put himself south of the enemy and follow him to the death." Stanton and Halleck raised questions about Grant's proposal, and at last Lincoln told Grant that his idea "will neither be done nor attempted unless you watch it every day and hour and force it." Grant quietly left City Point (refusing to relinquish command to Butler), and, after Hunter graciously stepped aside, personally installed Sheridan as "temporary" commander of the newly established Middle Military Division—the "temporary" designed as a sop to Meade, who pouted when he heard the news.[26]

Thus, once more Grant comported his preferences to political realities. Butler remained untouchable; Meade and his bruised ego continued in command of the Army of the Potomac. Only with Sheridan's appointment did Grant finally get his way. But few realized this. In Washington, members of the administration were becoming impatient with Grant. "A nation's destiny almost has been committed to this man," moaned Secretary of the Navy Gideon Welles, "and if it is an improper committal, where are we?" Halleck and Stanton joined the chorus of complaint. Halleck went so far as to suggest that Grant might have to abandon operations altogether in order to transfer soldiers north to quell expected outbreaks of violence against the draft—an idea Grant quickly squelched. Lincoln backed Grant, cheering him on with the directive, "Hold on with a bull-dog grip, and chew & choke, as much as possible." Grant's growing frustration with Halleck became evident when he proposed that Halleck be sent to California.[27]

August proved a difficult month for the Union cause, with only Farragut's victories at Mobile Bay providing hope. Grant maintained that victory was near: "We will peg away . . . and end this matter," he declared, "if our people at home will but be true to themselves." But unity and loyalty were in short supply. Democrats confidently looked forward to a November triumph as they nominated McClellan to head their ticket. Grant's refusal to permit prisoner exchanges on the grounds that such a policy would prolong the war by enlarging Confederate armies proved unpopular with families of Union prisoners, as did the efforts to raise more men for the army through the draft. "I fear the blood and treasure spent on this summer's campaign have done little for the country," reflected New Yorker George Templeton Strong. At the White House, Lincoln sensed defeat. At month's end, Grant had to relive the disaster at the Crater before a court of inquiry. One officer noted, "Grant is not at all well, & there are fears that he is breaking down."[28]

But then, at long last, Grant's strategy of continuous pressure on all fronts paid off. On September 2 he received news that Sherman had taken Atlanta. Grant ordered his men to celebrate by a cannonade on the evening of September 4. The next day he told his wife Julia that he was "feeling greatly better"; victories had a way of doing that with Grant. Within days he sought more. "We want to keep the enemy continually pressed to the end of the war," he told Sherman. "If we give him no peace while the war lasts the end cannot be distant." Toward that end he prodded Sheridan into action, visiting him on September 16. Three days later Sheridan defeated Early at Winchester and followed that victory with a second one at Fisher's Hill on September 22. Nearly a month later came news of a dramatic triumph at Cedar Creek. Winchester, Fisher's Hill, and Cedar Creek—three more good reasons, Republicans cheered, to reelect Honest Abe.[29]

Grant tried to contribute to the roster of victories by striking at Lee, but in a series of offensive thrusts succeeded only in tightening his hold on his foe. Meanwhile, he and Sherman discussed the wisdom of Sherman's proposed march to the sea, with Grant expressing some concern lest John Bell Hood wriggle loose to inflict damage, before agreeing to the plan in mid-October. Lincoln continued to harbor serious reservations about the idea, asserting that "a misstep by Sherman might be fatal to his army"—and, by extension, to Lincoln's chances in the fall contest. In the end, Sherman secured Grant's final approval—just before the election.[30]

Sheridan's victories and Sherman's capture of Atlanta redeemed the mistakes of the Virginia campaign and secured Lincoln's reelection. It was no accident that these two generals were Grant's men who shared their chief's vision. Their battlefield triumphs proved Grant a success as general in chief, for it did not matter where the decisive victory came but when. He had forfeited his preference to exercise command in the decisive theater of the West to accept the responsibility of nullifying Lee and withstanding the political pressures of the East. Subsequently, he had accommodated Lincoln in other ways, although in each case decisions made for political reasons threatened to prove counterproductive. He had struggled with the Army of the Potomac, and he discovered that in some cases he had overestimated the abilities of his generals. But Grant persevered. By placing continuous pressure on the Confederacy while adjusting to setbacks he achieved his goal of forcing the Confederacy to give way somewhere, all the while working within the constraints imposed by political considerations. In so doing, he proved that he was indeed Lincoln's general.

Notes

1. T. Harry Williams, *Lincoln and His Generals* (New York: Vintage, 1952), vii–viii, 300–307, 331–32, 336–37, 348–50. Among those studies that follow Williams's argument are Warren Hassler Jr., *Commanders of the Army of the Potomac* (Baton Rouge: Louisiana State University Press, 1962), which offers an especially dim view of Grant based on the writings of his enemies and critics; and Richard N. Current, *The Lincoln Nobody Knows* (New York: Hill & Wang, 1958). More recent commentaries that follow the Williams thesis include Mark E. Neely Jr., *The Last Best Hope of Earth: Abraham Lincoln and the Promise of America* (Cambridge MA: Harvard University Press, 1993), chapter 3; Joseph T. Glatthaar, *Partners in Command: The Relationship between Leaders in the Civil War* (New York: Free Press, 1994), chapter 7; and John Y. Simon, "Grant, Lincoln, and Unconditional Surrender," in *Lincoln's Generals*, ed. Gabor S. Boritt (New York: Oxford University Press, 1994), 163–223. Simon argues (p. 179) that Grant "ignored political realities tied to generalship." For an alternative view, see Brooks D. Simpson, "Lincoln and Grant: A Reappraisal of a Relationship," in *Abraham Lincoln: Sources and Style of Leadership*, ed. Frank J. Williams, William D. Pederson, and Vincent J. Marsala (Westport CT: Greenwood Press, 1994), 109–23.

2. Bruce Catton, "The Generalship of Ulysses S. Grant," in *Grant, Lee, Lincoln, and the Radicals*, ed. Grady McWhiney (Evanston IL: Northwestern University Press, 1964), offered the first revisionist statement, although Catton never explicitly stated that he was revising Williams. See also, Catton, *Grant Takes Command* (Boston: Little, Brown, 1969); Herman Hattaway and Archer Jones, *How the North Won: A Military History of the Civil War* (Urbana: University of Illinois Press, 1983); and Archer Jones, *Civil War Command and Strategy: The Process of Victory and Defeat* (New York: Free Press, 1992).

3. On Grant's proposal and the reaction to it, see Williams, *Lincoln and His Generals*, 291–97 (which speaks disparagingly of Grant's plans as "not too sound" and "faulty in several vital respects"); Hattaway and Jones, *How the North Won*, 510–15 (which speaks far more positively of it); and Brooks D. Simpson, *Let Us Have Peace: Ulysses S. Grant and the Politics of War and Reconstruction* (Chapel Hill: University of North Carolina Press, 1991), 54–56.

4. James H. Wilson to Ulysses S. Grant, February 25, 1864, in John Y. Simon, ed., *The Papers of Ulysses S. Grant*, 20 vols. to date (Carbondale: Southern Illinois

University Press, 1967–), vol. 10, 141–42 (hereafter cited as PG). For Lincoln's estimation of Banks's military ability, see Howard Beale, ed., *The Diary of Gideon Welles*, 3 vols. (New York: W. W. Norton, 1960), vol. 2, 26. During the Vicksburg campaign Lincoln expressed the opinion that Grant should have joined forces with Banks—which would have left Banks as the commanding officer of their joint column.

5. John Nicolay and John Hay, *Abraham Lincoln: A History*, 10 vols. (New York: Century Co., 1890), vol. 8, 335; Simpson, *Let Us Have Peace*, 51–54.

6. Ulysses S. Grant, *Personal Memoirs of U. S. Grant*, ed. William and Mary McFeely (New York: Library of America, 1990. Originally published in two volumes, 1885), 469–74; Lincoln to Halleck, November 27, 1862, in *Collected Works of Abraham Lincoln*, ed. Roy Basler, 10 vols. (New Brunswick NJ: Rutgers University Press, 1953–1990), vol. 5, 514–15. T. Harry Williams offers a different and ultimately unpersuasive account of the Grant-Lincoln conversation in *Lincoln and His Generals*, 304–5, an account made plausible by Grant's faulty recollection of the two rivers as emptying into the Potomac, not Chesapeake Bay. Lincoln's suggestion probably involved a landing between the Rappahannock and the York, most likely at West Point, where the Mattapony and Pamunkey Rivers meet.

7. Catton, *Grant Takes Command*, 138.

8. Catton, *Grant Takes Command*, 144–47.

9. The best summary of Grant's plan is in Grant to George G. Meade, April 9, 1864, PG 10:273–75. See also Grant to Benjamin F. Butler, April 19, 1864, PG 10:327–28. Lincoln's expression has become a point of some controversy. Grant said Lincoln offered it at their last conference before Grant took the field. T. Harry Williams declared that Grant in his *Memoirs* presented a "characteristically misleading account" of his last conference with Lincoln. Unfortunately, it is Williams who is misled by his assumption that Grant's last meeting with Lincoln occurred less than a week before Grant opened his campaign against Lee, an assumption accepted by Warren Hassler. However, Grant and Lincoln last met on April 4, 1864; Grant's use of the phrase appears in a letter of the same date to Sherman. See Grant, *Memoirs*, 480, 486; Tyler Dennett, *Lincoln and the Civil War in the Diaries and Letters of John Hay* (New York: Dodd, Mead, 1939), 179; Williams, *Lincoln and His Generals*, 308; Hassler, *Commanders of the Army of the Potomac*, 206; and Horace Porter, *Campaigning with Grant* (New York: Bonanza Books, 1961 [1897]), 46.

10. J. F. C. Fuller, *The Generalship of Ulysses S. Grant*, 2d ed. (Bloomington: Indiana University Press, 1929), 211, 275, 331.

11. William O. Stoddard Jr., *Lincoln's Third Secretary: The Memoirs of William O. Stoddard* (New York: Exposition Press, 1955), 199. In his "Lincoln, Grant, and

Unconditional Surrender," 170, Simon asserts that Grant feared becoming "McClellanized"—the meaning of which must be inferred from Simon's article—although he offers no statement from Grant to support this claim. Grant neither used the term nor expressed concern about being stifled by civil superiors. Grenville Dodge employed the term *McClellanized* quite differently—to describe officers who shared McClellan's political beliefs. See Catton, *Grant Takes Command*, 383.

12. Halleck to Grant, May 3, 1864, PG 10:375; Catton, *Grant Takes Command*, 141–42, 172–75; Hattaway and Jones, *How the North Won*, 524; Williams, *Lincoln and His Generals*, 309–10. Williams claims that Grant was "dodging the responsibility for removing Banks," but under law, the president appointed corps, army, and departmental commanders, so it was his responsibility to act. Simon in "Lincoln, Grant, and Unconditional Surrender," 181–87, shares Williams's misunderstanding.

13. See Hattaway and Jones, *How the North Won*, chapters 16 and 17.

14. On the opening battles in the Wilderness Campaign, see Gordon C. Rhea, *The Battle of the Wilderness, May 5–6, 1864* (Baton Rouge: Louisiana State University Press, 1994); Rhea, *The Battles for Spotsylvania Court House and the Road to Yellow Tavern, May 7–12, 1864* (Baton Rouge: Louisiana State University Press, 1997; William D. Matter, *If It Takes All Summer: The Battle of Spotsylvania* (Chapel Hill: University of North Carolina Press, 1988); and Gary W. Gallagher, ed., *The Wilderness Campaign* (Chapel Hill: University of North Carolina Press, 1997).

15. Halleck to Grant, May 17, 1864, PG 10:460. On the number of slightly wounded men, see *Wartime Washington: The Civil War Letters of Elizabeth Blair Lee*, ed. Virginia Laas (Urbana: University of Illinois Press, 1991), 381–82; Grant to Halleck, May 7, 1864, PG 10:405; Grant to Julia Dent Grant, May 13, 1864, PG 10:443–44; Charles A. Dana to Stanton, May 8 and May 10, 1864, Charles A. Dana Papers, Library of Congress; Porter, *Campaigning with Grant*, 192. See also James M. McPherson, *Battle Cry of Freedom: The Civil War Era* (New York: Oxford University Press, 1988), 720, 732, 741–42.

16. George G. Meade to his wife, June 4, 1864, in *The Life and Letters of George Gordon Meade*, ed. George Meade, 2 vols. (New York: Scribner, 1913), vol. 2, 200; Herbert M. Schiller, ed., *Autobiography of Major General William F. Smith, 1861–1864* (Dayton OH: Morningside, 1990), 114.

17. Halleck to Grant, May 17, 1864, PG 10:460; Grant to Halleck, May 21 and May 22, 1864, PG 10:475, 477; Grant to Halleck, June 5, 1864, PG 11:19. See Brian Holden Reid, "Another Look at Grant's Crossing of the James, 1864," *Civil War History* 39 (December 1993): 291–316.

18. Allan Nevins, ed., *Diary of the Civil War, 1860–1865: George Templeton Strong* (New York: Macmillan, 1962), 467 (entry of July 23, 1864); Lincoln to Grant, July 17, 1864, in Basler, *Collected Works*, 7:444.

19. Welles, *Diary*, 2:55, 58 (entries of June 20 and 24, 1864). Horace Porter to his wife, June 4 and 14, 1864, Horace Porter Papers, Library of Congress.

20. On Meade, see David S. Sparks, ed., *Inside Lincoln's Army: The Diary of Marsena Rudolph Patrick, Provost Marshall General, Army of the Potomac* (New York: T. Yoseloff, 1964), 386 (entry of June 19, 1864); Cyrus B. Comstock Diary, July 2 and 7, 1864, Cyrus B. Comstock Papers, Library of Congress. On Butler and Smith, see Comstock Diary, June 26 and 27 and July 2, 1864, Comstock Papers; on Washington defenses, see Comstock Diary, July 10 and 13, 1864, Comstock Papers.

21. Grant to Halleck, July 1, 1864, PG 11:155–56; Halleck to Grant, July 3, 1864, PG 11:156; Grant to Halleck, July 6, 1864, PG 11:176; Grant to Halleck, July 10, 1864, PG 11:205–6; Schiller, *The Autobiography of William F. Smith*, 116. Grant's letter of July 10 to Halleck bears careful reading. While it rejects the wording of General Orders 225 (PG 11:206), it merely suspends it and looks to place William B. Franklin (not Smith) in field command—a reading confirmed by Butler's comments to his wife (PG 11:206–7). This suggests that Smith's fate was separate from the ultimate fate of the effort to remove Butler from field command. See Comstock Diary, entry for July 17, 1864, Comstock Papers; George R. Agassiz, ed., *Meade's Headquarters, 1863–1865: Letters of Colonel Theodore Lyman from the Wilderness to Appomattox* (Freeport NY: Books for Libraries Press, 1970 [1922]), 192–93; Williams, *Lincoln and His Generals*, 321–24; Catton, *Grant Takes Command*, 326–35; and Sparks, *Inside Lincoln's Army*, 400 (entry for July 22, 1864).

For Butler on his political clout, see Sparks, *Inside Lincoln's Army*, 400–402 (entry of July 20, 1864). Smith swore that Butler forced Grant to rescind the order by threatening to reveal that he saw Grant intoxicated. Those who object to this interpretation argue that there was no truth to such stories. The truth is somewhere in between. On June 29, an ailing Grant, looking for relief on a hot, dusty day as he visited various commands, probably took several drinks, which only made him feel worse. That Butler could thus blackmail Grant is doubtful, however, and Smith's story does not fit the facts in other crucial respects. See PG 11:162–65, 206–10; Catton, *Grant Takes Command*, 326–35 (which muddles the sequence of events in critical ways); and Schiller, *Autobiography of William F. Smith*, 107–16. That stories soon circulated about Grant's drinking on June 29 is confirmed by Sparks, *Inside Lincoln's Army*, 415 (entry of August 15, 1864); they were spread by Smith's subordinates after his removal.

22. There is some debate over the exact wording of the proposed removal order; compare Williams, *Lincoln and His Generals*, 322–23, and PG 1:206. Butler contin-

ued to intrigue for a nomination well into the summer. See Dennett, *Lincoln and the Civil War*, 22; James G. Randall and Richard N. Current, *Lincoln the President: The Last Full Measure* (New York: Dodd, Mead, 1955), 211–12.

23. Grant to Abraham Lincoln, July 25, 1864, PG 11:309.

24. George K. Leet to William R. Rowley, August 9, 1864, PG 11:363; Grant to George G. Meade, August 1, 1864, PG 11:361.

25. Halleck to Grant, July 21, 1864, PG 11:286; Comstock Diary, July 15, 1864, Comstock Papers; Sparks, *Inside Lincoln's Army*, 409–10 (entry of August 5, 1864). Simon, in his "Lincoln, Grant, and Unconditional Surrender," 179–81, misrepresents the July 31 meeting by overlooking ample evidence concerning what Lincoln and Grant discussed—or that he did not wish to commit to paper his reasons for transferring Meade.

26. Grant to Halleck, August 1, 1864, PG 11:358; Lincoln to Grant, August 3, 1864, PG, 11:360n; Grant to Benjamin F. Butler, August 4, 1864, PG, 11:374n; Grant to Philip H. Sheridan, August 7, 1864, PG 11:380n; Meade to his wife, August 3 and 13, 1864, *Life and Letters of Meade*, 2:218–19, 221.

27. Welles, *Diary*, 2:92 (entry of August 2, 1864); Sparks, *Inside Lincoln's Army*, 403–4, 409 (entries of July 27 and August 5, 1864); Hattaway and Jones, *How the North Won*, 593; Catton, *Grant Takes Command*, 325–26; Halleck to Grant, August 11, 1864, PG 11:424–25; Grant to Halleck, August 15, 1864, PG 11:424; Grant to Stanton, August 15, 1864, PG 11:421–22; Lincoln to Grant, August 17, 1864, in Basler, *Collected Works*, 7:499.

28. Grant to Elihu Washburne, August 16, 1864, PG 12:16–17; Grant to Daniel Ammen, August 18, 1864, PG 12:36; Nevins, *Diary of George Templeton Strong*, 474 (entry of August 19, 1864); Grant to Julia Dent Grant, August 23, 1864, PG 12:77; Grant to Meade, August 25, 1864, PG 12:86; Grant to Julia Dent Grant, August 25, 1864, PG 12:91; and Sparks, *Inside Lincoln's Army*, 415 (entry of August 18, 1864).

29. Grant to commanders, September 2, 1864, PG 12:121; Grant to William T. Sherman, September 4 and 10, 1864, PG 12:127, 144; Grant to Julia Dent Grant, September 5, 1864, PG 12:130–31.

30. Grant to Julia Dent Grant, October 28, 1864, PG 12:362; Stanton to Grant, October 12, 1864, PG 12:303; Grant to Stanton, October 13, 1864, PG 12:302–303; Grant to Sherman, November 1, 1864, PG 12:370–71.

7 / Braxton Bragg and the Tullahoma Campaign

STEVEN E. WOODWORTH

For the Confederacy, May and June 1863 were the best of times and the worst of times. They saw both dramatic victory and dismal defeat. At the beginning of May, a large, powerful, well-equipped and -supplied Federal army advanced, turned its opposing Confederate army—and was roundly defeated and driven back in disgrace. At the end of June, another large, powerful, well-equipped and -supplied Federal army advanced, turned its opposing Confederate army—and without fighting a major battle sent the gray-clad defenders reeling back some eighty miles and almost out of the state they were supposed to defend. The May advance, of course, was that of Joseph Hooker's Army of the Potomac in Virginia; its defeat was the Battle of Chancellorsville, perhaps Robert E. Lee's finest hour as a commander. The June advance was that of William S. Rosecrans's Army of the Cumberland in Middle Tennessee; its result was what has become known as the Tullahoma campaign—definitely not Braxton Bragg's finest hour as a commander.

The essay that follows is not a tale of two commanders or of two campaigns. The reason for mentioning the Chancellorsville campaign is to demonstrate by way of contrast that something about the Tullahoma campaign requires explanation. Why was its result so dramatically different from what happened in Virginia six weeks earlier? True, this question could be dismissed simply by saying that Braxton Bragg was no Robert E. Lee, and certainly no one can dispute that fact. Nor was Bragg's Army of Tennessee the same as Lee's Army of Northern Virginia. But the differences between the two commanders and their subordinates are neither as obvious nor as simple as mere issues of good strategy and tactics or the lack thereof. The differences lie far more in less tangible factors, and Bragg's experience in the Tullahoma campaign illustrates how a commander can make the correct strategic and tactical decisions—and still lose.

When the Battle of Murfreesboro ended in January 1863, Bragg pulled his Army of Tennessee back about thirty-five miles to the southeast, across the Duck River, to the neighborhood of Tullahoma, Tennessee. Rosecrans kept his Army of the Cumberland around Murfreesboro. The turn-of-the-year battle had shaken him badly, and he was determined that matters of training, equipment, and supply in his army be brought to a state of absolute perfection before he ventured another brush with Bragg. So, to the immense frustration of Lincoln, Rosecrans and his army sat in Murfreesboro for five-and-a-half months. While on other fronts the war went on—Hooker advanced in Virginia and was defeated; Grant advanced in Mississippi and was victorious—neither bluster nor blandishment from Washington could budge the Army of the Cumberland from its camps around Murfreesboro.[1]

For Bragg, this "Sitzkrieg" had a different set of trials. He too had supply problems about which to worry, though his were matters less of neurotic perfectionism than of pure desperation. The Army of Tennessee was the shield of the Confederate heartland, and the Confederacy was an agricultural region; but the produce of the region this army protected was earmarked for the rations of another Confederate army—Lee's Army of Northern Virginia. That left the Army of Tennessee incapable—through its own government's policy—of drawing much in the way of supplies from its hinterland and made it dependent to a large degree on what it could draw from the immediate area around its camps and, almost incredibly, from what it could sneak around the flanks of the Union Army from areas that were theoretically behind Federal lines. Feeding an army this way was a remarkable accomplishment, but it was not conducive to the best deployment of the forces for the prospect of pitched battle. Bragg's cavalry had to maintain a far-stretched position on his right flank in order to screen the operations that were attempting to draw supplies all the way from Kentucky. Worse still, the main body of his army had to be dispersed across a wide front in order to maximize the area from which it could draw supplies and graze animals of its accompanying supply wagons and artillery. For this purpose, Bragg deployed his two infantry corps behind a range of hills about twenty miles northwest of Tullahoma and fifteen or so shy of the Union positions at Murfreesboro. The ridge, known as the Highland Rim, was rugged and could be crossed by an army at only a very limited number of gaps, but covering those scattered passes spread the army uncomfortably thin.[2]

If that had been the worst of it, though, Bragg would have had far less cause than he did for his chronic indigestion. Discontentment among the high command of the Army of Tennessee was approaching critical proportions. The ferment had several sources. Bragg's top subordinate, Leonidas Polk, had been an Episcopal bishop before the war and never seemed to reconcile himself to taking orders from anyone.[3] His military incompetence and his habitual disobedience of orders cost him the respect of Bragg, but his friendship with Confederate president Jefferson Davis, going all the way back to their West Point days, kept him in his position. Resenting Bragg's authority, as well as the fact that Bragg knew him for the incompetent he was, Polk became a bitter enemy of his commander.

Military acumen Polk might lack, but few could hope to excel him in persuasiveness. With his smooth ingratiating manner he won over a number of his fellow officers, the most important of whom was his fellow corps commander William J. Hardee. As a former West Point commandant of cadets and translator of the French tactics manual by which most young officers learned their trade, Hardee had enormous influence within the officer corps. Thanks to Polk, he was soon using it to undermine Bragg.

The Kentucky campaign of the previous autumn had only made matters worse. Bragg had pulled off a masterpiece of strategy, but the whole undertaking had been based on the belief that Kentuckians would rise en masse to support the Confederacy. They did not, and so the Confederate army withdrew, and the Kentucky officers within it—on many of whose overoptimistic assessments Bragg had based his campaign—vented their frustrations by blaming Bragg for all that was wrong in their world.

Other generals disliked Bragg because he was firm with their vices. A prevalent vice among high-ranking officers of the Army of Tennessee was alcohol, and Bragg was relentless in his attempts to rid the army of its ill effects. Generals such as B. Franklin Cheatham, whose drunkenness at Murfreesboro had been costly for the army, responded with intense resentment.[4]

As the Battle of Murfreesboro drew to a close, it had been Bragg's generals who had advised him to retreat, but in the days that followed newspapermen, writing as if they had inside sources, claimed Bragg had quit the field against the protests of his officers. Goaded to indiscretion, Bragg sent a circular to his generals asking if they had advised retreat and adding some vague and extremely ill-advised words about how he depended on his loyal officers and would gladly resign if he had lost their confidence in him.[5] That was all the invitation some of them needed, and they sweetened—for themselves—the bitter pill of admitting the advice they had given by adding some choice words on what they thought of Bragg and what they thought the army thought of him.[6] President Davis got wind of this disreputable affair, remarked that he could not imagine what possessed Bragg to send such a note to his generals, and ordered theater commander Joseph E. Johnston to hasten to Tullahoma and look to the matter.[7]

The months of recrimination that followed had been hard for Bragg and bad for the morale of the Army of Tennessee. Under the constant bombardment of complaints from Polk and others, Davis's confidence in Bragg, never as unquestioning as it has sometimes been represented, gave way, and he ordered Johnston to relieve Bragg and take over command of the army himself. Perversely, Johnston refused. Although he had claimed to want nothing better than to hold the position of army commander, Johnston now claimed that it would look bad for him to take the job in Bragg's place. In the face of orders from Richmond, he stalled and evaded until the president finally gave up and left Bragg in command.[8] When things turned sour for the Confederacy in Mississippi that spring, Davis ordered Johnston as theater commander to repair to that front and see what could be done.[9] Bragg was once again alone and in command—more or less—of his faithful lieutenants.

Thus armed with a weapon of very uncertain mettle, the Army of Tennessee, Bragg would have to parry the next thrust of the Army of the Cumberland—whenever Rosecrans felt good and ready to deliver it. The blow finally fell on June 24, 1863. The Army of the Cumberland advanced on a broad front with diversionary skirmishes flaring up angrily from one flank of Bragg's position to the other and beyond. Behind these elaborate diversions, Rosecrans aimed his main blow at Hoover's Gap, along the turnpike that ran from Murfreesboro to Manchester, a town a dozen miles northeast of Tullahoma from which the Federals could sorely threaten Bragg's supply line, such as it was.[10]

None of this was any particular surprise to Bragg.[11] For some months he had been alert to the possibility of a Federal stab at one or more of the gaps on his right center that were held by Hardee's Corps, and he had warned his cavalry commander, Maj. Gen. Joseph Wheeler, to be sure he had adequate force in front of the Highland Rim to delay a Federal advance and give ample notice of its approach.[12] That was the correct order, and if it had been carried out things might have been much different. Here, however, the first of the intangibles of the Tullahoma campaign intervened. Wheeler was an officer with some good traits but questionable overall merit as a top cavalry commander. For one thing, like Bragg, he had difficulty getting the cooperation of his subordinates; for another, unlike Bragg, he was not successful in maintaining good discipline in his command.[13] The result was that a certain slackness tended to characterize the regular cavalry operations of the Army of Tennessee.[14] On June 24 this meant that the Union force bearing down on vital Hoover's Gap confronted precisely one Confederate cavalry regiment, and that regiment made very little show at all. The leading Federal unit, a brigade of mounted infantry armed with the fearsome Spencer repeating rifle, obeyed literally its orders to ride through the gap, going through at a trot despite the overwhelming strength of the defile as a defensive position.[15] The Confederate cavalry stampeded through the gap ahead of them, and on reaching its southern mouth scattered to the four winds—or at least as many winds as would carry them away from the pursuing Federals—leaving their fine silken regimental colors behind them.

The Confederate horsemen apparently made no systematic attempt to alert other Southern units of the Union advance. Thus, General Bushrod Johnson, commanding a brigade stationed at Fairfield, five miles from the gap, learned of the penetration a full hour before General William B. Bate, who was commanding a brigade (of Stewart's Division) encamped a mile closer to the scene of the action—the force that was intended to plug the gap in case of just such a Union advance.[16] So inadequate was the information the cavalrymen supplied that the first Confederate units to respond to the penetration wasted crucial time and strength in trying to locate the enemy.[17]

Bate was the junior brigadier general in the Army of Tennessee, serving under a division commander who was the junior major general in the army. Both were able men, but both were having some teething problems in this campaign.[18] Furthermore, Bate's role as a rapid-response force for Hoover's Gap was one he had inherited just one month before when the unit previously charged with that duty had been transferred to Mississippi to help shore up sagging Confederate fortunes there.[19]

Somehow, amidst all the reshuffling, reassignments, and promotions, the interaction between the units and officers sharing responsibility for the defense of Hoover's Gap had never become as smooth as it should have. As if all that were not enough, Bate and most of his officers seem to have been enjoying themselves at a Masonic picnic that afternoon and were not immediately available for duty.[20] Despite the fact that the Federals had taken up a position just two miles from his camp it was late afternoon by the time Bate finally got around to launching his counterattack. Even then, he managed to get only half his troops into action.[21] Still, Bate was a fighter, and when he hit the Federals he hit hard. He gave the brigade of Union mounted infantry a few bad minutes that evening, Spencers and all, but by that time the solid infantry columns of the Army of the Cumberland were close by and had begun to bolster and extend the Federal line at the southern end of the gap. Before it was over that night, Bate had lost nearly a quarter of the men he led into action, but the opportunity of retaking the gap had passed.[22]

From the Confederate point of view, affairs that afternoon were only somewhat less discouraging five miles to the west at Liberty Gap. There, a slightly less formidable collection of Federals, assigned the task of merely making a demonstration, was slightly less aggressive than their comrades in arms at Hoover's Gap. Two regiments of Confederate cavalry performed with marginally more credit than their ill-fated comrades to the east and managed to preserve at least some semblance of order and decorum as they were, nevertheless, ejected from the gap in a very firm, prompt, and businesslike manner. The response force, here one of the brigades of premier Confederate division commander Patrick R. Cleburne, got into position somewhat more rapidly, but the end result was the same.[23] The Federals slept on their arms that night in firm control of both gaps, the doorways to the open rolling landscape of the interior of Bragg's position.

Phase one of the Tullahoma campaign was over less than twelve hours after it had begun and almost before Bragg knew it was in progress. Bragg's position had been strong and well selected. The deployment of his troops had been about the best that could have been devised under the constraints he faced. Yet he had lost round one. The reason? He had not managed to get the right commanders into the right positions of responsibility, nor had he succeeded in communicating to the key officers precisely what it was he expected them to do when the ball opened. His instructions and the exigencies of the situation seem clear enough in retrospect. Competent and experienced officers like those who led the Union advances through Hoover's and Liberty Gaps could probably have triumphed with Bragg's instructions, but Bragg's task was to triumph with the men he had.

The abject failure of the Confederate cavalry and the halting performance of Stewart's Division on the afternoon and evening of June 24 gave away the Confederates' strongest potential line of defense and made Rosecrans a winner in round one of the struggle for Middle Tennessee. Still, Bragg was not down for the count. His army now held viable defensive positions in front of each of the two gaps through which substantial Union forces were advancing. True, these positions were not as strong as the gaps themselves had been, but now Bragg could know, within a very small number of possibilities, the routes of the Union advance and could position his forces accordingly. The Army of the Cumberland might have difficulty deploying its superior numbers through the narrow gaps, and, though he was not aware of it, Bragg had an additional factor working in his favor.

The main Union advance was through Hoover's Gap toward Manchester. That meant the Federals would have to cross Garrison's Fork of the Duck River and then, still following the Murfreesboro and Manchester pike, ascend the plateau on the other side by way of an impossibly narrow draw known locally as Matt's Hollow. In some places, this thin slash in the rim of the tableland permitted a road wide enough for only a single wagon at a time.[24] Thermopylae itself could hardly have offered a better place for a small force to hold back a larger one almost indefinitely. Of course, the commander of the Union column, General George H. Thomas, could send a flanking force toiling up the rugged slopes to either side or wending their way up the ravines of any one of several small streams that cut into the shelf of higher ground with fair chances of turning the Confederates out of a position on the rim. But the arrangement offered Hardee, whose corps was assigned to hold this sector, a whole new set of opportunities, and best of all it promised a substantial amount of time. If Hardee could manage to win enough of that most precious of commodities, if he could delay the Federals long enough near the Highland Rim, Bragg believed he could prepare a little surprise for Rosecrans and his Northern friends.

Throughout June 25, both armies consolidated their positions and took stock of the situation. Much depended now on who could move first and seize the initiative. That was a problem for Bragg, who still had to struggle to make sense of the rapidly developing situation in front of him on the basis of the inadequate reconnaissance provided by his cavalry. By noon on June 26, he had sized up the situation and decided what to do. He summoned Polk to a conference at his headquarters in Shelbyville on the Confederate left-center, southwest of Hardee's positions. Bragg wanted Polk to march his corps up the Shelbyville and Murfreesboro pike that night and through broad and easy Guy's Gap. That would put him, by dawn of the twenty-seventh, on the north side of the Highland Rim, ready to turn eastward and sweep down on the rear of the Federal troops in Liberty Gap while Hardee pressed them from the other side.[25]

This plan never became reality; but was it realistic? Could Polk's troops have made such a march and fought such a battle under the circumstances then prevailing—incessant rain and muddy roads? We can test this hypothesis point by point by comparing this proposed movement to real movements carried out by those same troops during this same period. First, how long would it have taken Polk to have his command ready to march? In reality, at 11:00 PM that night Bragg gave Polk orders to march first thing in the morning in retreat toward Tullahoma. Polk's troops were on the road by 5:30 AM, just six-and-a-half hours later, and since the orders did not call for an earlier movement the possibility exists that the corps could have been ready even sooner.[26] Even accepting the need for a full six-and-a-half hours to prepare to march—and taking 1:30 PM on the twenty-sixth as the latest probable time for Polk's headquarters meeting with Bragg—yields 8:00 PM as the time at which Polk's corps could have begun its night march through Guy's Gap.[27]

In his actual march toward Tullahoma the next day Polk was hindered by cumbersome wagon trains, traffic snarls at the few bridges over the Duck River, and confusion created when Hardee mistakenly directed some of his units onto the same routes being used by Polk.[28] With these delays, he had covered only ten miles in eleven-and-a-half hours.[29] Yet even if his hypothetical march through Guy's Gap—presumably with the minimum number of supply wagons—had been equally slow, he still would have been through the gap and ready to turn eastward by approximately 6:00 AM, June 27.

Was a night march practical? And could troops who had marched all night still be fit to fight the next day? In fact, twelve weeks later the Union corps of George H. Thomas actually did march all night to reach a key position in time for the first day's battle at Chickamauga, where they did some very good fighting indeed. Clearly, such an operation was well within the capabilities of a Civil War army.

What would Polk have encountered during this hypothetical advance? In fact, he would have encountered no opposition whatsoever in Guy's Gap. Confederate cavalry continued to hold the gap until midmorning of the twenty-seventh. Three miles north of the gap at the town of Christiana was a force of eight thousand Union cavalry and sixty-seven hundred infantry. Elements of this force had clashed with the Confederate cavalry in front of Guy's Gap on the twenty-sixth, then pulled back to Christiana. At 6:00 AM on June 27, Union major general Gordon Granger, commanding the force at Christiana, received orders from Rosecrans to "feel the enemy at Guy's Gap." His troops did not actually leave Christiana until 9:00 AM and would not have made contact with the Confederate pickets at the gap until at least 10:00. Only after skirmishing for some two hours and perceiving that no Confederate infantry was present did Granger's men press on and drive the Southern horsemen out of the gap and back toward Shelbyville.[30] By the time Granger's skirmishers moved gingerly toward the entrance to Guy's Gap, Polk could, in his hypothetical attack, already have been at least four hours east of the gap and probably in contact with Federal forces there. A single one of Polk's eight infantry brigades, which he would almost undoubtedly have left behind him to cover Guy's Gap, would have deterred an all-out attack by Granger and, with the advantage of the terrain and the aid of the Confederate cavalry, might well have been able to hold the gap for several more hours even if Granger, perhaps goaded by a desperate Rosecrans, had launched such an assault after all.

That would have given Polk until at least midafternoon. What would he have encountered? And what might he have accomplished in that time? A five-mile march from the north side of Guy's Gap would have taken him into Liberty Gap from the north, behind the Federals who would at that time, according to Bragg's plan, have been resisting serious pressure by Hardee at the other end of the gap. He almost certainly would have covered that distance and been deployed for the attack by 10:00 AM, probably considerably earlier. On the morning of June 27 the Union forces in Liberty Gap consisted of a mere two brigades, and at about daylight that morning they received orders from Rosecrans to disengage, pull back, and swing over to join the concentration for the big push out of Hoover's Gap. In the event, they had little difficulty disengaging, but had Hardee been applying the pressure specified in Bragg's plan it would have been a different matter.[31] Polk would have struck these forces in flank and rear as they tried to withdraw. Even if, as is probable, he had detached another brigade to guard against any possible Union reaction from the direction of Hoover's Gap farther east, his remaining six brigades, which were larger than their Federal counterparts, would have given him a nearly four-to-one numerical superiority even without help from Hardee's troops, who could have been expected at that time to have been pushing up the gap to meet him.[32] The result would almost undoubtedly have been the destruction or rout of the Federals. That would have allowed Polk to reestablish his communications through Liberty Gap and, if necessary, dispense entirely with Guy's Gap.

And that would have put Rosecrans in a very bad situation. At the north end of Liberty Gap, Polk would have been closer to Rosecrans's base at Murfreesboro than Rosecrans was. He would thus have succeeded in turning the Federal general and forcing his retreat. While Rosecrans would probably have managed to extricate his army and escape back to Murfreesboro—Civil War armies were notoriously difficult to annihilate—the result would have been hailed as a great Confederate victory, and rightly so.

Even if Rosecrans had succeeded in breaking through Hardee's lines and taking position at Manchester so as to threaten Bragg's communications, the result would not have been negative from the Confederate point of view. While commanding in person at Tullahoma the previous March, Joseph E. Johnston had observed that the Confederates "could afford to exchange bases" with Rosecrans; the Union general, of course, could afford nothing of the sort.[33] In short, Bragg's plan for a flanking movement by Polk through Guy's Gap had the realistic potential to produce a major victory.

But the victory never happened, for the plan was never implemented. On hearing it Polk immediately complained about the "character of the country" he would have to traverse, "the heavy cedar growth, and the peculiar topography." Nothing like that had deterred Stonewall Jackson from making his flanking march at Chancellorsville eight weeks before, but Polk was no Jackson and insisted that "the position he was about being thrown in [was] nothing short of a man-trap."[34] How enthusiastically and efficiently he would have cooperated in the movement with this attitude is impossible to say, though his record then and later gives little cause for optimism. As it turned out, Bragg never had the dubious gratification of seeing him try it. Later that afternoon he sent a note to Polk calling off the whole thing. The reason, he explained, was that Hardee's forces had given way and were being driven by the Federals pouring out of Hoover's Gap.[35]

Bragg seems not to have considered the possibility that Hardee would fail to hold the Federals along the Highland Rim, at least until Polk could make his descent on the Union flank and rear. Back in January, Hardee had written Bragg that Tullahoma was vulnerable to a turning movement and could not be held once the Federals breached the wall of the Highland Rim.[36] In April, Hardee had written Bragg to say how impressed he was with the strength of the Highland Rim passes as defensive positions and to assure his commander that his central reserve was within good supporting distance of all three of the major gaps.[37] Surely, then, Hardee—whose nickname, after all, was "Old Reliable"—could be counted on to put up a tough fight on that front. Or could he?

In early June, he had written Bragg that his "command was too much scattered for easy concentration." Nothing had changed really, but this was vintage Hardee, who nervously desired maximum concentration of his forces whenever contact with the enemy threatened. It took nerve to maintain one's own deployments until the enemy was located and fixed and could be discomfited by a timely concentration of forces. That was Robert E. Lee's method, but few generals shared his audacity. Hardee was not one of them, and so he nervously urged Bragg to collect his forces at once, preferably withdrawing from the Highland Rim altogether and preparing to concentrate the army at Tullahoma in case of Union advance.[38] In view of the fact that Hardee considered the Tullahoma position untenable this was curious advice, and Bragg can be excused for failing to heed it. The problem was that Bragg also failed to see to it that Hardee understood precisely what he expected of him and that this campaign was going to be conducted according to the ideas of the general commanding and not one or both of his lieutenants. Making one's subordinate generals understand one's wishes was something they never thought to teach people at West Point. Now the hostility between Bragg and Hardee had led to an almost complete breakdown in communications.[39]

Yet even allowing that Hardee did not understand—or chose not to understand—what Bragg expected of him, his behavior is difficult to explain. Instead of reacting to the initial Federal assault through Hoover's Gap by rushing reinforcements to the scene and going there himself to provide experienced senior direction to the defensive effort Hardee remained at his Wartrace headquarters, eight miles from the front, and took no action to aid Stewart in any way. Indeed, that evening Hardee sent Stewart a dispatch directing, "If hard pressed tomorrow, you will fall back gradually toward Wartrace."[40] Thus, Hardee actually gave away the strong defensive position along the Highland Rim and the valley of Garrison's Fork of the Duck River. When they came out of Hoover's Gap on June 26, the Federals easily drove Stewart's three brigades because Stewart, true to his orders, pulled back rather than make a stand-up fight. That the action on this front was distinctly low grade is demonstrated by the low casualties among the attacking Northerners.[41] That evening, Hardee reiterated his instructions to retreat "if the enemy shows any disposition to press."[42]

By that time, Bragg had given up and ordered his army to take up the retreat across the Duck River and back toward Tullahoma the next morning, June 27.[43] So on a day when the Army of Tennessee could have been achieving a great victory it was instead embarking on a great retreat. Rosecrans had won the second phase of the Tullahoma campaign.

Still, all was not lost for Bragg, who at this point in the campaign could still have entertained realistic hopes of rolling back—or at least halting—the Federal advance. Tullahoma itself, toward which his forces were now moving from all along their previous Highland Rim positions, was by this time extremely well fortified. Rosecrans considered the works there a good deal stronger than those at Corinth, Mississippi, where eight months before he had slaughtered the Confederate army of Earl Van Dorn.[44] Behind such powerful works even Bragg's smaller army would have no difficulty administering an equally lopsided defeat to the Army of the Cumberland, should its commander be foolhardy enough to order an assault. On the other hand, if Rosecrans did not opt for a quick and decisive head-on attack, Bragg could reasonably expect to find other ways of making his life miserable.

Over the past year, Bragg had had much success in using cavalry to disrupt his opponent's supply lines. If his mounted troops were not much good for screening and scouting, they had an enviable record as raiders. Cavalry raids launched by Bragg had all but immobilized Union General Don Carlos Buell in the fall of 1862, defeated Grant's December 1862 drive on Vicksburg, and tormented Rosecrans in his operations around Nashville and Murfreesboro.[45] Bragg had had under his command some of the foremost cavalry raiders in American military history: Earl Van Dorn, John Hunt Morgan, and the incomparable Nathan Bedford Forrest. During the months preceding the Tullahoma campaign Bragg had, not unreasonably, counted on his cavalry as a major component of his strategy for stopping Rosecrans. The main force of his cavalry was stationed on both his flanks, Van Dorn and Forrest on the left, Wheeler on the center and right, and Morgan on the far right. If Rosecrans should advance, Bragg expected these powerful cavalry forces not only to give timely warning but also to swing down on the Federal rear, cutting supply lines and rendering advance impossible. This was particularly to be the case if Rosecrans should try to pass to Bragg's right, and in April Bragg had sent Wheeler a specific admonition to be ready. The Federals, Bragg hoped, might "be checked by the prompt movement of the main body [of Wheeler's cavalry] on the enemy's rear."[46]

Now, with precisely that case being played out in reality as Rosecrans drove in his right flank, Bragg pulled the trigger on his much vaunted cavalry weapon. What he got for his trouble was hardly a flash in the pan. Even as he struggled to assess the situation in his front and mature the plan for Polk's abortive flanking movement, Bragg sent word for Morgan's cavalry to strike.[47] By this time, however, Morgan was beyond the range of active intervention in the campaign and getting farther away by the hour. A few days earlier, Bragg had authorized Morgan to make a raid into Kentucky with a small force in hopes of throwing the Federals off balance. Bragg had added the caution, however, that Morgan was to remain alert to any sign of a Union advance toward Tullahoma and respond to it by slashing down on Rosecrans's supply line. Morgan had other ideas. Dreaming of glory and with an inveterate gambler's love of a risk he had merely used the pretense of a Kentucky raid to deceive Bragg into allowing him to depart on the most daring and dramatic cavalry raid of all—a bold thrust across the Ohio River into the free states. With that in mind, he took more than the authorized number of troops, leaving the right wing helplessly weak, and set off for the North with nary a backward glance. When Bragg less than a week later exercised his recall option in the face of Rosecrans's advance, Morgan had already ridden himself and a fifth of Bragg's total cavalry strength right out of the campaign.[48]

The rest of Bragg's cavalry proved equally disappointing. The quality of its leadership had declined. Van Dorn was dead, shot May 7, allegedly by a jealous husband.[49] Forrest too had been shot, though not fatally. His wound came on June 13, just eleven days before the start of the Tullahoma campaign, at the hands of a disgruntled subordinate (whom Forrest had then killed with a knife). The redoubtable Forrest was back in the saddle in time to ride against Rosecrans's advance, but he could hardly be blamed if he was less than his usual fearsome self. His command and what was left of Wheeler's ended up fighting a losing battle to delay the Federal pursuit across the Duck River and toward Tullahoma.[50] The dramatic results Bragg had hoped for from his cavalry never became reality. Once again, Bragg's strategic thinking had been sound, but somehow he had not been able to place in key positions the sort of intelligent, responsible officers that were needed. Or, to put it another way, he had failed to get the behavior he needed out of the officers he had to work with. The pattern was to become a familiar one for Bragg during this and other campaigns.

With the first and second rounds lost and his cavalry never even answering the bell for the third, Bragg had suffered a remarkable series of reverses despite good strategy and tactics. Yet, even then, if he could somehow manage to overcome the intangible factors that were working against him victory was still within his reach.

By June 28, the two armies faced each other across a gently rolling expanse of Middle Tennessee countryside known as "the Barrens" for its infertile soil. Bragg was firmly ensconced in the Tullahoma defenses, while Rosecrans was in possession of Manchester, a dozen miles to the northeast and astride the turnpike that was the most direct route from Murfreesboro to Chattanooga. Each general was now in position to threaten the other's communications: Rosecrans by a thrust to the southeast, Bragg by a similar movement to the northwest or by such cavalry strikes as he could manage, though Bragg could no longer hope for much in that department. The countryside between the two hostile armies was by now a soggy mess after several days of the heaviest rains in memory. It was a complicated situation, full of opportunities for the general with greater initiative, ingenuity, and ability to translate these qualities into action on the part of his army.

For Bragg, it was not entirely an unanticipated situation. Back when Johnston had been in Tullahoma in April, he and Bragg had discussed the issue of just such a scenario developing. Johnston had written to the authorities in Richmond that although the Confederate position could be turned on the right, he did not consider that a very serious problem since Rosecrans would have to expose his own communications as much as he threatened Bragg's. If Rosecrans detached a substantial body of troops for the southeastward lunge at the Confederate supply line he would be leaving his main body weakened and, Johnston hoped, vulnerable to Confederate counterattack. If, on the other hand, Rosecrans made his move with his entire army Johnston believed the Confederate could be well content to "exchange bases with him."[51] That is, Bragg, having traded places with the Army of the Cumberland, would still be able to draw supplies tolerably well from the rich farming district south and west of Murfreesboro, while Rosecrans, having cut Bragg's supply line probably somewhere in the neighborhood of the western slope of the Cumberland Plateau, would be completely unsupplied.

Throughout June 27 and much of June 28, both armies struggled through the rain and over the muddy roads toward the positions designated by their commander. By 8:00 AM on the twenty-ninth, Bragg had his entire army in line in the Tullahoma fortifications.[52] Rosecrans had spread his forces across a fair-sized expanse of country in his original—and successful—bid to keep Bragg guessing about the real point of attack. Now he was, in a sense, the victim of his own successful strategy as the unseasonable rainy spell transformed the dirt roads of the Barrens into an oozing muck that delayed the concentration of his far-flung columns. Neither the Twentieth Corps nor the Twenty-first Corps, wide on the two flanks, got all its elements up until very late on June 29, and even then their commander had to admit that the mud-spattered troops and animals were considerably worse for the wear.[53] On the morning of the twenty-ninth, Rosecrans had only about two-thirds of his army concentrated around Manchester, at most about thirty-five thousand men.[54]

The Federal commander gave orders for the remaining units to come up as rapidly as possible and chafed at the rain's interference with his plan of campaign. "Nothing but heavy and continued rain," he complained in a dispatch to Washington that day, "has prevented this army from reaching Tullahoma in advance of Bragg."[55] An audacious Confederate commander might have taken the opportunity to attack Rosecrans. Bragg could not have known the exact proportions of the forces but must have been aware that all the units of the Army of the Cumberland were not up yet. In fact, the ration of forces early on the twenty-ninth, thirty-two thousand Confederate infantry and artillery against thirty-five thousand Federal, was better than most Southern commanders could hope to enjoy most of the time.[56] Still, Bragg's inadequate cavalry was giving him only the sketchiest of reconnaissance information, and he understandably—and probably wisely—was in no frame of mind to undertake aggressive action. Thomas had a strong position around Manchester and would probably have beaten off any direct attack.[57]

That was small enough comfort to Rosecrans, who dared not leave Bragg's army intact at Tullahoma to threaten his own supply line if he should advance farther. The Federal commander would have to defeat Bragg at Tullahoma or halt his advance where he was. Since the latter course was out of the question, given the mood of his superiors in Washington Rosecrans prepared to attack.[58] While he waited for the completion of his preparations, Rosecrans made use of the time by dispatching his brigade of mounted infantry on a raid toward the Confederate supply line. The hard-hitting Midwesterners, under the resourceful Colonel John Wilder, ranged all the way onto the Cumberland Plateau, tearing up track, wrecking other facilities, and cleverly dodging the Confederate pursuit. Even the cunning Forrest was bested and left staring at a deserted river crossing where Wilder and his men should have been. By noon on June 30, the mounted infantrymen and their Spencers were back in the Federal lines and ready for more trouble.[59]

The raid had been a nuisance for Bragg, but tracks and facilities could be fixed and communications restored. As long as Rosecrans could not get onto Bragg's supply lines with a force too powerful to be driven off, Bragg's situation remained manageable. That day, Rosecrans finally got the last of his troops into position and prepared to advance on Tullahoma in the morning.[60] It would be a desperate undertaking. Besides the powerful fortifications, Rosecrans would have to contend with the soggy countryside through which his army would have to flounder as it made its deployment and approach.[61] Further, Rosecrans's 1.6-to-1 numerical superiority was not even close to the kind of leverage needed to carry even modest field fortifications if stoutly defended.

Bragg recognized his opponent's dilemma and settled down to enjoy it. When Polk stopped by headquarters about 9:00 AM on the twenty-ninth, Bragg mentioned Wilder's raid and said he just did not have enough cavalry to keep that sort of thing from happening now and then. Still, he believed he could fight successfully at Tullahoma and planned to do so.[62] Polk was of another mind. The bishop-general probably required no further reason for desiring not to fight at Tullahoma than to know that Bragg did desire to fight there. He hated taking orders and had started believing his own propaganda to the point of considering Bragg a strategic imbecile.[63] He now conceived the idea that, in effect, while the Confederate army might be tied to such mundane things as supply lines, Rosecrans's blue-clad phantoms were beyond such merely physical restraints and, as Ulysses Grant once quipped on another occasion, might "turn a double somersault and land in our rear and on both our flanks at the same time."[64] In short, Polk decided that Tullahoma was another one of those hopeless and dreaded "man-traps."

Determined to force his will upon Bragg, Polk went looking for fellow corps commander Hardee. Finding him, he related his fears regarding Tullahoma, and the two made an appointment for a conference with Bragg that afternoon. At 3:00 PM they met at Bragg's headquarters. Bragg got right down to business and asked Polk what was on his mind. Polk replied that their communications had been cut and that Bragg's first duty was to restore them. They were already restored Bragg replied, and so they were. That would have taken the wind out of most people's sails but not those of the glib bishop. The sneer in his response rings clearly through the dusty sources that have preserved it for us. "How," he demanded, "do you propose to maintain them?" Patiently, Bragg explained that he was going to station cavalry at key positions to chase off any future raiders before they could do too much damage, but Polk would have none of it. No, he insisted, within thirty-six hours Rosecrans would be sitting astride the Confederate line of communications with a force too powerful to be driven off. He then launched into an elaborate scenario of all the bad things that might happen to them then: a horrible retreat into northern Alabama, men and animals starving, the artillery and wagons all abandoned, the army finally going completely to pieces, and all the while Rosecrans romping happy and unmolested through Chattanooga, Atlanta, and the rest of Georgia and even the Carolinas. It sounded dreadful, but it was as unrealistic as it was apocalyptic. For it was all based on Rosecrans doing something impossible (abandoning his own supply lines) and Bragg neglecting to do something very possible (supplying his army from Middle Tennessee).

Still, delivered with grave dignity by the silver-tongued bishop, it must have been impressive. All these calamities, he intoned, could be avoided if Bragg would only "fall back."

"That is all very well," Bragg replied, "but what do you distinctly propose to have done?"

"Retreat immediately," Polk replied, there was not a moment to spare.

"Then," Bragg persisted, perhaps still a bit incredulously, "you propose that we shall retreat."

"I do," Polk answered, "and that is my counsel."

Hardee was less forthright when pressed for his opinion. He had formed a strong habit by now of always siding with Polk against Bragg, but he had an even stronger preexisting habit of never taking responsibility for anything if he could avoid it. So he temporized. Polk's arguments were certainly very weighty, but he was not quite ready to go on record as advising retreat. Maybe they could send some infantry back to guard the supply line. Confronted with the demands of both corps commanders, Bragg agreed to implement at least that halfway solution, and on that note the meeting broke up.[65]

Bragg had made the right decision and resolutely stuck to it despite the fears of his subordinates. If all that had been required was the successful solution of a strategic problem, Bragg's retreat would have ended here, and he would probably have administered a bloody repulse to Rosecrans in the bargain. But war is not that easy. Command is a lonely business requiring supreme self-confidence when all others are questioning one's decisions. Bragg possessed this intangible trait of personality to a certain degree but not quite enough to deal with the likes of Polk and Hardee, especially when Bragg was in poor health and had just suffered several military reverses that by all odds simply should not have happened. During the remainder of June 29 and the morning of June 30 (and perhaps the intervening night hours as well), Bragg fretted on Polk's dire predictions. As garbled bits and pieces of intelligence came in that day (as intelligence ordinarily does come to a general during an active campaign), Bragg tended more and more toward the mistaken belief that Rosecrans was indeed thrusting infantry toward the Confederate supply line.[66] By mid-afternoon of the thirtieth,

Polk's scary stories had finally conjured up out of the darkness of uncertainty in Bragg's mind the sort of monster he could no longer endure. At 3:00 PM, just twenty-four hours after his conference with Polk and Hardee, Bragg gave orders for the Army of Tennessee to retreat.[67] If he could have waited only another fourteen hours he might have had an opportunity to slaughter Rosecrans's troops in front of the Tullahoma fortifications. At daylight, July 1, the Army of the Cumberland advanced only to find the entrenchments empty.[68]

Southeast of Tullahoma the terrain offered no place for the Confederates to make a stand short of the Elk River, about ten miles from the town. With the Tullahoma position abandoned, the campaign thus became a race for the Elk River bridges. Bragg managed to get his army across the rain-swollen river and had the bridges burned behind him.[69] With the Elk River across his front, Bragg was in the last viable defensive position north of Chattanooga. It was the weakest of the three he had held within the past week, for it had none of the massive fortifications he had abandoned at Shelbyville and Tullahoma, and while the Elk might be high, turbid, and unfordable at present it was rapidly dropping and showed promise of soon resuming its accustomed character as a shallow meandering stream, easily fordable at any number of places.[70] Bragg could not hope to prevent Rosecrans from reaching the south bank, but he could perhaps hope to catch him at a disadvantage there, much as Lee almost did to Grant at the North Anna eleven months later.

It was not to be. Bragg was the only one of the top three Army of Tennessee generals who entertained any remotest idea of fighting along the Elk, and after the events of the past week and with the state of ill health to which the prolonged stress had brought him, he was none too sure about it himself.[71] At 7:00 PM on July 1, Bragg, who was now beginning to take on some of the characteristics of a whipped man, sent a note to Polk: "The question to be decided instantly, Shall we fight on the Elk, or take post at foot of mountain at Cowan?" Cowan was even farther to the rear, at the very foot of the Cumberland Plateau. Though Polk had previously advised fighting behind the Elk, now that he was here he quickly changed his mind. He replied that he would not only retreat to Cowan but would even send a good part of the army's wagon train on over the mountains toward Chattanooga. Hardee was still more agitated. With all the zeal of a new convert to Polk's fervent preaching of retreat Hardee now found it almost unendurable to think that Bragg might contemplate giving battle along the Elk and began to toy with the idea of mutiny. At 8:30 that evening he sent Polk a dispatch marked, "Confidential." He said he had been thinking a good deal about the army and its present condition and commander. Bragg, he suggested, was physically incapable of exercising command. In this case, he asked, "What shall we do? What is best to be done to save this army and its honor? I think we ought to counsel together. . . . Where can we meet?"[72] This has to be one of the most remarkable communications of this very remarkable war. Military organizations have been known to hang officers who meet secretly behind their commander's back to decide what to do with him and his army.

But it never came to that. Hardee belatedly received his own copy of the query from Bragg as to where the army ought to fight. He quickly answered, "Let us fight at the mountain" and then dashed off a note to Polk to cancel the clandestine meeting for that night. The delay involved in falling back toward the Cumberlands would give them at least another day to decide what to do with Bragg. Hardee added in his note to Polk that with Bragg in command he would rather not fight at all but go on retreating right over the mountains to Chattanooga.[73] As it turned out, Hardee was to get his way. At 3:00 AM, July 2, Bragg gave orders to fall back on Cowan, but with the Cumberland Mountains immediately at the army's back no real stand could be made there, so the retreat continued more or less without pause until the Army of Tennessee reached Chattanooga several days later. Rosecrans did not pursue vigorously beyond the foot of the Cumberlands.[74] By July 4, 1863, the North, had it needed any further cause for celebration amidst news of Gettysburg and Vicksburg, could also have celebrated the complete—and relatively bloodless—conquest of Middle Tennessee.[75]

Somehow Bragg had been defeated, despite the fact that his position was well selected and his strategy and tactics correct, at times even brilliant. If warfare were a game of chess, Bragg's performance might have brought triumph, or at least stalemate. But war is much more complicated than that, and somewhere in its intangible factors Bragg's generalship had fallen short. He had somehow failed in communicating to his subordinates precisely what he wanted them to do and motivating them to do it, and he had allowed his subordinates' carping, obstructionism, and lack of nerve to break down his own force of will. But while identifying Bragg's problem is simple enough—Bragg himself no doubt was aware of it—explaining how it could have been avoided is a much more difficult matter. One is reminded of the dictum of the famous German philosopher of war Carl von Clausewitz, "In war, everything is very simple, but the simplest thing is difficult."

So it is with the matter of how Bragg could have supplied himself with cooperative lieutenants. Bragg has long been depicted as a sour-spirited, acerbic, curmudgeonly man who alienated all those around him.[76] Yet considerable testimony suggests that Bragg could be kindly and patient. Clearly, Bragg did make a conscious and determined effort to lay aside his personal quarrels for the good of the Confederate cause.[77] Also contrary to legend, he had a considerable number of friends and supporters within the Confederate army.[78] The dislike of him was not universal, but it was widespread enough to destroy his effectiveness.

How might Bragg have avoided this? First, in a war in which each side suffered a surfeit of so-called political generals who were sometimes military disasters, Bragg might nevertheless have done well to be a bit more political himself. Bragg was an Old Army man, and he had Old Army ways that sometimes brought him into conflict with volunteers who knew nothing of the army and little of taking orders at all for that matter. Bragg might also have profited by stroking the egos of popular politicians-turned-general. One of these was John C. Breckinridge, who was transferred out of the Army of Tennessee just before the beginning of the Tullahoma campaign. Breckinridge was proud, undisciplined, unmilitary, and sometimes not at all easy for a regular army man like Bragg to put up with. But Bragg would have done well to have swallowed a bit more of his own pride and tried to cultivate the friendship of Breckinridge, not because he liked him or thought him a good general but because he was a popular politician whose friendship could do Bragg much good and whose enmity could do him much harm. The same might well have been true of Leonidas Polk. Feeding the egos and puffing the already badly overinflated senses of self-importance of men like Polk and Breckinridge would not have been enjoyable but could have been very useful. Doing this, at least insofar as he could consistent with honesty and the maintenance of his own firm control over the army, might have preserved Bragg's popularity, and thus his usefulness, for a longer time. It was much the sort of tactic Lincoln used with many of the difficult politicians he had to handle. Lee, too, possessed this skill.

Naturally, the most desirable course would have been as much as possible to get such characters out of the army—or at least out of *his* army. That was a course that Lee often pursued with incompetent or uncooperative generals, and the result was that the Army of Northern Virginia had a senior officer corps much superior to that of the Army of Tennessee. Yet this tactic required the careful cultivation of yet another politician: Jefferson Davis. For all Bragg's reputation as the intimate friend of Jefferson Davis he never possessed one half the friendship with and influence over Davis that Lee held throughout his command in Virginia. Bragg was always very respectful toward Davis, sometimes even flattering, but lacking from his correspondence with the president is that smooth, easy, graceful and constant cultivation that one finds in Lee's dispatches to Davis. Very likely it was a skill Bragg simply did not possess. Consequently, when Lee was determined to rid himself of an incompetent officer he always got his way. If the man was a friend of the president Lee might have to approach the matter gently and discreetly, but invariably when next the Army of Northern Virginia marched to battle the inadequate officer had long since departed for points west.[79] By contrast, Bragg was forced to deal with a number of generals whom he knew to be incompetent and insubordinate but whom Davis, despite Bragg's requests, would not allow him to remove.[80] Being a successful general in Bragg's case might thus have meant not only more successfully cultivating the generals with whom he had to work but also more successfully cultivating the president in order to have the choice of the generals with whom he would have to work.

A third thing Bragg might have had to do to retain the effective cooperation of his difficult generals was win more battles. That, of course, is easy to say but hard to do. Nevertheless, the fact remains that nothing succeeds like success, and a number of impressive early victories would have been immensely beneficial to Bragg's reputation and his degree of acceptance among his generals. He might have done considerably better if he had been accorded the opportunity of winning more small, relatively easy victories shortly after taking command, not so much for what they would accomplish strategically, but for their beneficial effect on the army and its morale. Again, this is easier said than done. Instead, his first campaign was the enormously ambitious Kentucky venture. It had to be since Confederate public opinion would never have forgiven Bragg if he had not attempted it. Yet when it failed, many, including the army's large and powerful Kentucky faction, turned bitterly against Bragg. With respect to Kentucky, Bragg probably could not have won no matter what he did. Its conquest by the Confederacy was possible only if its people rose in revolt against Federal authority. The people of Kentucky, as a whole, would not do this, and the large and influential clique of Kentucky officers in the Army of Tennessee would almost undoubtedly have vented its frustration over this on whatever officer held Confederate command in Tennessee, be he Braxton Bragg, Joseph E. Johnston, or Robert E. Lee.[81] Still, Bragg might have weathered that storm a little better with a few more small successes to his credit. In part, however, there was simply no escaping the fact that a general who suffered a highly publicized major reverse, particularly one early in his tenure as army commander, was probably more or less ruined in his service to a democratic government—at least nine times out of ten.

The final quality that Bragg lacked was probably the most important, for it lay behind several of the others. It was an intangible quality: the ability to inspire and motivate those around him. One might call it charisma, or simply a winning personality. Many, though far from all, great generals have had it. Bragg did not, and in his case that was a serious handicap. President Davis himself recognized Bragg's deficiency in this regard, remarking that "another Genl. might excite more enthusiasm."[82] Yet Davis did not take the steps necessary on his part to preserve the fragile usefulness of a general who needed only hearty cooperation to make his excellent strategy and tactics effective but whose lack of the intangible trait of charisma made him incapable of winning that loyalty on his own.

Thus Bragg suffered defeat in the Tullahoma campaign, not for any lack in the more obvious skills of war, but rather for want of some elusive quality of personality that would have enabled him to win and keep the loyalty, confidence, and cooperation of the difficult collection of men that it fell to his lot to have as fellow Confederates.

Notes

1. Archer Jones, *Civil War Command and Strategy: The Process of Victory and Defeat* (New York: Free Press, 1992), 165–66; William M. Lamers, *The Edge of Glory: A Biography of William S. Rosecrans, U. S. A.* (New York: Harcourt, Brace & World, 1961), 275; Freeman Cleaves, *Rock of Chickamauga: The Life of General George H. Thomas* (Norman: University of Oklahoma Press, 1948), 138–39, 142.

2. Thomas Lawrence Connelly, *Autumn of Glory: The Army of Tennessee, 1862–1865* (Baton Rouge: Louisiana State University Press, 1971), 112–15; Don C. Seitz, *Braxton Bragg* (Columbia SC: The State Company, 1924); "A Staff Officer," *Synopsis of the Military Career of General Joseph Wheeler*, ed. George R. Steward (N.p.; reprint, Birmingham AL: Public Library Press, 1988), 11; Timothy H. Donovan Jr., Roy K. Flint, Arthur V. Grant Jr., Gerald P. Stadler, *The American Civil War* (Wayne NJ: Avery, 1987), 169–70.

3. For details on Polk and his negative impact on the Army of Tennessee, see Steven E. Woodworth, *Jefferson Davis and His Generals: The Failure of Confederate Command in the West* (Lawrence: University Press of Kansas, 1990).

4. Christopher Losson, *Tennessee's Forgotten Warriors: Frank Cheatham and His Confederate Division* (Knoxville: University of Tennessee Press, 1989), 89–91.

5. Connelly, *Autumn of Glory*, 74–75.

6. U.S. War Department, *The War of the Rebellion: A Compilation of the Official Records of the Union and Confederate Armies*, 128 vols. (Washington DC: Government Printing Office, 1881–1901), 1st ser., vol. 20, pt. 1, pp. 682–84, 689–99, 701–2 (hereafter cited as OR; all references are to series 1 unless otherwise noted) OR.

7. Dunbar Rowland, ed., *Jefferson Davis, Constitutionalist: His Letters, Papers, and Speeches*, 10 vols. (Jackson: Mississippi Department of Archives and History, 1923) vol. 5, pp. 420–21.

8. Woodworth, *Jefferson Davis and His Generals*, 196–98.

9. OR 23, pt. 2: 825.

10. Donovan et al., *The American Civil War*, 171–72; Donn Piatt, *General George H. Thomas: A Critical Biography* (Cincinnati: n.p., 1893), 353; Cleaves, *Rock of Chickamauga*, 144; Francis F. McKinney, *Education in Violence: The Life of George H. Thomas and the History of the Army of the Cumberland* (Detroit: Wayne State University Press, 1961), 210–11.

11. McKinney, *Education in Violence*, 211; Johnston had in March predicted Manchester or McMinnville, even farther on the Confederate right, as the most likely targets of a Union advance. OR 23, pt. 2: 724.

12. OR 23, pt. 2: 794–95.

13. Donovan et al., *The American Civil War*, 170–72.

14. This does not, of course, include Forrest, whose operations were usually anything but ordinary. Forrest, however, was serving out on the other flank beyond the Confederate left.

15. Cleaves, *Rock of Chickamauga*, 144.

16. OR 23, pt. 1: 602, 611; Connelly, *Autumn of Glory*, 126–27.

17. OR 23, pt. 1: 602–3, 611–14.

18. OR 23, pt. 1: 886.

19. OR 23, pt. 1: 848–49.

20. Connelly, *Autumn of Glory*, 126.

21. OR 23, pt. 1: 458, 611–14.

22. OR 23, pt. 1: 430, 454–55, 458–59, 611–14.

23. OR 23, pt. 1: 465–66, 483–84, 486–87, 586–89; Craig L. Symonds, *Stonewall of the West: Patrick Cleburne and the Civil War* (Lawrence: University Press of Kansas, 1997), 129.

24. Lamers, *The Edge of Glory*, 276–78; Cleaves, *Rock of Chickamauga*, 144; McKinney, *Education in Violence*, 211.

25. OR 23, pt. 1: 618.

26. OR 23, pt. 1: 618–19.

27. Since Bragg canceled the proposed movement on the basis of a dispatch dated 2:00 PM on the twenty-sixth, it follows that the conference with Polk would probably have been substantially earlier. OR 23, pt. 1: 618.

28. OR 23, pt. 1: 619–20, pt. 2: 796.

29. OR 23, pt. 1: 619.

30. OR 23, pt. 1: 410–11, 536, 539.

31. OR 23, pt. 1: 471.

32. In this essay I am using the figures given in OR for troops present for duty, since both sides used this figure and thus it offers some reasonable degree of comparability. The June 20 return of the Army of Tennessee assigned some 15,728 present for duty to Polk's eight brigades (OR 23, pt. 1: 585–86). This gives an average of 1,966 men in each of Polk's brigades. The returns of the Army of the Cumberland showed 14,096 present for duty in the nine brigades of the Twentieth Corps, to which belonged the two brigades in Liberty Gap on June 27 (OR 23, pt. 1: 410–11). If they were average brigades for the corps, they would have had 1,566 men each. Thus, six of Polk's brigades would have numbered 11,796, while the two brigades of the Twentieth Corps could have mustered only 3,132, making a 3.8-to-1 numerical superiority for Polk. He might have had difficulty deploying that much of an advantage on the terrain there, but, especially with the aid of Hardee's force, he should have been able to get the job done.

33. OR 23, pt. 2: 724.

34. OR 23, pt. 1: 618.

35. OR 23, pt. 1: 618.

36. Connelly, *Autumn of Glory*, 117.

37. OR 23, pt. 1: 790.

38. OR 23, pt. 1: 790.

39. Connelly, *Autumn of Glory*, 119.

40. OR 23, pt. 2: 884.

41. OR 23, pt. 1: 419–24.

42. OR 23, pt. 2: 886.

43. OR 23, pt. 1: 618–20.

44. OR 23, pt. 1: 403.

45. James Lee McDonough, *War in Kentucky: From Shiloh to Perryville* (Knoxville: University of Tennessee Press, 1994), 30–60; OR 30, pt. 2: 403; Robert G. Hartje, *Van Dorn: The Life and Times of a Confederate General* (Nashville: Vanderbilt University Press, 1967), 269.

46. OR 23, pt. 2: 794–95.

47. OR 23, pt. 2: 885.

48. James A. Ramage, *Rebel Raider: The Life of General John Hunt Morgan* (Lexington: University Press of Kentucky, 1986), 158–62.

49. Hartje, *Van Dorn*, 308–17.

50. Brian Steel Wills, *A Battle from the Start: The Life of Nathan Bedford Forrest* (New York: Harper Collins, 1992), 122–29; Robert Selph Henry, *First with the Most: Forrest* (Indianapolis: Bobbs-Merrill, 1944), 142–44; OR 23, pt. 1: 620; John P. Dyer, *From Shiloh to San Juan: The Life of "Fightin' Joe" Wheeler* (Baton Rouge: Louisiana State University Press, 1941), 83; "A Staff Officer," *Synopsis*, 12; T. C. De Leon, *Joseph Wheeler: The Man, the Statesman, the Solder* (Kennesaw, GA: Continental Book Co., 1960; originally published 1899), 101; Seitz, *Braxton Bragg*, 310.

51. OR 23, pt. 2: 741.

52. OR 23, pt. 1: 619.

53. OR 23, pt. 1: 407.

54. Lamers, *The Edge of Glory*, 281; OR 23, pt. 1: 410–11.

55. OR 23, pt. 1: 402.

56. OR 23, pt. 1: 585–86.

57. OR 23, pt. 1: 426.

58. OR 23, pt. 1: 402, 407; Donovan et al., *The American Civil War*, 173; McKinney, *Education in Violence*, 215–16. As these sources make clear, Rosecrans intended and expected to fight a great battle at Tullahoma. Some scholars have suggested that Rosecrans actually intended nothing more than a feint toward Tullahoma. Lamers, *The Edge of Glory*, 284.

59. OR 23, pt. 1: 460–61.

60. OR 23, pt. 1: 407.

61. Lamers, *Edge of Glory*, 284.

62. OR 23, pt. 1: 621; Connelly overestimated Rosecrans's threat to Bragg's communications because he underestimated the degree to which Bragg, at least potentially, threatened Rosecrans's communications. Connelly, *Autumn of Glory*, 129.

63. Joseph H. Parks, *General Leonidas Polk, C.S.A.: The Fighting Bishop* (Baton Rouge: Louisiana State University Press, 1962), 349; Woodworth, *Jefferson Davis and His Generals*, 239.

64. Grant was referring to the inflated opinion of Robert E. Lee held by many officers in the Army of the Potomac. Bruce Catton, *A Stillness at Appomattox* in *Bruce Catton's Civil War* (New York: Fairfax, 1984; originally published, 1953), 513.

65. OR 23, pt. 1: 621–22.

66. Connelly, *Autumn of Glory*, 127.

67. OR 23, pt. 1: 622.

68. OR 23, pt. 1:402.

69. OR 23, pt. 1:623.

70. Donovan et al., *The American Civil War*, 173.

71. Peter Cozzens, *This Terrible Sound: The Battle of Chickamauga* (Urbana: University of Illinois Press, 1992), 19.

72. OR 23, pt. 1:623.

73. OR 23, pt. 1:624.

74. OR 23, pt. 1:624–27; Cozzens, *This Terrible Sound*, 19.

75. The Army of the Cumberland suffered fewer than 600 killed and wounded during the Tullahoma campaign. OR 23, pt. 1:419–24.

76. A prime example is the anecdote Ulysses S. Grant related in his memoirs. Bragg, as a junior officer in the prewar U.S. Army, so the story goes, actually got into an argument with himself. Ulysses S. Grant, *Personal Memoirs of U. S. Grant*, 2 vols. (New York: Charles L. Webster, 1885), vol. 2, pp. 86–87. Of course, no other evidence exists to corroborate this highly improbable tale, and Grant probably did not really intend it to be taken seriously.

77. Not least among the quarrels he laid aside was one of long standing with Jefferson Davis himself. Grady McWhiney, *Braxton Bragg and Confederate Defeat*, (Tuscaloosa: University of Alabama Press 1991; originally published 1969), vol. 1, 135–40. For additional incidents of Bragg's acting counter to his reputation, see Ramage, *Rebel Raider*, 134–35; Joseph H. Parks, *General Edmund Kirby Smith, C. S. A.* (Baton Rouge: Louisiana State University Press, 1954), 245; Woodworth, *Jefferson Davis and His Generals*, 243–44.

78. McWhiney, *Braxton Bragg*, 379–83.

79. The only exception to this involved regimental officers. Rowland, *Jefferson Davis*, 5:345–46, 367; Clement Eaton, *Jefferson Davis* (New York: Free Press, 1977), 249; William C. Davis, *Jefferson Davis: The Man and His Hour* (New York: Harper Collins, 1991), 426–27; OR 19, pt. 2: 643–55, 681, 683–84, 697–98; OR 21:1029–30, 1045; Douglas Southall Freeman, *R. E. Lee: A Biography*, 4 vols. (New York: Scribners, 1934), vol. 2, 418–19; Douglas Southall Freeman, *Lee's Lieutenants: A Study in Command*, 3 vols. (New York: Scribners, 1944), vol. 2, 414. See also Steven E. Woodworth, *Davis and Lee at War* (Lawrence: University Press of Kansas, 1995), 178, 203–4.

80. OR 17, pt. 2: 627–28, 654–55, 658, 667–68, 673.

81. True, Lee was forced out of Maryland and did suffer criticism for that episode, but he already had behind him an impressive string of victories and, more important, the Maryland influence in the Army of Northern Virginia was not as strong as the Kentucky influence in the Army of Tennessee.

82. Roland, *Jefferson Davis*, 5:356–57.

The Contributors

Professor Donald E. Collins of East Carolina University is a historian of diverse interests, his fields of study ranging from Japanese-Americans during the Second World War to regional history in the southeast, particularly in eastern North Carolina. He is the author of two books and a dozen articles, including several on the Civil War.

Professor William B. Feis of Buena Vista University is the author of several articles and book chapters on the Civil War. He is currently working on a book studying Ulysses S. Grant's use of military intelligence.

William J. Miller is editor of *Civil War* magazine, the publication of the Civil War Society. His books include *The Training of an Army: Camp Curtin and the North's Civil War* (1990), *The Battles for Richmond, 1862* (1996), and *Mapping for Stonewall: The Civil War Service of Jed Hotchkiss* (1993), winner of the New York Civil War Round Table's Fletcher Pratt Award as the best nonfiction Civil War book of 1993. He has taught writing at the University of Delaware and at George Mason University in Fairfax, Virginia.

Philip L. Shiman received his B.A. from Yale University and his Ph.D. from Duke. Along the way he has achieved a distinguished academic record that includes the Dissertation-Year Fellowship of the U.S. Army Center of Military History and the Lee and Evelyn Combs Dissertation Prize of the American Blue and Gray Association. He has served as a lecturer at Duke, and he has been a contract historian for the North Carolina Department of Cultural Resources, the Fort Branch Battlefield Commission, and the U.S. Army Corps of Engineers. He has written several articles, and his book, *Engineering Sherman's March: Army Engineers and the Organization of Modern War, 1861–1865*, is forthcoming.

Professor Brooks D. Simpson of Arizona State University is a respected Civil War scholar whose books include *Let Us Have Peace: Ulysses S. Grant and the Politics of War and Reconstruction, 1864–1868* (1991; a selection of both the History Book Club and the Book-of-the-Month Club), *The Political Education of*

Henry Adams (1996), and *America's Civil War* (1996). He has written over a score of scholarly articles or book chapters.

Professor Craig L. Symonds of the United States Naval Academy is a Civil War scholar of well-established reputation. His five Civil War books have received three Book-of-the-Month Club selections, four History Book Club selections, and two Military Book Club selections. *Joseph E. Johnston: A Civil War Biography* (1992) was a 1993 runner-up for the prestigious Lincoln Prize. He has edited or coauthored more than half a dozen Civil War books and is the author of over one hundred articles, review articles, and book reviews. He has been an invited lecturer at the U.S. Naval War College, the U.S. Army War College, Oxford University, and other institutions. His most recent book is *Stonewall of the West: Patrick Cleburne and the Civil War* (1997).

Professor Steven E. Woodworth of Texas Christian University is author of *Jefferson Davis and His Generals: The Failure of Confederate Command in the West* (1990) and *Davis and Lee at War* (1995), both History Book Club selections and winners of the Fletcher Pratt Award. His other works include *The American Civil War: A Handbook of Literature and Research* (1996) and *Six Armies in Tennessee: The Chickamauga and Chattanooga Campaigns* (1998).

Index

Holmes, Theophilus, 9

Holt, Judge Advocate General Joseph, 72–73, 75

Hood, Gen. John Bell, 5, 13, 94, 151

Hooker, Joseph, 157, 158

Hotchkiss, Jedediah, xii, 121, 133; background of, 122–23; and the Shenandoah Valley campaign, 119, 124–26, 127, 128–29, 130, 131, 132

Huggins, W. S., 66

Hunter, David, 146, 147, 150

information maps, 98, 99, 105, 108–9

Innes, Col. William P., 102

intelligence, x–xi, 17, 18, 21–23, 25–26; and balloons, 109; and information, 43 n.3

Irving, William, 61, 62

Jackson, Gen. Thomas J. "Stonewall," 3, 76, 166; background of, 122; and Frémont, 126–27; and Hotchkiss, 121, 123, 125, 127, 128, 133; and personal character, xii, 119–22, 132–33, 134; personality of, 120, 121, 133; and religion, 121, 122; and the Shenadoah Valley campaign, 123–32; subordinates selected by, xii, 119–20, 122, 133, 134, 135–36 n.30, 136 n.30

Johnson, Andrew, 46 n.31, 71, 74, 75; Southern leaders punished by, 71

Johnson, Brig. Gen. Edward, 127

Johnson, General Bushrod, 161

Johnston, Gen. Albert Sidney, 5, 26, 29, 34, 142; and Grant's intelligence operations, 31, 33, 47 n.63

Johnston, Beverly, 11

Johnston, Gen. Joseph E., xii, 70, 71, 124, 177; and Bragg, 8–9, 12; in Confederate congress, 5; and Davis, x, 5, 7, 9–10, 11–12, 13, 14,

160; in Georgia, 12–13; as military genius, 14–15 n.5; and Pemberton's Army of Mississippi, 8–9; personal traits of, 7; at Tullahoma, 166, 170, 179 n.11; and Vicksburg, 9–11; and Wigfall, x, 6–8, 10, 11, 12, 13, 14

Johnston, Lydia, 7, 9

Jomini, Antoine Henri, 17

Jones, Archer, 4–5, 6–7, 14 n.2

Jones, David, 56, 59, 60–61, 77

Jones, Stephen, 60, 62

Jones, William, 62, 65

Jordan, Capt. Macon, 126

Justice, Lt. John G., 63

Kellum, Elijah, 56, 66, 69, 70

Kernstown, Battle of, 123, 124

King, Adm. Ernest, 118, 119

King, Sgt. Blunt, 59, 61, 72

Kinston hangings, 50, 60, 62–63, 64–65, 68–77

L., Mr., 26, 46 n.31

Ledlie, James, 149

Lee, Robert E., 1, 2, 12, 174, 177; and Beech Grove, 57; and Chancellorsville, 157; in Confederate congress, 5; and Davis, 13, 176–77; desertion viewed by, 51, 52, 77, 80 n.40; and Grant's campaign maneuvers, 137, 138, 139, 140, 142, 143, 144, 145, 146, 147, 151, 172, 174, 153 n.9, 181 n.64; indictment of, 71; in Maryland, 182 n.81; personality of, 5, 167, 176; Richmond viewed by, 124; and undesirable generals, 176–77, 182 n.7; viewed by the Army of the Potomac, 181 n.64

Leith, First Lt. Samuel, 57, 58

Lellyett, John, 46 n.31

Lexington, 22